EXETER CITY F.C.
A GRECIAN ANTHOLOGY

By Mike Blackstone

Published by Mike Blackstone
First published in October 2008
© Mike Blackstone and Exeter City Football Club

The right of Mike Blackstone to be identified as author of this work has been
asserted by him in accordance with the Copyright, Designs & Patents Act, 1988.

ISBN 978–0–9548201–1–4

A catalogue record for this book is available from the British Library.

A number of photographs appear throughout this book.
Our thanks in particular go to the *Express & Echo*; Keith Stone (www.cheggerspics.co.uk),
and the Dave Fisher Collection. Other photographs are from the author's own collection or as indicated.

Cover design by Lynda Braithwaite.

Page design by Kevin Bovey.

Typeset, printed and bound by Kingfisher Print & Design Ltd, Wills Road,
Totnes Industrial Estate, Totnes, Devon TQ9 5XN.

All enquiries concerning this publication should be directed to:
Exeter City Football Club, St James' Park, Exeter, Devon EX4 6PX.

DUST JACKET ILLUSTRATIONS
Front cover:
Exeter City's promotion-winning team of 1963–64
Celebrating promotion back to the Football League in 2008
Back cover:
The Cowshed, St James' Park
The Flybe Stand that replaced the Cowshed

CONTENTS

DEDICATION

To the directors, players and supporters of Exeter City Football Club 1904–2008. And more latterly to those who saved the club from oblivion – the Exeter City Supporters' Trust.

To Lynda, who makes everything worthwhile (yes, even taking preference over Exeter City F.C.!). As ever, massive thanks for her great encouragement, assistance and love, before, after and during the writing of this book.

ABOUT THE AUTHOR

Born in the summer of 1951, so as not to miss the start of the new football season, and Exeter City's opening Third Division South fixture against Crystal Palace, Mike Blackstone hails from Exmouth, Devon, where he lived until December 2002, when he took the monumental decision to move 'up north' to Heysham, Morecambe in Lancashire. He moved from the land of pasties and cider to the land of pies and flat caps.

Mike took his first tentative steps through the turnstiles at Exeter City's St James' Park in the 1959–60 season for the visit of Rochdale in the Fourth Division of the Football League. It proved to be a successful start as he saw City go through the rest of the season – what there was left of it – unbeaten at the Park. Little did he know at the time that following the fortunes of Exeter City F.C. wasn't always as good, or as easy! This had been the start of a lifelong love affair with the Grecians, which is still as strong in 2008 as it was in that initial season.

An Exeter City statistician and avid programme collector, Mike started to contribute to the club's match programme in 1969 and became the editor during the 1992–93 season, and continues to be so, having won a string of honours, several years in succession, including best programme in the country on more than one occasion.

Having contributed to numerous books, magazines and newspapers, and the programmes of many other clubs, he is also the author of three books prior to this one.

Mike's enthusiasm for the game, together with his love of reading and writing about it, as well as visiting 'new' grounds (especially non-league), shows no signs of diminishing.

He currently still lives in Heysham, sharing a house and attending to the needs of Merlyn the cat, who thankfully has never quite mastered the art of walking across the computer keyboard, or selecting the delete key, which many would doubtless thank him for if he did!

ALSO BY MIKE BLACKSTONE

- *Exeter City: a File of Fascinating Football Facts,* ISBN 0–946–65153–1, Obelisk Publications, 1992.
- *Plymouth Argyle: a File of Fascinating Football Facts,* ISBN 0–946–65165–5, Obelisk Publications, 1993.
- *The Brown Sauce Is Off: a North West Non-League Odyssey,* ISBN 0–954–82010–X, Mike Blackstone, 2004.

EXETER CITY SUPPORTERS' TRUST
(SPONSORS OF *A GRECIAN ANTHOLOGY*)

Founded during 2000, the initial meetings of the Trust were held at any available venue, often in a corner of the St James' Centre bar. The Trust grew slowly in years one and two, and raising money was difficult, as was convincing people that there was a real threat to the existence of the club, let alone committing themselves to financial involvement in a very slow-growing organisation, and one that had little apparent guarantee of success for its aims.

In 2001 the Supporters' Trust decided that it would ask the board of the club to be represented by an associate director, and an election was held to decide between the two candidates Norman Warne and Bill Palmer. A sum of £6,000 was given to the club to facilitate this post. Norman Warne was elected in summer 2001 although he didn't attend his first board meeting until September 2001.

During late summer 2002 the Trust became increasingly sure, especially after the appointment of two new directors, that it needed to make plans for the future, though at this time the aims of the Trust were still to 'assist and help' the club. The decision to alter the aims to 'purchase the majority shareholding of the club' was taken as a result of an open meeting of the Trust on 1st February 2003 that was addressed by John Russell (then vice-chairman of the club).

Having decided to alter the aims of the Trust to include ownership of the club, Trust membership, which had been at 211 in March 2003, began to grow quickly. The Trustees formulated two further immediate aims. Firstly to press the existing board for an active role for the associate director post and secondly to recruit business sponsors with a view to developing a more 'professional' look for Trust documentation.

In March 2003 six club directors resigned following a visit and report by the F.A. Financial Unit, which suggested that the club was trading insolvently. The Trust also instigated a meeting at the Buckerell Lodge Hotel where three businesses agreed to become the first commercial sponsors of the Trust. Events on (and off) the pitch at St James' Park made the case for Trust membership easier to promote, and by the end of April 2003 membership stood at just over 500.

By the end of season 2002–03 it had become clear to Trustees that the club was in terminal decline and could be heading towards relegation. Membership of the Trust was growing but the Trustees started to make contingency plans to put in place a 'shadow cabinet' that could act as an interim regime if the worst happened and the club was left without an administration.

The arrest of two directors during May 2003 left the then chairman in a situation where he was the sole director, and he looked for help to run the club on a day-to-day basis. It became evident to the three Trust members who were appointed as directors that the club was in an even worse state than had originally been thought. Not only was the financial situation dire, but it also soon became obvious that uncertainty extended to management of the playing side of the club as well.

In these circumstances the decision of the Trust board to press ahead with the purchase of a majority shareholding retrospectively seemed foolhardy. However the new directors were convinced that it was the only way that the club could possibly continue to trade, let alone put a competitive side out for its first season in the Football Conference. In September 2003 the Trust, after much negotiation, acquired a majority shareholding, and set about planning to move the club into a CVA with the hope of reducing the club's debts.

The Trust and the football club have faced many challenges in the years that followed 2003. The board of society would like to thank everybody who has assisted the football club over the last five years, with special thanks to the club directors who have run the football club on behalf of the Trust and who have embraced the community ethos of the Trust in administering Exeter City F.C.

The Trust is proud of the achievements of the club over the last five years and looks forward to a similarly rewarding and successful future as a fan-owned football club back in the Football League.

FOREWORD

Over a long career in football, I have been fortunate enough to have travelled to many places, met many people and made enduring friendships. I worked hard enough, had enough talent and steered clear of enough injuries to tread hallowed turf, lay claim to historic silverware and play with and against some of the legendary names in world football.

The greatest footballer of them all, Pele, called football, 'The Beautiful Game' and whilst one understands his point, it isn't always such a joy to be involved in. Malpractice, lack of ethics, disloyalty, incompetence, injury, bad luck, bad timing, officialdom, the pressure of economics and the sheer heartbreak that can be involved, all have to be weighed against the far fewer moments of real joy. Thanks is a rare commodity for those in football. For every letter of congratulation we receive for winning, we get four times the number when we lose.

I moved to the West Country not for football but for the joy of living in a beautiful part of the world and, having settled in the area, becoming involved with Exeter City was just a way to put something back into a game that has been good to me and that is so important in the lives of so many people. I saw a club struggling and that clearly needed help. I found, as I returned from a period in Japan, a club that had been bankrupted and had dropped out of the Football League.

I also came across a club that its fans had come together to save. I saw a band of dedicated coaches and management battling against a mountain that seemed insurmountable. I also saw a heart that wouldn't die within those people and, for better or worse, I offered my help. It seemed the right thing to do – and history has proved that it was.

As I look now at the facilities and backroom set-up and staff being built at the Cat and Fiddle, at the wonderful playing surface being developed at St James' Park, at the professional playing management and the professionalism of the forward planning, as I think of a club that has been to Wembley for the last two seasons, the 50,000 fans that cheered the team on during those Wembley trips, I look back on this club with its 104 years of history and see the start of a new period in that history. A period probably filled with the same optimism as those early pioneers of the club felt. This is a new beginning and one that I believe the club is better prepared for than for many years previously.

That the club faces a future of optimism is a tribute to those that went before with good intent and to those that carry the mantle now. This book celebrates the past and is a milestone for the future history of the club. It is a testament of the support that has carried the club and of those who truly love it, uncomplainingly and forgivingly. I am therefore proud to have been involved in my small part and to have been asked to write this foreword.

Steve Perryman MBE

PATRONS' LIST

(1)	Exeter City Supporters' Trust
(2)	Stephen R. Weston
(3)	Mark Bendell
(4)	Matt Young
(5)	Rachael Sanders
(6)	Dominic Sanders
(7)	C. P. Baker
(8)	K. G. Baker
(9)	The Parkhouse Family
(10)	David Baker
(11)	Paul Morrish
(12)	Robert Carter
(13)	Jacob Oliver John Woollacott
(14)	The Aplin Family
(15)	Paul Barnard
(16)	Chris Henley
(17)	Ivor Morrish
(18)	Diane Hawkings
(19)	John Hawkings
(20)	Vic Allen
(21)	Francis Welland
(22)	Bill Gubb
(23)	In Memory of William Edward Gubb
(24)	In Memory of Kathleen Gubb
(25)	Alastair Young
(26)	Alex Young
(27)	In Memory of Derek Broom
(28)	David Morgan
(29)	Nick Rendle
(30)	Jim Shepherd
(31)	In Memory of Nina Wills
(32)	The Yates Family
(33)	The Marks Family
(34)	Graham Tooth
(35)	Charles Neary
(36)	William Tucker
(37)	Sarah Penfold
(38)	Derek Richardson (Wallsend)
(39)	Reg Palmer, 1903–1997, 'City Til He Died'
(40)	Colin Williams
(41)	John Williams
(42)	In Memory of Gwen Hoare
(43)	Percival Worner Founder 1884–1916
(44)	Di Lee
(45)	John Lee
(46)	Paul Howard
(47)	Tania Howard
(48)	Vince Davies
(49)	Max Davies
(50)	In Memory of Tony Davies 1944–2006 'City Till I Die'
(51)	Roger Walker
(52)	Neil Rogers
(53)	Mellissa Rogers
(54)	Brian Peeke
(55)	Derrick Peeke
(56)	Steve Bennett
(57)	Adrian J. Kavanagh
(58)	Debra Silverberg
(59)	Michael Clayson
(60)	Lewis Jones
(61)	Richard Jarvis
(62)	In Memory of Leslie Jarvis
(63)	The Ellis Family
(64)	Tony Brooks
(65)	Keith Eaglestone
(66)	Tom Eaglestone
(67)	Frank Sealey
(68)	Adrian Shand
(69)	David Vincent
(70)	Tim Long
(71)	Andrew Long
(72)	Ben Long
(73)	Stephen McAndrews
(74)	In Memory of 'Mac' Hodder
(75)	Sarah Flower
(76)	Rebecca K. Jackson
(77)	Rodney Boulton
(78)	Ian Bishop
(79)	In Memory of Bert Bishop
(80)	Stafford Spurway
(81)	Darryl Thomas
(82)	Dave Gumm
(83)	In Memory of Jim Gumm
(84)	Grant Coleby
(85)	Jon Carr
(86)	Dave Gibbs
(87)	Cliff Mingo
(88)	Peter Davis – Ley Lane Stores Kingsteignton
(89)	Dan Hall
(90)	Kate Hall
(91)	Roger Fearn
(92)	Giles E. L. Ashman
(93)	Ted Ashman
(94)	In Memory of Sally Ashman
(95)	George Bruce
(96)	David Edmonds
(97)	The Raffells
(98)	Bill Jarman
(99)	Jim Tucker
(100)	Mark Morrell
(101)	Denise Watts
(102)	Ross Watts
(103)	In memory of my Mum Janet Gobey 09/06/31–23/11/84
(104)	Reg Gobey, my brilliant Dad, 80 years young on 27/9/08
(105)	In Memory of James Brimblecombe
(106)	Dr Roger Brimblecombe
(107)	Frances Farley
(108)	Paul Farley
(109)	Matthew Farley
(110)	Thomas Farley
(111)	Tim Spencer

(112) In Memory of Frank Conway
(113) In Memory of Ken Sansom
(114) Bill Short
(115) Paul Sussex
(116) In Memory of Jim Blackstone
(117) Lynda Braithwaite
(118) Paul A. Layton
(119) Jack A. Layton
(120) Jon Smith
(121) Alan J.G. Southwell
(122) Glenn P. Southwell
(123) Gyles B. Southwell
(124) Peter J. Southwell
(125) John McCormack
(126) Ann Guest
(127) Robert Blackhall
(128) Will Linsdell
(129) John Butcher
(130) Ron Baker
(131) James Denslow
(132) Nik Tucker – Happy 50th Birthday
(133) Christopher Wickens
(134) In Memory of The Far Post, Bedford Street, 2003–2005
(135) Mark Thorne
(136) Catherine Jowitt
(137) George Jowitt
(138) Marcus John Munro
(139) Nigel Beer
(140) Ian Andrews
(141) Bill Field
(142) Peter Holding
(143) Nathan Spillings
(144) Andrew Wiseman
(145) Paul Davy
(146) Phil Vigar
(147) Tom Higgins
(148) Ron Harris
(149) In Memory of David White
(150) Ron Page (Grandad)
(151) Chris Clipson
(152) George Edward Prouse
(153) Linda Prouse
(154) Darren Parr
(155) Michael Hinton
(156) Charlotte Braund
(157) James Vickery
(158) Ian Jubb AKA Jubby
(159) Stephen James Morris
(160) Chris Howes
(161) Graeme Lovell
(162) Robert Taylor
(163) Clive Taylor
(164) In Memory of Jeff Taylor
(165) Christopher Morris
(166) Rob Doidge ECFCST
(167) Kevin Bamsey
(168) Dr. David Treharne
(169) Ian Townsend
(170) Wayne C. R. Brice
(171) In Memory of Albert T. Brice
(172) Sally Cooke
(173) Michael Cooke
(174) Stephen Cooke
(175) Rory Driscoll
(176) Andrew Gardner
(177) Ian Totterdell
(178) Steve Rippin & Family
(179) Simon Carnall
(180) Ian Webber
(181) Edward Sowton
(182) The Pidsley Family
(183) Paul Hunkin
(184) Graham Needs
(185) Esko Peltomo
(186) Leonie Welch
(187) Roger Hamilton-Kendall
(188) Exeter City Supporters Club
(189) A.J.J.S. Beer
(190) Ashley Bickham
(191) Richard Cousins
(192) Morris Elliott
(193) Paul Elliott
(194) Quinn George Elliott
(195) Graham Jiggens
(196) Mr Philip H. Wilmot
(197) Miss Fiona Mackay
(198) Christopher Vickery
(199) Jo-Anne Vickery
(200) The Tripp Family
(201) Betty Radford
(202) Thierry Stortenbecker
(203) Theunis Stortenbecker
(204) Timothy Adkin
(205) Martin Weiler
(206) The Wedlake Family
(207) D. R. & A. R. Phillips
(208) John Treleven
(209) Russell Smith
(210) Fullsy (Barry Fulls)
(211) Andy & Margaret Gillard
(212) Jane, Gordon, James & Thomas Souter
(213) Ted & Maureen Liddell
(214) Graham & Jonathan Kirk
(215) Stuart James
(216) Terry Palmer
(217) Stephen Palmer
(218) Sue Perryman
(219) Jim Farrant
(220) Gary Moore
(221) Barry Blackmore
(222) Mike Phillips AKA Colonel
(223) Andrew John Madge
(224) Brian Moore
(225) Sam Bigwood
(226) Red Army Junior Supporters Club
(227) Mick Escott

INTRODUCTION AND ACKNOWLEDGEMENTS

Firstly I would like to thank Exeter City Football Club for their enthusiasm for the book, and therefore being written with their 100 per cent support. In particular, grateful thanks to Paul Morrish and Bruce Henderson, Commercial Director and Business Development Manager respectively.

In writing the book I have constantly referred to the written history of the Grecians, which runs to hundreds of pages, compiled by my late father Jim Blackstone and myself. Without that, it would have taken a lot longer to have completed.

The book covers only selected incidents, matches, players etc. throughout the 104-year history of the club. It has been difficult to decide what to include and leave out as there has been so much material! It is purely my own personal selection. The book is in a chronological format as far as possible.

Much of that material was based on press cuttings, notably from the *Express & Echo*, and to a lesser degree the *Western Morning News*. There were also other sources for historical material, both written and oral (former directors, players, supporters etc.).

I have used various reference books to check documented facts etc., and these are listed in the Recommended Bibliography. Web sites have also proved to be a very useful source of material.

Exeter City match programmes, handbooks and ephemera have formed an invaluable record of the club's history and they have proved to be a constant source of reference.

I would like to thank Steve Perryman MBE, Exeter City's Director of Football, for kindly writing the foreword to the book.

My thanks also go to Tony Ellis, a mine of information about all things Exeter City since the 1950s. I have 'tapped' his knowledge of the club on several occasions during the past few years.

Thank you to Exeter City fan Sarah Willis for painstakingly checking and rechecking proofs and for her invaluable suggestions for changes etc.

Finally, a huge thank you to the 'team' at Kingfisher Print & Design in Totnes, Devon, for their professionalism and undoubted expertise, which is second to none, and also for their patience when handling numerous phone calls and emails from me!

Mike Blackstone, October 2008

There's no place like home! St James' Park, Exeter City F.C.

Imagine the scene. The players of Exeter United and St Sidwell's United are gathered for an end of season social at the Red Lion public house in Sidwell Street, Exeter.

The game of football had grown tremendously in popularity in the previous 12 months, although rugby union was still very much in the ascendancy at the County Ground in Exeter.

However, someone suggested that it would be a good idea to take the next step in promoting football by merging the teams of Exeter United and St Sidwell's and giving the team an identity that could be associated with Devon's premier city – that of Exeter City Football Club.

OK, maybe this is all supposition and there is certainly no firm evidence to suggest one way or the other, however, it is true to say that the plan did go ahead in the summer of 1904 and that the new Exeter City club held its meetings at the Red Lion.

The St Sidwell's club had gone out on a high, with their last appearance of the 1903–04 season being in the final of the East Devon Cup.

The match was actually staged at the County Ground, mainly because it was the only venue in the city big enough to accommodate the expected high numbers going along to the game.

Facing United on Saturday 30th April 1904 were the 110th Battery, and honours went to them as they won 2-1.

Many of the St Sidwell's players were to go on and play for the new Exeter City club and ironically the first game for the City was against ... 110th Battery!

Exeter City had entered the East Devon League and a local newspaper report stated: 'This was City's first engagement for the season and great interest was shown by the Soccerites. A large attendance assembled at St James' Field to witness the encounter.'

City's first-ever team on Saturday 10th September 1904, lined up as follows: Peters, Ashford, Aplin, Wallage, Davidson, Morgan, Sellick, Thomas, Rev. Reid, Eveleigh, Horner.

One familiar name in that fledgling City team was that of Sidney Thomas. He was to be associated with the Grecians for very many years and eventually became the club secretary, after undertaking pretty well every other task.

One aspect of the new club that would horrify present-day supporters of Exeter City was the fact that team wore green and white shirts!

It proved to be a good start for Exeter City as they won 2-1, with goals from Eveleigh and Thomas, and although the Battery pulled a goal back after trailing 2-0 at one stage, luck was on Exeter's side as the 'Soldiers' also contrived to miss a penalty that would have given them a share of the points, had they scored.

Life as Exeter City, and their first-ever season in the East Devon League proved to be a good one, for after just one season they decided to take a step up the local footballing ladder and join the Plymouth and District League.

This was the result of winning the East Devon League championship, sustaining only one defeat all season, that being at the hands of Dawlish who won 4-2 at St James' Field.

Top scorer was Reverend Reid, who in between praying for others, managed to crack 16 goals in just 11 East Devon League outings.

Exeter City Football Club were here to stay! If only they could predict what would happen to them during the next 100-plus years.

SEASON 1904–05 – EAST DEVON SENIOR LEAGUE

Appearances: Morgan 14; Thomas 14; Davidson 13; Peters 13; Sellick 13; Horner 12; Wallage 12; Reid 11; Ashford 10; Russell 10; Eveleigh 9; Campbell 4; Fenwick 4; Andrews 3; Coles 3; Keech 2; Wells 2; Aplin 1; Bailey 1; Henderson 1; Smeath 1; Sturge 1.

Goalscorers: Reid 16; Thomas 12; Sellick 5; Andrews 2; Ashford 1; Coles 1; Davidson 1; Eveleigh 1; Russell 1.

Up until Exeter City joined the Southern League in 1908, the team played its league matches in the East Devon Senior League (1904–05) and the Plymouth and District League (1905–08). However, there were simply not enough teams in either competition to enable a full season of matches to be staged.

As a result there were numerous friendlies arranged by City, some against well-known sides of the time, others less so, and slightly unusual perhaps, including the likes of the 1st Rifle Brigade and the Plymouth Garrison Choir!

In the very first season of the club's existence, City played no fewer than 17 friendlies, commencing with a 5-0 home thrashing of Torquay United on 24th September 1904. Indeed, the Grecians were to lose just two of the 17 matches, being beaten 3-0 at the 112th Battery Royal Artillery and also 3-0 at Holsworthy.

There were some high-scoring matches, notably, 8-0 wins over the North Devon School and the 111th Battery Royal Artillery. The Plymouth Garrison Choir were definitely not on song as City won 6-3 at St James' Park, and they also beat Torquay United by the same score.

Add to those impressive scorelines the 6-2 home win over Friernhay and a 5-1 romp over the Devon County School at the Park, it was pretty obvious that the City team were more than a match for their friendly opponents!

Onto season 1905–06, and whilst the team were finishing in sixth place in the Plymouth and District League, there were also a further 19 friendlies staged. The opposition must have been a lot tougher than the previous season for City suffered defeat in no fewer than seven of them, although on occasions they played anything but their first-choice team.

They suffered a humiliating 6-1 defeat at home to an East Devon League XI on 9th December 1905, and St Luke's also managed to win 4-1 on their own ground.

On the positive side, City recorded a 6-2 home win over the Royal Marines and did even better on their visit to Holsworthy, where they won 7-2. They played neighbours Exmouth United for the first time on 13th January 1906 and defeated the 'Seasiders' 4-1.

With more matches being played in the Plymouth and District League in 1906–07, a season in which the Grecians finished in ninth place, there were only 11 friendlies played, two of which were staged at the County Ground, Exeter against Green Waves (on Christmas Day – City winning 3-2) and the 15th Brigade Royal Artillery (the 'Soldiers' winning 6-3).

The best win of the season came on the road at Barnstaple on 22nd September 1906, with City winning 7-0, one of just four matches that they did win, the others being against Taunton Casuals, Friernhay and the previously mentioned festive success against Green Waves, who were a Plymouth-based team.

So onto the last season as a truly amateur club – 1907–08 – before the Grecians took the bold step of joining the Southern League. With a fifth place in the Plymouth and District League, City arranged nine friendly matches, and again one was played at the County Ground, Exeter, that being a 3-3 draw against an East Devon XI, once more played on Christmas Day.

Only two matches were to end in defeats as the 1st Rifle Brigade won 3-1 at St James' Park on 28th September 1907, and the 15th Brigade Royal Artillery also triumphed at the Park, winning 3-1.

Goalscoring, unlike previous seasons' friendly encounters, was a bit more restrained, and the best victory recorded by Exeter City was a 4-1 home win over Exmouth United.

Once the Grecians entered the Southern League in 1908, there was a full programme of matches to fulfil and virtually no friendly matches at all were played, although the reserve team did undertake such games from time to time.

With the County Ground in St Thomas, Exeter, now a memory, so with it went a little of the long and varied history of Exeter City Football Club.

Traditionally the home of Exeter Rugby Club and for many years the Exeter Falcons Speedway team, the Grecians used the stadium for several matches in their early years.

Apart from St James' Park, the County Ground has the distinction of being the only other venue where home matches were played by Exeter City, unlike many other clubs who have moved from ground to ground.

It was as far back as 24th April 1905 that Exeter City first used the County Ground for a home fixture.

That was to welcome a team from Plymouth called 'Triumph' in a friendly fixture. It proved to be no triumph for the visitors though, as City ran out 2-0 winners.

Their first competitive fixture played there was an F.A. Cup fifth qualifying round replay against Stoke in 1909.

Having drawn the first match 0-0 in the Potteries, the replay was unable to be staged at St James' Park due to the ongoing alterations being made to the grandstand, therefore it was off to the County Ground.

An attendance of 5,500 saw yet another stalemate as the teams drew 1-1. City's goal was netted by former Chorley player, Percy Hartley.

The third meeting was played on the neutral ground of Craven Cottage, Fulham, where Exeter lost 2-1.

Controversy reigned the following season – 1910–11 – when it was found that the pitch at the Park did not meet the minimum required length and therefore teams objected to playing there in the F.A. Cup.

First to do so were Reading for a fourth qualifying round replay. After the teams had drawn 1-1, the replay went back to the County Ground.

Ironically with just ten minutes of the tie remaining to be played and the sides locked at one goal apiece, the match was abandoned due to an

Exeter City played a handful of matches at the County Gorund, home of the Exeter Rugby Club. The photograph shows the County Ground just prior to its recent demolition. (Martin Weiler)

ever-thickening bank of fog that had descended on the area.

Five days later, on 28th November 1910, the teams were back at the County Ground and this time the Grecians booked their place in the next round with a 1-0 win and a goal from Spencer Bassett.

City's next opponents were Nelson, at home, who also refused, as was their right, to play at St James' Park.

Exeter Rugby Club saved the day once more and offered the use of their ground where goals from Archie Hughes (2), Bob Watson and Edwin Jones gave City a 4-3 win over their Lancashire visitors. It would be the last time that City played at the County Ground.

The Grecians were then paired with Burnley, and despite lengthening the St James' Park pitch at the Big Bank end, the Turf Moor club still refused to play there and also turned down the alternative venue of the County Ground.

City therefore had little alternative but to switch the tie to Burnley, giving up home advantage, and in doing so lost 2-0.

Great interest centred on Exeter City's Plymouth and District League match with Millbrook Rangers on Saturday 14th December 1907.

It was purely due to the fact that the City were fielding former West Bromwich Albion and Plymouth Argyle wing-half, Jack Banks, and thus it was first time that the team had used a professional player in their ranks.

Professionalism had arrived very quickly at Exeter City, for only the previous season they had at times been relying on players stationed at the nearby Topsham Barracks to make up the numbers for some of their games.

There was some doubt as to whether the registration forms for the player would be received in time to permit Banks to make his debut; however, on the morning of the match the all clear was given.

Banks went on to feature in 17 matches for the City, two of which were in the Southern League in 1908–09.

Born in West Bromwich in May 1874, Banks had played for Oldbury Broadwell before joining West Bromwich Albion in 1893.

He stayed with the Albion for seven years making 119 appearances and scoring five goals. In 1901–02 he linked up with Newton Heath (later to become Manchester United) where he featured in 40 matches. From there he signed for Plymouth Argyle, and then onto Exeter City.

It wasn't the ideal day weather wise, for heavy rain had turned the pitch into a sea of mud. The expected higher than usual attendance didn't materialise either with the inclement weather putting a lot of people off.

Goalless at half-time, Millbrook then took the lead 15 minutes into the second half, before the game turned into pure farce!

A few minutes after the goal was scored, the game was abandoned, not because of the weather, or the state of the pitch, but due to the fact that there was a problem with the balls being used.

Two balls had burst in the pre-match warm up and then a third one met the same fate during the course of the match.

The referee, Sergeant Major Adams, waited impatiently for City officials to find another ball, but none was forthcoming.

The Millbrook players elated over their one goal lead, questioned the referee as to how long he was going to wait before the game could no longer be restarted and were told ten minutes.

Unfortunately the ten minutes passed, and still no sign of a replacement ball, which left the referee with no alternative but to abandon the game.

The Millbrook team immediately left the field, and the crowd, disgusted with what had happened, made their way out of St James' Park.

As they did so, lo and behold, the City officials had somehow managed to procure another ball, but it was simply too late.

The local newspaper report stated: 'It was the most ridiculous farce ever known at St James' Park and the City management are greatly to blame for their failure to provide for an emergency, when two balls burst in the practice kick about before the start of the game.

'The Rangers will no doubt claim the points and the matter will have to be settled at a meeting of the Plymouth and District League to be held in Plymouth.'

The one redeeming feature of the afternoon was that Banks was described as showing every promise of being a fine 'general' for the team and would be just the man that Exeter City wanted to assist with improvement to the side.

A few weeks later the Plymouth and District League announced their verdict as regards to the abandoned match at the Park, and ordered the game to be replayed with Exeter City to pay the expenses incurred by Millbrook Rangers.

The rearranged match was played at St James' Park on 14th March 1908 and there was no repeat of not being enough balls available as Massey scored a hat-trick for City, as they won 3-0.

A public meeting was held in April 1908 to gauge the interest of Exeter City Football Club becoming a fully professional club and to apply to enter the Southern League. A report of the meeting appears below:

'The promoters of the Exeter City professional team could not have wished for a better or more enthusiastic public meeting, which was held in the Royal Public Rooms at the bottom of Northernhay Place, Exeter.'

Captain F.J. Harvey presided, and was supported on the platform by the Reverend Philip Williams, Messrs Nat Whittaker (Secretary of the Southern League), R. Knight (Secretary of the London League), R.F. Davis (Chairman of Plymouth Argyle), Louis Crabbe (Secretary of Plymouth Argyle), Sydney Cole and J. Jacques (both of Plymouth Argyle), E. Arnfield (Southampton F.C.), J. Skeggs (Millwall F.C.), Mr Robinson (Sports Traffic Manager, Great Western Railway), Mr Bickford (Great Western Railway), J.T. Howcroft (well-known referee of Bolton) and Exeter City representatives – Mr M.J. McGahey, Norman Kendall, W. Fenwick, A.M. Alford, T. Oliver, A. Collingwood and Sydney Thomas.

The hall was packed some time before the start, the interval being occupied with musical selections by the City Orchestra.

The chairman read letters from those regretting absence from the meeting, as well as one from Mr F.T. Wall (Secretary of the Football Association), who wished the scheme every success and said that 'a professional team in the city would no doubt popularise soccer throughout the entirety of East Devon'.

Mr Crabbe told the meeting that ever since he had brought the Argyle Reserves to Exeter three years ago for the first time, he was struck by the possibilities of professional soccer in East Devon. It was said that the public want first-class soccer and the first step towards that was taken when Exeter City engaged Jack Banks as a professional player-coach.

Mr Skeggs pointed out that in general Cathedral centres were not good sporting centres, but now he was convinced that the city of Exeter was an exception.

The enthusiasm of the meeting showed it and the presence of the Reverend Williams on the

The first Exeter City professional squad of players: 1908–09
Back row: Arthur Chadwick (Manager), Albert Ambler, Joe Bulcock, James Fletcher, John Crelley, Jack Banks, Levi Copestake, William Wake.
Middle row: Tom Drain, Thomas Craig, Samuel Johnson, Robert Watson, Andrew McGuigan, James Bell, Thomas White.
Front row: Herbert Tierney, Frederick Parnell.

platform, he regarded as a particularly healthy sign. 'Get the parsons with you', remarked Mr Skeggs (amid loud laughter) 'and you are bound to succeed!'

He went on to give facts and figures as a comparison to other clubs, such as Swindon Town and said that Exeter City could therefore easily make a Southern League club pay its way.

Nat Whittaker pointed out that if Exeter City made friends with the Great Western Railway Company, they might get substantial help from them as regards special excursion trains to matches, both home and away.

Whittaker added that he saw the fine prospect of a first-class club in Exeter, and candidly speaking, he might say at once that he would use his influence in the direction that the Exeter public would like.

Exeter City's Norman Kendall proposed the following motion:

'That this representative meeting of the Citizens of Exeter pledges its support to the Exeter City Football and Athletic Company Limited in its endeavour to enter the professional Southern League.'

The Reverend Williams seconded the motion and spoke of the growth of soccer in recent years in Exeter. The resolution was carried unanimously.

It was said that the City promoters can therefore now proceed in the full and complete assurance that the club will secure admission to the First Division of the Southern League, providing that at the meeting of the League they provide proof of the possession of a suitable ground, financial support and a strong team.

The meeting of the Southern League was held at the Charterhouse Hotel in London, on Friday 29th May 1908 and Exeter City were duly elected to the competition.

There were five vacancies and six applicants, namely, Leyton, New Brompton, Exeter City, Croydon, Southend United and Coventry City. The voting went as follows: Exeter City 33; Leyton 32; New Brompton 31; Southend United 26; Coventry City 25; Croydon 10.

Norman Kendall put forward Exeter City's case at the meeting and had made a good impression with his report on the team and the ground, and remarked that the club had the assistance of the Great Western Railway, and were the club elected they would be ever loyal to the Southern League.

EXETER CITY'S RESULTS – SOUTHERN LEAGUE 1908–09

Sep 2	Millwall	A	2-2		Feb 27	Brighton & H.A.	H	1-0
Sep 5	Bristol Rovers	H	3-3		Mar 6	Crystal Palace	A	0-0
Sep 12	Watford	A	1-3		Mar 8	Southend United	H	2-1
Sep 19	Norwich City	H	3-2		Mar 10	Plymouth Argyle	A	0-4
Sep 26	Reading	A	2-1		Mar 13	Brentford	H	1-2
Oct 7	Swindon Town	A	1-2		Mar 17	Swindon Town	H	1-4
Oct 10	Leyton	A	2-4		Mar 20	Luton Town	A	2-0
Oct 14	Southampton	H	1-2		Mar 22	Coventry City	A	1-0
Oct 24	Brighton & H.A.	A	2-1		Mar 24	Southend United	A	0-0
Oct 31	Crystal Palace	H	1-1		Apr 1	West Ham United	A	1-4
Nov 11	Plymouth Argyle	H	2-1		Apr 3	Portsmouth	A	0-2
Nov 14	Luton Town	H	2-1		Apr 13	Southampton	A	0-2
Nov 16	Brentford	A	2-0		Apr 17	Northampton Town	H	2-1
Nov 28	Portsmouth	H	4-1		Apr 21	West Ham United	H	1-0
Dec 12	Northampton Town	A	0-1		Apr 24	New Brompton	A	1-3
Dec 19	New Brompton	H	1-3					
Dec 25	Millwall	H	2-1					
Jan 2	Bristol Rovers	A	1-5					
Jan 9	Watford	H	1-0					
Jan 23	Norwich City	A	0-2					
Jan 30	Reading	H	5-1					
Feb 8	Coventry City	H	0-3					
Feb 13	Leyton	H	3-1					
Feb 20	Queens Park Rangers	A	1-1					
Feb 24	Queens Park Rangers	H	1-0					

City appearances (Southern League only):
Bell 39; Watson 39; Craig 38; Ambler 35; Copestake 32; Wake 30; Parnell 29; Robinson 29; McGuigan 28; Bulcock 23; Johnson 23; Chadwick 19; White 19; Crelley 18; Drain 14; Fletcher 11; Tierney 11; Banks 2; Plant 1.
City goalscorers (Southern League only):
Bell 22; McGuigan 16; Copestake 6; Watson 6; Parnell 3; Chadwick 2; Drain 1.

Arthur Chadwick was given the task of taking Exeter City into the professional era as manager of the team that was elected to the Southern League in 1908.

A former England centre-half, Chadwick had many contacts in Lancashire, having been born in Church, near Accrington, and it was from that county that many players came to Devon during his 14-year reign as Grecians' boss.

His first task was to assemble a side capable of playing in the Southern League for the 1908–09 season, and this he did with remarkable speed, relying heavily on northern players.

As well as having played for England, making his debut against Wales in 1900, Chadwick had also worn the colours of Church, Accrington, Burton Swifts, Portsmouth, Southampton and Northampton Town.

He continued to play in his first two seasons as manager at St James' Park, making his debut in a 3-2 home win over Norwich City in September 1908, scoring one of the goals from the penalty spot.

Chadwick was actually known as 'Advisor' rather than manager for the first two seasons at the Park. He gained the title of 'Manager' in the summer of 1910.

His last league outing for Exeter was against Plymouth Argyle in a Boxing Day fixture at St James' Park in 1911. This was his only appearance that season, and City lost 1-0.

The City team ended their first season as a professional club by finishing in 19th place in the Southern League, which considering the huge jump in playing status was quite respectable.

It was a constant battle for Chadwick to build a team at Exeter City with finances, or the lack of them, dictating what he could or could not do.

With the First World War calling a halt to competitive football until 1919–20, Chadwick had to virtually rebuild from scratch again, and the fact that the club was quickly accepted into the Football League made it an even more daunting task.

Unfortunately it was still a struggle off the field as players were sold to balance the books. Legendary goalkeeper Dick Pym departed for Bolton Wanderers, although the fee received for him didn't go back into the playing budget, but was used to purchase St James' Park outright instead.

Centre-forward Billy Goodwin was another City

Arthur Chadwick.

player to depart for financial reasons, as Chadwick managed to sell him to Manchester United.

The departure of star players meant that Chadwick become disillusioned with life at Exeter City, and after a couple of indifferent seasons in the Football League, he decided to relinquish the post of manager in December 1922.

After leaving the Grecians, Chadwick became manager of Reading in January 1923, a post he held until October 1925. He was then appointed manager at Southampton the same month and stayed at The Dell until May 1931.

One of the best achievements of his managerial career was taking Southampton to the semi-finals of the F.A. Cup in 1927.

He is still in the record books as the longest serving manager ever at Exeter, and did much to promote the Grecians in the early formative years as a professional club.

Chadwick retained a strong link with Exeter City and occasionally watched them in later years. It was whilst sitting in the grandstand at St James' Park for a City match against Clapton Orient in March 1936 that he sadly died.

His name will always live on, however, as the man who guided the club from being a humble Plymouth and District League outfit to a Football League team.

Wouldn't it be great if you were able to travel back in time for perhaps just a few hours, giving you an opportunity to watch an Exeter City match played in their very first season of professional football in 1908?

It is an era that is none too well documented, for even the club minute books for those pioneering days seem to have disappeared – even though they were definitely in existence in the 1990s.

They would certainly make fascinating reading to any historian of the club and provide a valuable insight as to what life was like at St James' Park.

Imagine going back to that historic first home match in the Southern League, when Bristol Rovers were the visitors on 5th September 1908.

You would take your place on the rudimentary terraces or banking along with 8,000 other football fans, keen to get their first glimpse of the professional game at the ground.

The Grecians had already opened their Southern League campaign three days earlier and had got off to an excellent start as they shared the spoils at Millwall, drawing 2-2.

Both City goals were netted by James Bell – otherwise known as 'Daisy' – a player who was to become the fans' first goalscoring legend. Imagine the modern-day chants had he been playing now – 'Daisy, Daisy give us a wave'!

So what would you have found at St James' Park in 1908? Well, it would certainly have been very different to what we have today.

A wooden grandstand, where the current 'old grandstand' is now, a structure that was to be consumed by a disastrous fire in 1925.

The covered Big Bank terrace was nothing more than shale banking and much shallower than the modern-day version.

The banking was extended at the same time as the pitch was lengthened to meet the minimum requirements so that F.A. Cup matches could be staged at the Park.

Flybe (the stand named after the company), and indeed the concept of air travel as we know it today, was unheard of and along that side of the pitch was a small covered area, which was not

Flat-capped City supporters.

extended for many years, into what then became known as the Cowshed.

For quite some time that area was known as the Flowerpot Stand, although it would be fascinating to know why!

There is no record or account of quite what the St James' Road end of the ground was like, although there was certainly standing accommodation for matches.

One of the houses overlooking the ground was used by the club directors' wives, who were not allowed inside the hallowed confines of the boardroom. How times have changed!

The other thing you would notice with great certainty, would be the lack of females in general, for the crowd would consist almost entirely of men, with the majority wearing their trademark flat caps.

There are several excellent postcards in existence of 'crowd scenes' at St James' Park, and all are an example of how the sales of hats and caps must have been a highly profitable business!

So, we are back at St James' Park for the game between Exeter City and Bristol Rovers. The score? Well, there were plenty of goals. Six of them. But they were shared between the teams, so another draw.

Fred Parnell, who had been signed from Leeds City (a club long gone out of existence), scored twice for Exeter, whilst the other goalscorer was former Woolwich Arsenal forward, Bob Watson.

To score double figures in any match is an achievement, but for Exeter City it came very early in their existence, the very first season the club had entered the F.A. Cup, and the first tie that they took part in.

The unfortunate opponents were Weymouth, who visited St James' Park for a first qualifying round tie on 3rd October 1908.

The Grecians had made a very good start in what was their first season as a professional club, playing in the Southern League.

An attendance of around 5,000 was present at the Park, and none of the spectators could have forecast what they were about to witness.

The local newspaper report stated: 'Exeter City's first venture into the English Cup was farcical in the extreme. The play resolved itself into a continual and long drawn out bombardment of the Weymouth goal.'

By half-time City were leading 10-0! They added another four goals without reply in the second half with every one of the forward line netting at least once as the 14-0 scoreline remains to this day the club's record win in the F.A. Cup.

Up until that point, only Preston North End, Wanderers, Bristol Rovers, Darwen, Notts County, Queens Park and Royal Engineers had scored more goals in an F.A. Cup tie than Exeter City.

The Grecians lined up: James Fletcher, Thomas Craig, Joseph Bulcock, Albert Ambler, Arthur Chadwick, William Wake, Frederick Parnell, Robert Watson, Andrew McGuigan, James Bell, Levi Copestake.

Bell scored six goals, and there were four for McGuigan, two for Copestake and one each for Parnell and Watson.

In the next round – the second qualifying – City travelled to Dorset side Longfleet St Mary's, and drew 1-1.

Then for the replay they once again hit double figures as they hammered Longfleet 10-1, with the scorers being Watson (3), McGuigan (2), Bell (2), Copestake, Johnson and an own goal.

The Grecians went on to enjoy a good run in the cup, beating Whiteheads 4-0 in the third qualifying round at the Park, and then going to Bristol club Kingswood Rovers in the following round, where they won 2-0.

In the fifth qualifying round they made their longest trip so far, winning 3-0 at Barnet Alston, thus booking themselves a place in the first round proper, which was quite an achievement.

After drawing 1-1 at Wrexham, Exeter then proceeded to beat them in the replay back at the Park, winning 2-1.

Round two of the cup and a local derby, as the Grecians made the short trip to Plymouth Argyle, where the Home Park club ended the Grecians' adventure by winning 2-0.

Exeter City would have to wait until the 1913–14 season before they again reached round two of the F.A. Cup, but by then they didn't have to battle their way through the qualifying stages, instead entering the competition in the first round proper.

CITY'S F.A. CUP MATCHES 1908–09

First qualifying round:
Exeter City 14 Weymouth 0
City scorers: Bell 6, McGuigan 4, Copestake 2, Watson, Purnell.

Second qualifying round:
Longfleet St Mary 1 Exeter City 1
City scorer: Copestake.

Second qualifying round replay:
Exeter City 10 Longfleet St Mary 1
City scorers: Watson 3, McGuigan 2, Bell 2, Copestake, Johnson, own goal.

Third qualifying round:
Exeter City 4 Whiteheads of Weymouth 0
City scorers: Watson 2, Chadwick, McGuigan.

Fourth qualifying round:
Kingswood Rovers 0 Exeter City 2
City scorers: McGuigan, Watson.

Fifth qualifying round:
Barnet Alston 0 Exeter City 3
City scorers: Bell, Parnell, Chadwick.

Round one: Wrexham 1 Exeter City 1
City scorer: Watson.

Round one replay: Exeter City 2 Wrexham 1
City scorers: Chadwick, McGuigan.

Round two: Plymouth Argyle 2 Exeter City 0

There have been good ones, bad ones, tall ones, short ones, unforgettable ones. Goalkeeper is the one position where you cannot afford to make a mistake, for it inevitably leads to the opposition taking advantage. Some Exeter City keepers have been a little eccentric as well, such as Jack Robinson.

The former England international played for the club during its first professional season in 1908 and was something of a character to say the least. He was no friend of referees, for he had the habit of disputing their decisions.

One one occasion, after conceding a goal, Robinson walked out to the referee on the halfway line to protest to him, saying that an opposition player had been offside.

Robinson was told to return to his goal by the official, but before he did so, the charismatic keeper promptly picked the ball up and kicked it over the St James' Park grandstand and out of the ground, amid much laughter from the supporters.

Surely today, if he had done that, a red card would have been the certain outcome. However, on this occasion the referee decided that all was needed was a severe lecture.

Robinson also had the rather strange super-stition of having to eat rice pudding before games. This he said, was to avoid the repetition of the occasion when he conceded eight goals at Sunderland! One assumes that he forgot to eat his rice pudding that day!

Outfield players have on a number of occasions replaced goalkeepers for one reason or another whilst playing for Exeter City. It is doubtful, however, if anyone will beat the record held by City winger Charlie McClelland.

He first took over as goalkeeper when Barney Singleton was injured in City's match at Bournemouth on Friday 23rd March 1951. There were no substitute keepers then. The game ended 1-1.

Just eight days later Singleton was again injured at Norwich City, and once more McClelland stood in between the posts. Exeter lost 2-0.

The following month, 14th April, McClelland was called on yet again to keep goal, this time for only the final two minutes of the City reserves fixture at home to Tonbridge, when Ken Salter sustained an injury. City won 1-0.

The McClelland goalkeeping saga did not end there though. The City winger must have performed so well between the posts that he actually volunteered to play in goal for a complete game when the Grecians' reserves were short of their usual choice.

He took to the field as goalkeeper when City played a Southern League fixture at Merthyr Tydfil on 14th February 1953. Perhaps he may have had second thoughts about changing positions permanently from winger to that of goalkeeper, however, as the Welshmen ran out 7-0 winners!

One City goalkeeper who achieved the opposite of McClelland was Alan Barnett. The Grecians were so short of recognised forwards in April 1965 that keeper Barnett played centre-forward in their Western League fixture at Weston-Super-Mare. City lost 3-1. The Exeter scorer? ... Yes, it was Barnett!

Another scoring goalkeeper was Grecian trainee Jamie Day. He made a substitute appearance in the club's reserves South West Counties League fixture at Swansea City in November 1989, after just four minutes of play. He replaced the injured Ben Rowe and went on to score one of the City goals in a 2-2 draw.

Goalkeeper John Smout almost 'scored' a crazy own goal to end all own goals. Smout who played for City between 1966 and 1968 went to throw the ball to a colleague. Somehow though he just managed to throw it towards his own net as he bowled his arm around. Fortunately he raced back quick enough to dive on the ball before it entered the net, thus preventing a very embarrassing moment.

Goalkeeper Richard Smeath was pressed into service as one of the substitutes in Exeter City's match at Leyton Orient in October 1988. Defender Scott Hiley failed a late fitness test and striker Jamie Harris was taken ill on the journey to London.

This left City with just eleven outfield players and two goalkeepers in the travelling party. Smeath, who was not called upon, did not make another first-team Football League appearance and was subsequently released.

In 2007, a team of consultants was brought in by Exeter City Football Club to investigate the implications and costings of the club either remaining at St James' Park for the long term, or moving to a new stadium, including the possibility of ground sharing with the Exeter Chiefs.

Talk of moving ground is of course not new, nor is the possible ground share with City's rugby counterparts.

As long ago as 1908, when Exeter City became a professional outfit and joined the Southern League, there was much discussion then as to whether St James' Park would be a suitable venue at which to stage games.

Mention of moving the club to the County Ground, home of the rugby club, was suggested, although it was felt that this would be morally wrong, even though football had been played there, as rugby was firmly established.

St James' Park was developed to meet the necessary standard for Southern League football, and Exeter City have remained there ever since.

More recently, in 1990, the possibility of selling St James' Park and moving to a brand new stadium on the outskirts of the city was discussed.

Plans to move to Matford Marshes were thrown out by the city council following objections, and a move to the Exeter Arena athletics stadium was even mooted, but not progressed.

Had it not been for the intervention of the city Member of Parliament in the 1910–11 season, then City may well have been playing at a completely different venue by now.

It had been discovered that the St James' Park pitch was not long enough to stage F.A. Cup ties and games were either switched to the County Ground or the ground of City's opponents.

The club had no joy persuading landowners behind what became known as the Duke Bank, and latterly the Big Bank, to sell some of their land so that the pitch could be lengthened.

However, Mr Duke, Member of Parliament for Exeter, intervened and his persuasive powers were successful, which resulted in the lengthened pitch being used for the first time in a game against West Ham United in the Third Division South.

Ten years later the football club purchased St James' Park outright for the princely sum of £5,000 – what would it be worth today?

They were able to do so thanks to receiving a sizeable transfer fee for goalkeeper Dick Pym, who joined Bolton Wanderers.

Since then, of course, City have gone through the well-documented near collapse of the club; the sale of the ground to Beazer Homes and then on to Exeter City Council, who undoubtedly kept the club in existence by purchasing the land.

Despite suggestions over the years that Exeter City might move to a new ground, they still play at St James' Park.
(www.cheggerspics.co.uk)

Exeter City have endured many occasions when they have had to battle against financial troubles, not least of course prior to the takeover of the club by the Exeter City Supporters' Trust.

But long, long before that, as early as the summer of 1911, there were very real fears for the future of the club, which had only been formed seven years before and had only played three seasons as a full professional outfit in the Southern League.

Rumours surfaced about the club's perilous financial position shortly after the 1910–11 season had ended and it was suggested that the very future of Exeter City was a gloomy one.

The club tried its best to dispel the rumours by stating that the financial position, whilst a 'problematical one' was no worse than 12 months earlier.

The proposal was that no players were to be re-engaged by the club thus saving on summer wages up until August 1911, but this unfortunately didn't meet with the 100 per cent approval of manager Arthur Chadwick, who delayed signing a new deal with the Grecians because of it.

Chadwick felt it was imposing an unfair responsibility to ask him at the end of July, when every other club had signed players, to seek further players of sufficient quality for City who would keep the flag flying as far as Southern League football was concerned at St James' Park.

There simply was not enough income to enable the players to be paid during the summer months. However, once the story became public knowledge, the supporters rallied round and at a well-attended meeting nearly £100 was promised towards the wages. Shortly afterwards it was reported that a further £160 was forthcoming.

The difficulties for the club, however, didn't end there, for the pitch at St James' Park was a few feet short of the required dimensions for F.A. Cup ties, which was one cause of the financial problems, as any 'home' fixture had to be either switched to their opponent's ground or moved to the County Ground in Exeter, thus causing a reduction in income.

Efforts to secure a strip of land at the Old Tiverton Road end of the ground had proved to be unsuccessful, as the owner would only sell all the land, or none at all.

The club therefore had to face up to the fact that they wouldn't be able to stage F.A. Cup ties at St James' Park, and even considered the possibility of moving to County Ground, which would become their home ground.

Then Mr Duke came to the rescue and through his good offices the club were able to add 20 feet to the length of the St James' Park pitch by means of buying the previously mentioned land.

Mr Duke was asked to nominate someone to represent him on the Exeter City board of directors and the choice fell upon Mr F.G. Hill, who for many years had been involved with the game of football in the city of Exeter.

Suffice to say that Mr Duke had come to City's aid when no one else did as regards the problem with the pitch. He certainly earned the gratitude of Exeter City, and by his timely action, together with the finance raised by supporters to meet the summer wage bill, the outlook for season 1911–12 was far better than it had been just a couple of months or so previous.

The *Express & Echo* reported: 'Exeter City stands at the threshold of what should prove to be a new era in its affairs, and for that reason interest in the coming season's doings will be much more acute than public interest has previously been.'

The club had even introduced its first-ever mascot as the *Echo* added: 'Several prominent football clubs had gone in for adopting pet dogs as "mascots." Exeter City are one such club and the new mascot is a large English sheepdog called "Laddie" which is owned by City goalkeeper Walter Whittaker.'

Like many football clubs, Exeter City have unfortunately had to endure crowd problems during their history, although thankfully it is a very rare occurrence.

As early as September 1910, the Grecians were ordered to post warning notices around the St James' Park ground by the Football League following an incident involving the Crystal Palace team.

They had been pelted with mud as they left the Park on their way back to St David's Railway Station by a group described in the local press as 'rowdy youths'.

The local Constabulary had to intervene at the Exeter City versus Aston Villa F.A. Cup tie in January 1914. An hour before kick off a fight broke out between two people on the Shilling Bank – now the Big Bank. The persons involved were described as 'having a lively two rounds before the Police got to them'.

It was a case of the opposition not being too benevolent when during the City reserves 8-1 win over Plymouth Argyle in a friendly match at St James' Park, a spectator jumped the railings onto the pitch.

He had been incensed by a series of alleged heavy tackles on City players. The spectator was quickly removed by a rather persuasive policeman.

The game was being played to raise funds for the Football League Jubilee Benevolent Fund! Passions don't run quite so high these days when the Grecians and Argyle meet at reserve team level.

On another occasion an irate spectator had to be restrained by several policemen and the two trainers as he invaded the pitch and made an attempt to reach an Exeter City defender during their cup tie against Bournemouth and Boscombe Athletic in November 1946.

A serious fracas took place in front of the main grandstand at the East Devon Divisional Cup Final played at the Park between The Loyals and The Royal Navy Transport Depot on 21st April 1945.

After the final whistle, players indulged in a free for all. Spectators became involved and the referee was pushed to the ground. Several received injuries during the fight before order was eventually restored.

Warning notices had to be posted at the ground again on the orders of the Football League, both in 1948 and 1955.

The former incident occurred when missiles were thrown at match referee, Mr Walkely, who had ordered off Exeter City forward Ron Johnston for attempting to strike an opponent.

Seven years later Aldershot centre-half Charles Billington was struck by a spectator as he entered the tunnel for the half-time break at St James' Park. Several other spectators had to be restrained during the unsavoury incident.

Exeter City secretary Dick Miller wrote the following in the match programme for the home game against Swindon Town in October 1965:

'At St James' Park we have always been proud of the conduct of our supporters, but more recently I have been concerned about the behaviour here, such as the throwing of toilet rolls, slow hand clapping etc. Let me give fair warning to those people inclined towards such action that the Police have strict instructions to remove from the ground anyone who is seen to throw toilet rolls onto the pitch.'

During the 1970s and 1980s, football hooliganism became a major problem all over the country, and Exeter City did not escape this unwanted infiltration of a minority group, who captured all the headlines.

Some of the worst scenes ever witnessed at St James' Park followed the F.A. Cup tie with Wolverhampton Wanderers in 1978. Visiting fans invaded the pitch, broke the crossbar at the Big Bank end of the ground and then set about smashing windows of various properties outside the ground.

A number of incidents that resulted in unacceptable injuries to police officers occurred during the Exeter City versus Bristol Rovers match in January 1984.

This again started with an end-of-match pitch invasion as the Rovers contingent rushed the Cowshed where City supporters had been standing.

Cardiff City supporters have twice been involved in crowd problems. After the home match against the Welshmen in November 1985, some of the visiting fans damaged grandstand seats, invaded the pitch and then tried to get hold of their own team manager, who had to be escorted back to the dressing room by police.

In September of the following year, 21 arrests were made before, during and after the Cardiff game, again at the Park, as numerous incidents took place mainly outside the ground.

The Exeter City board of directors decided they had enough. They were so disgusted that the Cardiff fans were immediately banned from future matches at St James' Park.

The ban of Cardiff fans by Exeter City was later lifted as the football hooliganism problems generally subsided. Even neighbours Torquay United had banned the Cardiff fans, so Devon had become something of a no-go area for them for a short time.

A packed St James' Park – and no sign of trouble! (www.cheggerspics.co.uk)

Exeter City recorded their then record Southern League score, winning 8-1, as they trounced Kent side, New Brompton at St James' Park on 9th September 1911.

In later years the New Brompton club's name was changed to the now more familiar Gillingham.

This was the second game of the season for the Grecians, having started off by drawing 0-0 at Watford, and they fielded an unchanged line up as follows:

Walter Whittaker, Nolan Evans, Arthur Coates, Spencer Bassett, Charlie Pratt, Fred Prideaux, Enos Whittaker, Robert Watson, Arthur Rutter, Henry Lockett, James Garside.

The afternoon was notable for the fact that work had been undertaken on the ground and the match report of the day noted:

'Naturally a great deal of interest was taken in the huge alterations which have already been effected at the lower end. The trees have gone, and excavations have been carried out half way across.'

The 6,000 crowd could not have predicted that they were to see nine goals scored, eight of them by the Grecians.

City could not have made a better start after they took the lead in just 30 seconds when Watson's powerful shot, although parried by the keeper, was still strong enough to end up in the net.

Five minutes later New Brompton were rocked when they conceded a second, Watson again scoring when following up after his initial shot had been blocked by the keeper.

Exeter were well on top, playing some excellent football and it was 3-0 after 15 minutes when Rutter fired home an unstoppable shot.

The visitors looked a demoralised side and fell further into arrears as Rutter finished off a cross from Enos Whittaker.

Amazingly there was still time before the interval for City to make it 5-0, Watson completing his hat-trick after a mesmerising run that took him past three defenders.

There was one glimmer of hope for the Kent side in the 35th minute as they reduced the arrears

City supporters waiting for kick off, standing in front of the main grandstand at St James' Park, believed to be prior to the year 1914.

through Whiteside, and shortly afterwards they almost scored again when Westwood's shot skimmed the top of the crossbar.

The second half was a case of New Brompton trying to stem the tide and limiting further 'damage'. But they still conceded another three goals.

The sixth City goal saw Lockett hit a rising shot into the net. Garside got their seventh with a lobbed effort over the keeper's head, and the same player netted again with a header from Whittaker's cross.

Whiteside, who was the visitors' best player, won a penalty in the closing minutes when he was tripped in the area, but although he took the spot-kick himself, it was a very poor effort that Whittaker had no trouble in comfortably saving.

The 8-1 scoreline was easily the best of the season for the Grecians, but the early-season optimism failed to materialise during the rest of the campaign and indeed City were to win only three more Southern League fixtures out of the next 20.

Needless to say City eventually finished low down in the league table, in 15th place, whilst New Brompton ended their season three places below them, despite winning the return meeting back in Kent by 4-1, to at least gain some revenge for the heavy beating at St James' Park.

The very thought of it, let alone seeing photographic evidence, is enough to put every die-hard Grecian off their food for days.

But there is no getting away from the fact that Exeter City did play in green and white in their early years of existence.

Quite why the committee of the club chose the same colours as those worn by a football team representing the other city in Devon is indeed strange.

However, thankfully the club did eventually see sense and decided on an identity of their own, thus changing the colour of the shirts worn by the City players.

It wasn't until November 1910 that the green and white was ditched, following a deputation by some of the players who felt that green was proving to be unlucky.

The directors made what had become an excellent choice, as they opted for red and white striped shirts, which were worn for the very first time for a Southern League fixture against West Ham United.

City's luck on the field didn't immediately change though as they were held to a goalless draw by the Hammers in front of a crowd of around 6,000.

In fact, if it was meant to be bad luck wearing green, then it was a little ironic that the team eventually finished the 1910–11 season in, unlucky for some, 13th place in the Southern League table!

Since then City have continued, in the main, to always wear red and white, whether it be striped shirts, or ones with hoops.

There have been a few occasions where the kit has been changed, all white, all red and various combinations of colours for both shorts and socks, but in general it is pretty well unthinkable to watch City not in their traditional red and white stripes for matches at St James' Park.

So it must have been a bit of a shock to some to see the City wear their black and gold outfit for the visit of Grimsby Town and Manchester United in the F.A. Cup in November 2004, but it has to be said, the kit looked extremely smart and the radical change was fitting to celebrate the club's centenary.

Perhaps the black and gold was not quite as radical as the shirts worn by the Grecians for the visit of Southampton to St James' Park in December 1913 though.

So that City's kit did not clash with the red and white of the Saints, the Grecians decided to wear a fetching chocolate shirt with yellow sleeves!

As far is as known, it was the only occasion that the particular shirt was worn by the team, which was probably just as well!

There were only minor changes to the look of the kit once football resumed after the Second World War, but not before City supporters got used to seeing their heroes in red and white hoops instead of stripes for a few years, simply because the latter were unobtainable.

It wasn't long before the striped shirt returned, and apart from tinkering with the kit here and there, that has remained the case until this day.

One other unusual kit that City wore was for their first round F.A. Cup tie at Brentford in November 1958.

With the Bees wearing red and white striped shirts, City's directors splashed out and bought a completely new look kit.

On that occasion City must have surprised home and away fans as they wore tangerine shirts with black edgings, white shorts and socks.

One wonders what happened to that kit after the Grecians lost 2-3 to Brentford. Unlike the splendid black and gold centenary shirts, it is doubtful whether anyone, other than the players, actually got the chance to wear the tangerine variety as there was no such thing as replica shirts then, which maybe was no bad thing.

It could have been worse had City still been wearing their green shirts with white sleeves from the early 1900s. Just imagine trying to sell those as replica shirts in the club shop today!

15 City Fined: Director Suspended

On 29th April 1912, Mr T. Oliver, a director of Exeter City Football Club, reported to the Football Association certain irregularities that had taken place in connection with the club, and supported it by the signed statements of fellow directors, Mr W. Fenwick and Mr W.H. Cook.

The books of the club were asked to be seen by the Football Association and it was found that they had only been partially written up. The cash book was incomplete and generally the books were not in a satisfactory condition.

An F.A. Commission was appointed to further investigate the charge and met at Exeter on 1st June 1912.

Those present, in addition to the members of the Commission were Messrs Norman Kendall, J.M. McGahey (Exeter City chairman) and Exeter City directors J.I. Pengelly, F.G. Hill, T. Oliver, W.H. Cook, F. Parkhouse and W. Fenwick. Also present were Sidney Thomas (Exeter City secretary) and S. Spooner (president of the Devon County Football Association).

Statements were made by each of the directors and officials, also by Captain Harvey (chairman of the Exeter City board of directors in 1908, the first year of the club's existence as a professional outfit).

It was admitted that in season 1908–09 bonuses were paid to players. It was also admitted that in season 1910–11 bonuses were paid for the F.A. Cup ties against Reading.

The bonuses came within the amnesty proclaimed by the Football Association on 9th March 1909. The Football Association had no rules prohibiting bonuses, but the payments were matters affecting the rules of the Southern League.

It was further admitted that after a home match against New Brompton on 9th September 1911, a portion of the gate receipts had been put aside as a reserve fund, and therefore not shown in the accounts.

The inquiry found that this was done with the prior knowledge of Messrs Cook, Fenwick, Parkhouse, Oliver and Thomas, and without the sanction or knowledge of the other club directors.

The charge was made by Mr Oliver who said this was done to pay bonuses, As soon as that came to the knowledge of Mr McGahey, he brought it all before the directors meeting and the practice was discontinued, and the money placed in club funds. No bonuses were paid and no illegitimate use was made of the money.

The Commission approved of the action of Mr McGahey and the other directors, but censured Messrs Fenwick, Cook, Parkhouse and Thomas for their improper and irregular action.

The Commission further stated that the books were not up to date, nor kept in accordance with the regulations and considered that in connection with a club of the standing of Exeter City, this was most unsatisfactory.

The club was at once ordered to update their books in accordance with regulations and submit them again for inspection. Furthermore Exeter City would be fined £20.

In the course of the inquiry, the Commission were satisfied that Mr T. Oliver, who did not report the irregularities until eight months after the date, though himself aware at the time, had been the prime cause of dissension among the directors, players and officials, and that in the interest of Exeter City his official connection with the club should cease.

Mr T. Oliver was therefore suspended as a director or from fulfilling any other official capacity with Exeter City.

'Things could not have continued as they were', reported the *Express & Echo*. 'Mr. McGahey, Chairman of the club, will naturally welcome the fact that he has been entirely exonerated even on the matter of technical irregularities.

'Another who would find the report not altogether distasteful, will be manager Arthur Chadwick. He has in the last two seasons had too many discouragements, and often to use his own words, he felt ready to "chuck the whole thing", but the outlook will be changed from now on.

'Exeter City are making practically a new start, sweeping changes having been made in personnel of the team whilst during the summer the Club has loomed very prominently in the public eye and the F.A. Commission which is still very fresh in the minds of all.'

It proved to be the biggest day in the fledgling history of Exeter City, as they were to entertain Aston Villa in the F.A. Cup second round on 31st January 1914.

Such was the interest in the tie that a record attendance was set for St James' Park as 9,500 were present, producing gate receipts of £910.

The build up to the game was very, very different to what you may expect for a similar cup tie being staged in 2008. And the style of reporting in the local press was very different as well, as can be seen from the extract below:

'All roads led to St James' Park today. From noon, when the gates to St James' Park were opened, a stream of spectators, all the while increasing in numbers, converged upon Exeter City's ground.

'It was a record day for the club, a record in almost every sense of the word. Ever since the draw was made and it was known that the Grecians' opponents were to be none other than holders of the F.A. Cup and probably the most famous of all clubs, Aston Villa, little else had been talked about in the city and for miles around.

'Cup fever gripped the city. Everywhere the club's colours have been flown, while scarcely any tradesman's window carried no decoration, and quite a number of shops, as a matter of fact have devoted one whole window to the cup tie display. No football event in Exeter has ever aroused over so wide an area the excitement and anticipation of this tie between Exeter City and Aston Villa.'

The Villa team were welcomed at St David's Station at 8.12 p.m. on Friday evening by about 200 enthusiasts, who cheered them to the echo. Outside the Rougemont Hotel, another small crowd waited for the party of about 30. They had travelled by the Great Western Railway route through Yate, Standish and Cheltenham, having left home at 3.55 p.m.

All the players visited the Exeter Hippodrome, and the Exeter City team were also there. A packed house applauded the theatre manager, Mr Fitchett, when he came forward to welcome the teams and thank them for their attendance.

On the morning of the match, even from the early hours, wearers of claret and blue were to be seen parading the city streets, and these followers of the Villa had evidently left nothing to chance of a late excursion arrival, preferring instead to pay the extra on the ordinary trains.

The City's colours were flying everywhere, and two ebullient spirits spent the whole morning riding on the top of a tram car waving red and white umbrellas.

The mascot, a goat, which had been bought for presentation to Jimmy Rigby, the Exeter City captain, by the city taxi drivers, was marched through the main streets at about 11 a.m., decked out in Grecians' colours and favours.

The Villa players walked to St James' Park from the Rougemont Hotel early in the morning and spent some time on the pitch, They subsequently walked back to the hotel for light lunch, served at about 11.45 a.m.

About that time the cinema operators began their work in the city streets and despite the miserable weather conditions, it was obvious that this was to be the day of days in Exeter sport.

Streams of people made their way to St James' Park. Every tram car carried its full freight of enthusiasts. Many arrived early for fear of the gates being closed on a full ground.

A few youngsters climbed on to the top of 'Football Express' scoreboard, but were promptly ordered down in case of accidents. Red and white umbrellas were waved form the Shilling Bank, and intermittently 'City war songs' rang out.

The first fight was seen on the Shilling Bank at 1.55 p.m. The two combatants had a lively two rounds before the police got to them.

The Villa players arrived at the ground at 2 p.m., having been conveyed from the Rougemont Hotel in six of the Exeter Blue Taxis. The City players had arrived some time earlier.

So the scene was set for a colourful and noisy afternoon. What was the outcome of the game? Was the pre-match expectation justified? It was a case of the experience and status of the Villa team proving to be too much for the unbounded enthusiasm of the Exeter City players, although the game proved to be a lot closer than may have been suggested.

Villa won the tie 2-1, but they had a fright especially as City's Jack Fort missed from the penalty spot, his shot grazing the post and going behind for a goal kick. The one success of the afternoon for the Grecians was the goal scored by Henry McCann.

One wonders what happened to the City mascot. Was the goat gracefully retired to a farm perhaps?

Much has been recorded and written about Exeter City's tour of South America in 1914, but there were several incidents of note that took place that are well worth recalling.

City actually played eight matches in Argentina and Brazil with the following results: Argentine North (lost 0-1), Rosarian League (won 3-1), Fluminese (won 5-1), Argentine South (drew 3-3), Combinadoes (won 5-0), Brazil (lost 0-2), Racing Club Buenos Aires (won 2-0), Rio de Janeiro (won 3-0).

The game against Brazil was that country's first-ever international fixture. The teams on that day, 21st July 1914, were:

Brazil squad: Marcos, Pindaro, Nery, Lagreca, Rubens, Salles, Rolando, Abelardo, Oswaldo, Gomes, Friedenreich, Osman, Formiga.

Exeter City team: Reg Loram, Jack Fort, Sammy Strettle, Jimmy Rigby, Jim Logan, Fred Marshall, Harry Holt, Fred Whittaker, William Hunter, William Lovett, Fred Goodwin.

The match referee was a Mr Harry Robinson, who also played cricket for the Brazilian club, Paysandu.

When the Grecians scored in their game against Racing Club Buenos Aires, the secretary of the home team brandished a revolver and threatened to shoot the match referee!

Not surprisingly the game was stopped and it was only after a good deal of persuasion that the match official decided to restart the fixture, with City winning 2-0.

Against the Rosarian League, City were leading 3-0 at one stage. The hosts were then awarded a penalty from which they scored.

Such was the excitement of the crowd that they went wild with delight letting off fireworks, screaming and shouting. This was immediately followed by a band marching onto the pitch to play the Argentine National Anthem, preventing the game from continuing not once, but a dozen times!

Exeter City goalkeeper Dick Pym broke two ribs in the very first game of the tour and his understudy Reg Loram played in goal for the rest of the matches.

Pym did not enjoy the best of sea journeys from England to South America, as he suffered badly from sea sickness on the outward crossing.

This was quite remarkable in view of the fact that Pym used to spend hours fishing on the River Exe near his home in Topsham and was something of an accomplished sailor.

In another incident, several City players were arrested for 'indecent exposure' on the beach at Rio de Janeiro. They had decided to go sunbathing and removed their shirts, as well as taking a dip in the sea, just clad in their football shorts.

But this was regarded by the Brazilian police as being indecent and they were soon arrested for the offence much to their surprise. The players were taken off to the local police station for questioning, being transported there by tram!

After a good deal of explaining through an interpreter, the players were eventually allowed to go their own way without any charges being brought.

The tour, despite it being a huge success as far as the results were concerned, was not quite so good according to one of the Exeter City directors who had accompanied the players.

On the last day in South America he was reported as saying: 'I shall be glad when we have gone. I have had a wretched time and so have the players. We are sick and tired.'

Goalkeeper Pym actually brought a gift of a parrot back to England with him. The bird survived quite happily for a few years at St James' Park.

On the bird's death it was decided to give it a decent burial behind the goal at the St James' Road end of the ground. After a short while it was pointed out that since the bird had been buried, City had not won a game!

So, with footballers being a superstitious group, the poor, deceased parrot was unceremoniously dug up again and buried elsewhere. The story goes, of course, that City's fortunes changed immediately for the better and they started winning again.

Another item brought back from the tour was the actual football used in the Racing Club versus Exeter City fixture. This again was looked after by Pym – for 71 years! For in 1985 Pym offered the ball to the Topsham Youth Club so they could auction it to raise much needed funds.

The ball was purchased by the then Exeter City chairman Byron Snell for £100, and could be seen on display in the Royal and Albert Museum in Exeter, during an exhibition detailing Exeter City Football Club's history in 1991.

In July 1984 a Brazilian television company, Global TV, visited Exeter to make a documentary about the game between the Grecians and their national side.

They interviewed Pym, who was still in fine form at the age of 91, and they also filmed at St James'

Park, and in and around the city centre.

Pym died in September 1988, and as mark of respect, the Grecians observed a minute's silence before the start of their next home game against Torquay United a few days later.

ASOCIACION ARGENTINA de FOOT-BALL

Exeter City Team

1.a Fila: S. Greeneway (Trainer), A. Norman Kendall, A. Chadwick (Manager), J. S. Pengally, W. Norman, G. A. Middlewick, S. M. Thomas (Sec.).
: .la: E. Lewis, R. Loram, R. Gerrish, W. Kirby, R. Pym, S. Shettle, A. Evams, F. Munt. J. Manatan Groundsman.
..a Fila: J. Whittaker, J. Fort, J. Rigby, M J. Mc. Gamey (Chairman-), W. Smith, F. Marshall, M. M·Gann, J. C. Lee.
Frente: M. Holt. C. Pratt, F. Lovett, J. Lagan, M. Orr, J. Goddard.

PROGRAMA OFICIAL de los **Partidos Internacionales de Foot-Baal** que se jugarán en el **Stadium de Palermo** con el concurso del Team Ingles **Exeter City F. C.**

Although only an image of a photocopy, this is a very rare programme from Exeter City's game against Argentine North, which was played on their tour of South America in 1914.
It was the first game of the tour, with the Grecians losing 1-0.

With the outbreak of the First World War, Exeter City's trip home from their tour of Argentina and Brazil was, to say the least, adventurous!

The team had journeyed aboard the steam packet *Alcantara* whose maiden trip it was, and three shots were fired across her bows after she had left Lisbon.

The first shot came from an English man-of-war and the next two from French vessels.

Mr M.J. McGahey, the Exeter City F.C. chairman gave the following account to the *Express & Echo*:

'The Royal Mail Steam Packet *Alcantara* left Rio de Janeiro on 3rd July 1914, having on board a mixed company of English, French, German, Brazilian and Argentine passengers.

'The ship is of course, the very latest of the Royal Mail fleet, being her finest and fastest boat, and of over 18,000 tonnage. She had on board a large quantity of bullion, and also a full cargo of frozen meat for Southampton.

'The new of declaration of War between Germany and France caused great excitement between the mixed body of passengers, and at last, about 12 midnight, when the wireless message was received as to the declaration of War between England and Germany, the news had a most sobering effect.

'Everybody felt that the world was fated with a terrible ordeal, the end of which no man could forsee.

'With the declaration of War came a realisation of danger in which the vessel was now placed. She would be a valuable capture for any German cruiser, and whilst it might be difficult to dispose of, they could take all of her gold and sink her, after landing the passengers or sending them into port in boats.

'It was known that there was at least two German ships in the vicinity of Madeira, and accordingly for two nights the *Alcantara* steamed at her utmost capacity, probably at 18 knots, with all the lights out, a precaution of as unusual character as to forcibly bring home to the minds of the passengers the particular danger in which they were placed.

'Madeira was reached safely and every ounce of

The City players on board ship, returning from their South American tour.

coal possible that could be obtained was got on board speedily, and away she went towards Lisbon. After a night of steaming we reached the Portuguese port in early morning.

'In the Lisbon harbour lay 19 large German vessels from the Cape, South America, China and elsewhere that had sought refuge in the port and were unable to leave for fear of capture by the English or French Men-of-War.

'All the English passengers from these boats were transferred to the *Alcantara* joining the Exeter City players who by now were very concerned for their safety. We set sail for Southampton and then late on that evening we met with a startling adventure.

'Away on the horizon appeared a column of smoke, and slowly four funnels of a Man-of-War was seen. This vessel, despite our speed, was rapidly overhauling us. There was signalling, and then a gun was fired, passing over us.

'The lady passengers became hysterical and everyone thought she was a German ship. She manoeuvred alongside us and it was instantly realised she was English, much to the relief of the City players and the rest of the passengers. She had been flying no flags. A tremendous storm of cheering went up from the passengers.

'The ship was HMS *Vindictive* and all her decks were cleared for action. We received instructions from her and steamed off once more. A little later we met a huge tramp steamer, and signalled to her.

We got near enough for her skipper to use a megaphone. It was rather amusing to hear the tramp's skipper ask: "Am I to understand from your signals there is a war between Germany and England?" ... "Yes, it was declared two days ago", was the reply sent back. ... "Good heavens!", came the voice from the tramp, and the last we saw of her she was lumbering on beyond us with a cargo for Glasgow.

'The next morning another Man-of-War hove in sight, and again a shot was sent over us. This boat proved to be the *Kieber* of the French Royal Navy and when she was alongside, the French sailors cheered the English vessel enthusiastically and we Englishmen felt very proud, with the City players stating how much more impressive HMS *Vindictive* had been in comparison to the French vessel.

'The *Alcantara* approaching Start Point off the South Devon coast, was surrounded in thick fog. The Exeter City party were in jubilant mood, knowing that they were nearing Exeter and home.

'At that stage, however, the ship was instructed to make for the port of Liverpool and in rough weather had to round Lands End and on towards the Lancashire coast.

'Despite this change of plan and the disappointment of the players who now had to travel south by train to Exeter, they were all in good spirits, fit and well, and all had got over their injuries they had suffered whilst in South America. The players were looking forward to the start of the 1914–15 season, which was in a few days time.'

DID YOU KNOW?

The ship, SS *Alcantara*, which the Exeter City players were aboard had not long been built. The ocean liner was built by Harland & Wolff for Royal Mail Lines and launched in October 1913, making her maiden voyage in June 1914 on the Southampton to South America route.

It was converted to an armed merchant cruiser in 1915 and fitted with eight six-inch guns, anti-aircraft guns and depth charges, being recommissioned as HMS *Alcantara*.

The ship was 'lost' when sunk by the German cruiser *Grief* on 29th February 1916. There were 72 crew on board when the order to abandon ship was made.

The Grecians had made an average start to their 1914–15 Southern League season, having won four and drawn two of their opening ten fixtures.

Southend United were the visitors to St James' Park on 7th November 1914, and having only conceded seven goals all season, it seemed the City would have a difficult afternoon. How wrong that proved to be!

Only one change was made to the Exeter team that had lost the previous match 4-0 at Swindon Town, with former Blackpool inside-forward Stan Cowie losing his place, after what was to be his only first-team match for the club.

City team: Dick Pym, Fred Marshall, Sammy Strettle, James Rigby, James Lagan, William Smith, Harold Holt, Alf Green, Billy Goodwin, William Lovett, Fred Goodwin.

Exeter were to enjoy an excellent afternoon as they just failed to equal their Southern League record win, this coming three years earlier, when winning 8-1 against New Brompton.

City were two goals to the good inside the first ten minutes, Green scoring the first after Billy Goodwin had missed a centre from his namesake Fred. Billy Goodwin made it 2-0 after receiving a pass from Holt, one of 23 Southern League goals that he was to score that season.

The Southend side was described as 'feeble' and it was no surprise when City got a third goal through Fred Goodwin who took advantage of some poor defending.

However the visitors themselves took advantage of a defensive blunder after the normally reliable Pym allowed a centre from Young slip from his grasp and Burrell pushed the ball into the net from close range.

The 5,000 watching spectators must have wondered just how many goals the Grecians would go on to score as half-time was reached with their team winning 6-1, as further goals were all netted by the returning Green to complete a fine four-goal haul.

City supporters had not been able to fathom out why Green had been dropped from the team for the previous match, and his reintroduction was more than justified as the bustling forward gave the Southend defence many problems.

The match report stated: 'Exeter City's exhibition during the first half was brilliant and little exertion was needed to score. There was little or no understanding between the Southend defenders.'

As is often the case, having enjoyed such dominance in the opening 45 minutes, the second half proved to be a bit of contrast as far as the Grecians were concerned, as they never reproduced the same flowing football that had earlier been seen.

They did, however, add one further goal as they rallied once more towards the closing stages of the match, when Lovett fired home a superb shot that gave the keeper no chance whatsoever.

Southend were described as being the poorest team seen at St James' Park that season as the report stated: 'Their failure was extraordinary.'

For Spencer Bassett in the visitors team, it had been a most unhappy return to his former club, having originally left Exeter for Swansea Town in 1913.

City ended the season in a mid-table position, whilst Southend were three from bottom.

SOUTHERN LEAGUE FIRST DIVISION – FINAL TABLE: SEASON 1914–15

	P	W	D	L	F	A	Pts
Watford	38	22	8	8	68	46	52
Reading	38	21	7	10	68	43	49
Cardiff City	38	22	4	12	72	38	48
West Ham Utd	38	18	9	11	58	47	45
Northampton T	38	16	11	11	56	51	43
Southampton	38	19	5	14	78	74	43
Portsmouth	38	16	10	12	54	42	42
Millwall	38	16	10	12	50	51	42
Swindon Town	38	15	11	12	77	59	41
Brighton & H.A.	38	16	7	15	46	47	39
EXETER CITY	**38**	**15**	**8**	**15**	**50**	**41**	**38**
QPR	38	13	12	13	55	56	38
Norwich City	38	11	14	13	53	56	36
Luton Town	38	13	8	17	61	73	34
Crystal Palace	38	13	8	17	47	61	34
Bristol Rovers	38	14	3	21	53	75	31
Plymouth Argyle	38	8	14	16	51	61	30
Southend Utd	38	10	8	20	44	64	28
Croydon Common	38	9	9	20	47	63	27
Gillingham	38	6	8	24	43	82	20

It was announced in May 1920 that Exeter City could find themselves playing in the Football League the following season. This was a result of a meeting held in Sheffield on 18th May between representatives of the Football League and the Southern League, when the following resolution was proposed by Watford F.C. and seconded by Norwich City F.C.:

'That this meeting of the First Division Southern League clubs is of the opinion that the time is opportune for an application to form a Third Division, consisting of a Northern Section and a Southern Section. Further, the clubs comprising of the Southern League First Division be selected to form the Southern Section.'

A vote was duly taken at the meeting by the Southern League clubs where 19 were found to be in favour of the resolution, one against and one abstention.

Eleven days later at the Annual General Meeting of the Football League, it was agreed 'that subject to the consent of the Football Association, a Third Division of the Football League be formed. The clubs present forming the First Division of the Southern League comprise the Third Division for season 1920–21.'

Exeter City manager Arthur Chadwick had no doubts that the step up into the Football League would be a good one.

'It is the finest thing that could have happened', he said, when he heard the news of the Football League decision, and club secretary Mr S.H. Thomas added that it was biggest and most revolutionary step in football for many years.

It wasn't just on the pitch that the Grecians would now have to find themselves being more competitive, but off it there had to be improvements made to St James' Park.

At the meeting of the Exeter City Supporters' Club in June 1920, it was unanimously agreed that they should give the City directors a sum of £180 with a request that it be used towards covering the cost of enclosing the playing field with iron railings.

In attendance at the meeting were City chairman Mr M.J. McGahey, and directors Mr J. Pengelley, Mr N. Kendall and Mr E. Head

Mr Pengelley explained that it would be impracticable to proceed with the building of a new grandstand that summer, and the directors had instead decided to concentrate on general ground improvements.

The popular bank would be stepped with timber and cinders, whilst the enclosure at the St James' Road end had been widened by taking a strip of turf. The pitch would be enclosed by iron railings, four foot high.

Mr Pengelley further stated that the popular bank would consist of 24 steppings of 15 inches wide, each with six-inch steps, which would give every person a good view of the play.

If the club had a further successful season, then more improvements could be undertaken. The fencing around the ground was to be completed by a supporter, free of charge, who wished to remain anonymous.

Mr McGahey said that the improvements to the ground would be completed during the summer months in time for the start of the Football League season and would involve expenditure of close on £1,000, but this would 'greatly improve the comfort of the spectator'.

By the middle of July the improvements to the popular bank had almost been completed, which prompted a report in the *Express & Echo*:

'The stepping of the popular bank is well under way and will ensure increased comfort and a good view to every spectator who takes up position there. At the same time it will give room for another 2,000 people.

'The extension to the St James' Road end and right along the stand will prove to be another big improvement, The new iron railings fronting the enclosure have still to be fixed.

'Thanks to the copious rain fall, the turf is knitting up wonderfully and there should be a splendid carpet for all this season.'

The City directors also released details of the cost of season tickets for attending Football League matches at St James' Park as follows:

'Ground season tickets £1 7s 6d; Enclosure £2; Lady's tickets £1 10s; Stand season tickets £2 5s; Lady's tickets £2; Centre stand £3; Lady's tickets £2 10s.'

Admission on the day to matches would be 1s 3d for adults. At the same time the players' bonuses were announced at £2 for a win and £1 for a draw.

Exeter City 1920–21.

Exeter City Football Club became one of the founder members of the Football League Third Division in 1920. It consisted almost entirely of clubs who had previously played in the Southern League and proved to be such a success that 12 months later a Northern Section was formed, Exeter then playing in the renamed Third Division South.

They were to remain members of that division until the regionalised sections were split into the Third and Fourth Divisions in 1958.

The Grecians' first Football League match took place on Saturday 28th August 1920 when Brentford were the visitors to St James' Park.

Liverpudlian William Wright had the distinction of scoring City's first-ever Football League goal as the Grecians went on to win 3-0 in front of an enthusiastic crowd of 6,000. Also on target for Exeter were Charlie Vowles and Jack Feebery, the latter from the penalty spot.

The City team on that historic occasion was: Dick Pym, Joe Coleburne, Jack Feebury, Cyril Crawshaw, James Carrick, James Mitton, Len Appleton, James Makin, William Wright, Charlie Vowles, John Dockray.

City remained unbeaten in their opening five league fixtures, but after such a promising start things turned out to be a good deal harder as the season progressed. They had to wait until 16th April before recording an away victory – this being a 2-1 success at Reading.

The Grecians had to be content with an eventual finishing position of 19th, and although they were obviously disappointed after the start they had made, they nevertheless voted the first season in the Football League as being a big success.

One unusual match they did play in was against Crystal Palace. The City were due to play at Selhurst Park, but Palace's ground was then ordered to be closed because of crowd disturbances, and the match was switched to The Dell at Southampton. Vowles was again on target as City lost 2-1.

Vowles and Wright ended the season as the club's leading goalscorers, with nine goals each in the league, but goalscoring in general was a problem throughout the campaign as the Grecians were only to find the back of the net on nine occasions in their last 16 matches.

Goalkeeping duties were shared between by the talented Dick Pym and Charles Waller, although the latter, signed from Plymouth Argyle, only made three appearances.

The mainstay of the rest of the team consisted of full-backs Joe Coleburne and Jack Feebury, and half-backs Cyril Crawshaw, James Carrick and Alf Green.

Coleburne had been recruited from Lancashire non-leaguers Swinton, whilst Feebury had been signed from Bolton Wanderers.

Crawshaw was in the first of two spells with the City, leaving the club in 1921 for Accrington Stanley, only to return two years later.

Carrick was yet another Lancastrian, having played for the delightfully named Plank Lane club, before going back north to link up with Oldham Athletic.

Right-winger Len Appleton only missed a handful of matches after being signed from Blackpool, but he was never happy in Devon and returned north to play for Southport in 1921–22.

The inside-right berth was filled mainly by James Makin, but he too left the club at the end of the season to sign for Accrington Stanley.

Centre-forward was something of a problematical position for City, with William Wright playing in the first half of the season, and Robert Shields, in an exchange deal that took Wright to Huddersfield Town, playing in the second half of the season.

Charlie Vowles was a regular at inside-left, whilst the skilful John Dockray was an ever-present on the left-wing.

Vowles had starred in Services football in India during the First World War, joined Exeter City and stayed for three seasons until moving on to play for Barrow.

Carlisle-born Dockray, arrived at the Park from Bury in 1920 and had four seasons with the Grecians prior to moving to Bideford.

Other players who featured in the City team during the historic season were William Betteridge, Walter Brayshaw, Tom Hesmondhalgh, Sydney Hetherington, Percy Hilton, John Hinton, William Laken, Thomas MacIntyre, Henry Pollard, Jimmy Rigby and George Taylor.

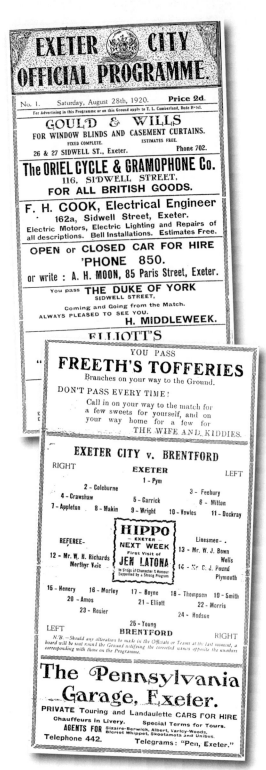

The purchase of St James' Park was completed on Friday 24th June 1921. Exeter City F.C. chairman Mr McGahey said that the major portion of the ground was the property of the trustees of Lady Anne Clifford's charity.

The residue of the ground at the back of the popular bank and a house abutting onto Old Tiverton Road was the property of Sir Henry Duke.

It should be remembered that it was Duke, when he had been the Member of Parliament for Exeter, who purchased the land in order to permit the extension of the playing area in order that F.A. Cup ties could be played at St James' Park. Prior to that the pitch had not been long enough.

Since the time of the purchase the club had been paying Duke a rental in respect of the land occupied by them.

Mr McGahey said it would have been useless for the directors to have bought the ground from the charity and for the other part still to be owned by someone else.

Therefore they approached Sir Henry Duke with regard to the acquisition of the property owned by him. He met with the club directors 'in a very reasonable spirit' and sold them the ground owned by him for the sum of £2,500.

Duke was quite a prominent member of society and in 1923 chaired a committee to establish a Department of Law at the University of Exeter. He was the Chief Secretary for Ireland after the Easter Rebellion of 1916–18 and was made first Baron Merrivale in 1925.

The price given by the club for the remainder of the ground to the Lady Anne Clifford charity was also £2,500.

At one time (way back in the 1650s), Lady Anne Clifford rented the site of the present St James' Park for fattening pigs. The proceeds went to a charity set up to pay for the apprenticeship of a poor child from the parish of St Stephen, an arrangement that was supposed to be renewed 'yearly to the world's end'.

In documents still extant, relating to the historic lease of 1904, between Lady Anne Clifford and Exeter City, it was stipulated that 'no menageries, shows, circuses or steam roundabouts' were to be allowed on the premises.

The purchase, Mr McGahey pointed out, was a very wise move by the club's directors, because unless they bought the terms of the lease, they could easily be subject to severe difficulties when that lease came to an end.

This could have led to grave increases in rent, and if they had given up the occupation of St James' Park every penny they had spent on the ground and structural improvements would have been thrown away.

As one of the conditions of the lease, it was stated that if the club gave up possession of St James' Park, the ground must be restored to its original state.

Considerable improvements were planned for the future and for a very long time the directors had been considering the construction of another covered stand.

Now that the ground had been bought by the club, this meant that any money spent on it would be spent in their own property rather than someone else's.

With the transfer of goalkeeper Dick Pym to Bolton Wanderers a few weeks after the purchase of the ground, the fee of £5,000 covered the overall cost of acquiring St James' Park.

DID YOU KNOW?

Henry Duke, who did much for Exeter City Football Club, was originally elected to the House of Commons for Plymouth, a seat he held until 1906 when he was defeated. He returned to Parliament in the January 1910 General Election as the representative for Exeter. He retained the seat in the December 1910 election by only a single vote (after a scrutiny of the votes), and held it until 1918. Duke sat on the front opposition bench during the early years of the First World War.

In July 1916 he was appointed as Chief Secretary to Ireland with a seat in the Cabinet. Duke's tenure as Chief Secretary saw the troubles in Ireland continue and he resigned in May 1918. After his resignation Duke was knighted. In 1925 he was raised to the peerage as Baron Merrivale of Walkhampton in the County of Devon.

You just had to pinch yourself, because Exeter City were going to play at Wembley Stadium in the Conference Play-off Final in May 2007.

With both of Devon's other senior clubs having already graced the hallowed turf, it was about time the Grecians joined them.

However, Exeter City would be the first of the county's trio to have played at the new Wembley Stadium. Could anyone really believe it?

Had anyone mentioned this possibility back in the 1950s, 60s, 70s, or even later, then you would have dismissed it as pure fantasy. No way would the name of Exeter City be seen at football's premier stadium.

And whilst the club may never have played there, there had been three notable players who started their careers at St James' Park and went on to play under the famous old twin towers.

You had to go back many years, but the three in question were goalkeeper Dick Pym, winger Cliff Bastin and centre-forward Harold Blackmore.

Bastin, who shot to prominence with the Grecians as a 16-year-old before being transferred to Arsenal in 1929, played at Wembley on many occasions for the full England team, as well as in the F.A. Cup Final for the Gunners.

Prior to his appearance at Wembley though, were the F.A. Cup outings of former Grecians, Pym and Blackmore.

The first-ever Cup Final to be staged at Wembley in 1923 became known as the 'White Horse Final' as a lone mounted policeman attempted to control the crowd that had spilled onto the pitch prior to kick off.

The scene must have seemed a million miles away to Pym, who liked nothing more than spending hours on his fishing boat on the Exe near his Topsham home.

The keeper had made his debut for City in 1911–12 and was a member of the party that toured South America in 1914.

He went on to make 209 appearances for City before being transferred to Bolton in the summer of 1921, the fee being used to purchase St James' Park.

Pym then went on to play in three F.A. Cup Final victories for the Trotters, without conceding a goal.

England honours came his way as he played three times for his country as well as totalling 301 league matches in ten years at Bolton.

After a brief spell with Yeovil Town, Pym returned to his roots and resided in Topsham until his death in September 1988, aged 95.

Blackmore, who hailed from Silverton, became his Bolton team mate, but the forward made his Exeter City debut against Swindon Town in October 1924.

He was soon to make his mark in the City team and in 1926–27 ended the season as the Grecians' record scorer, up to that point in time, with a total of 25 goals in 33 league appearances.

Blackmore, in fact, didn't complete the season with City, as Bolton paid what was a large fee at the time of £2,150 for his services.

Joining Pym in the Bolton team, Blackmore went on to score in the F.A. Cup Final victory over Portsmouth at Wembley.

Blackmore then played for Middlesbrough, Bradford and Bury, before, like Pym, he followed a completely new 'trade', that of being a butcher.

Blackmore died in 1989, and it is certain that he, along with the likes of Pym and Bastin, would have been very proud of the achievement of their old club, Exeter City, playing at Wembley Stadium.

DID YOU KNOW?

Bolton Wanderers undertook a tour of Devon in March 1927, winning 1-0 at Plymouth Argyle and losing 3-2 at Exeter City. Two of the Grecians' goals were scored by 21-year-old Harold Blackmore and after the game he signed for the Wanderers in a £2,150 deal. He quickly made his Bolton debut on 2nd April, scoring after only five minutes, in a 3-2 home win over Sheffield Wednesday.

The grandstand at St James' Park was destroyed by fire on the afternoon of Tuesday 17th November 1925, and with it all the club's playing kit. Damage was estimated at the time to have cost over £60,000, which was quite a sum in those days.

The fire broke out shortly after 2 p.m. and developed along the whole structure of the stand at such a rate that only a few of the club books and chairs from the boardroom were saved.

The City players had been training at the ground in the morning, but all had gone by 1 p.m. Even an hour later things appeared to be quite normal from inside and outside St James' Park, for groundsman Mr Orchard had just returned from his lunch break.

He went into the ground via the St James' Road entrance and made his way to the stand. There was nothing unusual in this until he almost reached the players' entrance to the pitch, when he noticed that the stand interior was filled with smoke.

The City groundsman dashed around the back of the stand via the manager's office, where he encountered Fred Mavin, the Grecians' team boss, who, having seen some smoke billowing from the rear of the stand as he had approached Well Street from his home, had hurried along investigate the cause.

Unlocking the doors to the stand, it soon became obvious that there was quite a serious fire taking hold. With a sudden rush the windows at the back of the structure burst outwards, showering glass all over the ground, and great volumes of black smoke belched out and swept away across the railway cutting, borne on a brisk easterly breeze.

Orchard immediately rushed for the higher entrance and contacted the fire brigade, the telephone in the stand being inaccessible.

Unfortunately the effects of inhaling the smoke proved to be too much for him and he collapsed on the ground just as City trainer Andy Tucker arrived on the scene.

Tucker lost no time in running to the call box at the top of Sidwell Street, but as it happened the fire brigade had already been informed and were on their way.

Back at St James' Park, Mavin, assisted by Mr Hawkins of Howell Road, Exeter, made a desperate attempt to save some of the club's property and actually managed to get the account books and a few chairs out of the office.

But this work had to be abandoned very quickly, for in less than three minutes, the whole of the grandstand burst into flames and blazed furiously from end to end.

Crowds of people collected in Well Street and at the popular entrance to the Park where they stood on the terraces, as the players, returning from lunch, also arrived. They watched the doomed structure burn out like a giant torch.

The fire brigade were at the Park within three minutes of receiving the call, but a considerable amount of time elapsed before they could get to tackle the fire. The heat was so intense that when hoses were run up to the ground by way of Well Street, they too burnt.

Remains of the fire-damaged grandstand.

There was no way the stand could be saved. The flames had secured a firm hold and the timbers were well ablaze. The huge arched roof crumpled at the back and sank lower. Fears were voiced that the roof would slide off into Well Street, but fortunately the girders held fast.

The flooring of the stand was quickly engulfed and the dressing rooms and offices became a raging and roaring inferno. A big area of the playing surface was scorched by the flames, but slowly the firemen were able to control the fire.

The most likely theory as to the cause of the blaze was that the coke stove in the training room, near to which some shirts were drying, had overheated.

A large force of police were present to give any help they could, along with members of the St John's Ambulance Brigade. City trainer, Tucker, required treatment for shock, whilst groundsman Orchard was slowly recovering from the ordeal.

Sid Thomas, the Exeter City Football Club secretary, said that the grandstand was insured, but not for its full value to cover rebuilding costs. It was believed to have been insured for the sum of £5,000 with the Commercial Union.

City manager Mavin had one big regret from the playing point of view, and that was the loss of all the kit and boots. He said that his players would have to appear 'in strange attire' and that would be a serious handicap for the team.

It was to be 12 months before the grandstand was completely rebuilt and, in 2008, it is still standing!

The grandstand at St James' Park, built to replace the one destroyed by fire in 1925, still standing and in use in 2008.

Exeter born and bred, Clifford Sydney Bastin, served his footballing apprenticeship at Exeter City to go on to win every conceivable honour during a glittering career with Arsenal.

'Boy Bastin' as he became known, first played for the Grecians at the age of 16 and made his First Division debut for Arsenal at 17. By his 20th birthday he had won a League Championship and an F.A. Cup winners' medal, as well as a full England cap.

Bastin was to win 21 caps in total for his country between 1931 and 1938, and remained a regular with the Gunners right up until his retirement in January 1947.

Born in Exeter on 14th March 1912, Bastin attended the Ladysmith Road School in the city and was in the Exeter Schoolboys side at the age of 11.

An appearance for England Schools followed at 14 in 1926, as did further experience with two Exeter junior sides, St Marks and St James.

Naturally enough Exeter City kept a keen interest in his rapid progress and not surprisingly signed him in 1926 on amateur forms. Bastin spent his time working as an electrician whilst learning his football trade with the Grecians' junior side.

His magical ball skills and legendary shooting quickly became noticed by City manager David Wilson, and on 14th April 1928, when Bastin was exactly 16 years and one month old, he made his Football League debut, the match being a goalless draw in the Third Division South at Coventry City.

The following week he scored the first of two of a total of 271 first-class goals when netting in the 5-1 home drubbing of Newport County. A week later he was on target again, as City themselves slipped to a 5-1 defeat at Walsall.

Bastin signed professional forms for Exeter City in October 1928 and made a further 14 league outings that term scoring six goals. Word soon got around that Bastin possessed exceptional ability and on 17th May 1929, Arsenal manager Herbert Chapman signed him for the Gunners for a fee of £2,000.

The Arsenal, under Chapman, were about to enter a glory period and Bastin was right in at the beginning of it, making his debut in a 1-1 draw at Everton on 5th October 1929 when still only 17 years old.

He gained a regular first-team spot over the Christmas period in 1929 and from there on went from strength to strength. He played in Arsenal's F.A. Cup winning side of 1930 against Huddersfield Town then becoming the youngest ever player to appear in a Final at 18 years and 43 days.

Bastin was ever-present in the Arsenal 1930–31 Championship side and then won the first of his England caps against Wales.

His international career was to span seven years, during which time he scored 12 goals. His last appearance for England was against France in Paris in May 1938, a game that was won 4-2, with Bastin scoring one of the goals.

The silverware quickly accumulated for both Arsenal and Bastin during the 1930s and following another F.A. Cup Final appearance in 1931–32, the Championship was again won in 1932–33, a season when Bastin set a wingers' goalscoring record of 33 in 42 games.

The league title was repeated in each of the following two seasons and again in 1937–38, with the F.A. Cup being won once more in 1936 as Arsenal continued to dominate the footballing scene.

The late 1930s were not quite so fruitful for the Gunners but Bastin remained a major force in their side continuing to score with great regularity.

He made in excess of 200 appearances for the Gunners during the war years and gained a Football League War Cup runners-up medal in 1942–43 as well as a Football League South Cup winners' medal in 1943.

His best days were behind him, however, and after a short spell back in the First Division with Arsenal in 1946–47, he decided to retire. His decision was influenced due to a condition that was leading to increased deafness.

The last of his 370 Football League outings took place at Maine Road on 28th September 1946, as Arsenal went down 5-2 to Manchester United, who were then ground sharing at Manchester City's ground due to bomb damage sustained at Old Trafford.

On leaving the game Bastin worked for a while as a Sunday newspaper journalist and later owned a restaurant in Edgware, London. He then returned to Exeter where he became landlord of the Horse and Groom in Heavitree.

Bastin died in Whipton, Exeter, 1991, but he remains to this day, and will continue to do so for a long while, the greatest ever footballer to be produced by Exeter City Football Club. He was honoured by the club by having the Big Bank terracing at St James' Park named after him recently.

Although not in this picture of the 1928–29 Exeter City team, Cliff Bastin will have played alongside all of the players at one time or another during the season
Back row: Reg Clarke, Dave Wilson (Manager), Wilf Lowton, Thomas Holland,
Charlie Miller, William Jones (Trainer), Leslie Dennington.
Front row: George Purcell, Billy McDevitt, Arthur Doncaster, Harold Houghton, William Death, Alexander Pool.

CLIFF BASTIN: EXETER CITY PLAYING RECORD
(Football League matches only)

Season 1927–28: Bastin played against Coventry City (away), Newport County (home – scored 2), Walsall (away – scored).

Season 1928–29: Bastin played against Southend United (home), Charlton Athletic (home and away), Newport County (home – scored and away), Queens Park Rangers (away), Bristol Rovers (home – scored), Merthyr Town (home – scored and away), Watford (home and away), Walsall (home), Brighton and Hove Albion (home), Crystal Palace (home).

Matches and performances sandwiched between two F.A. Cup ties are notorious for not proving to be particularly good. However, on this occasion on 4th December 1926, Exeter City disproved that theory and enjoyed a goal feast to record what was then their record Football League victory.

The previous week the Grecians had entertained Aberdare Athletic at St James' Park in the first round of the F.A. Cup and goals from William Compton (2) and George Purcell gave then a comfortable 3-0 win over the Welshmen to earn a second round tie, again at home, to Northampton Town.

In between those games though, City had the matter of a Third Division South fixture to contend with, as Coventry City were the visitors to the Park.

Exeter hadn't exactly enthralled their supporters so far that season, with only six wins in the league, nonetheless, 6,000 spectators were present to watch a City team that lined up:

Harry Bailey, Robert Pollard, Stan Charlton, Robert Pullan, Alexander Pool, John Garratt, George Purcell, Billy McDevitt, Harold Blackmore, Fred Dent, William Compton.

Coventry were a mid-table side but they were shocked when conceding a goal after just four minutes as Dent headed past their keeper following a cross from Compton.

The Grecians went 2-0 in front in the 11th minute. McDevitt weighted a superb pass along the ground to Blackmore, who swivelled to net the ball with a terrific drive that went just under the crossbar.

It was Exeter who were in rampant mood and they had the opportunity to go further ahead when Compton was fouled in the penalty area, but Charlton's spot-kick was fisted away to safety by the Coventry keeper.

They didn't have to wait too long though for goal number three when Compton hit a glorious drive from just outside the area on the half-hour mark, which went into the net via the underside of the crossbar.

A minute later Compton almost scored again, but his shot struck a post with the keeper well beaten, and Blackmore, following up, just failed to convert the chance.

There was a standing ovation for McDevitt at the interval, and the Irishman well and truly deserved it, for his play had borne the hallmark of a player appearing at a much higher level than the Third Division South, and he had been the inspiration behind most of City's attacks.

It was much the same in the second half, but this time the Grecians turned all their attacks into goals as Dent (52nd minute), Blackmore (54th), Compton (76th) and Purcell (85th and 89th) all hit the target to take the Exeter tally to eight.

For the first and only time in Exeter City's history, four players had each scored two goals, with Blackmore eventually heading the goalscoring charts at the end of the season with 25 from 33 matches, even though he left the club for Bolton Wanderers for a fee of £2,150, where he linked up with former Grecian, Dick Pym.

Coventry were completely outplayed, although they did manage to salvage something as they netted once through Heathcote.

For the record, the following Saturday, City duly beat Northampton Town in the second round of the F.A. Cup, McDevitt scoring the only goal of the tie and thus earned a third round chance at St James' Park against Accrington Stanley.

EXETER CITY IN THE F.A. CUP 1926–27

27th November 1926: round one: Exeter City 3 Aberdare Athletic 0 (Attendance: 9,000)
11th December 1926: round two: Exeter City 1 Northampton Town 0 (Attendance: 11,314)
8th January 1927: round three: Exeter City 0 Accrington Stanley 2 (Attendance: 13,647)

This was a day when both the Exeter City first and reserve team found their shooting boots, as they hit no fewer than 16 goals between them.

The Grecians' first team were at home to non-league opposition in the first round of the F.A. Cup as Southern League Aberdare Athletic were the visitors on 26th November 1927.

This was the second season running that the teams had met at the first round stage, with City winning 3-0 on the previous occasion.

Sporting their colours of black and amber, the Darians supporters who had made the trip to Exeter were in high spirits prior to kick off, as they took their places on the terraces at St James' Park amongst a crowd of 9,378, which produced match receipts of £573 14s.

Before the teams came onto the pitch, City secretary Sid Thomas had received a telegram from former Exeter manager Fred Mavin, who had recently left the club to take charge of Crystal Palace, wishing his old team the best of luck.

A similar message of goodwill had been sent off by the City to Mavin in the course of the morning of Palace's cup tie with Dartford.

The City team lined up: Thomas Holland, Robert Pollard, Stan Charlton, Arthur Phoenix, Alexander Pool, Harold Gee, George Purcell, Billy McDevitt, Fred Dent, William Vaughan, William Compton.

It soon became clear that the difference between the two teams was vast, and Aberdare's plight was hopeless from very early on, the match being as good as won by the City in the first 25 minutes when Dent, Vaughan and Dent again, all scored.

Vaughan added a fourth goal on the half-hour, but Aberdare did reduce the arrears when three minutes later Edwards netted with a simple cross shot.

Throughout the first half McDevitt had been a great source of inspiration to the other City forwards and the tall Irishman's clever play and cunning passes kept the opposition guessing all the time.

Almost on the stroke of half-time, Dent created a perfect opening for Purcell to fire home a splendid goal to make the half-time score 5-1.

The goals continued to come City's way in the second half as Dent hooked the ball into the net from Compton's 57th-minute cross.

Five goals in front, Exeter seemed content with their lead and took things easy for a while, but whenever they did attack, it rang alarm bells in the Aberdare defence.

With 15 minutes remaining, Purcell scored the Grecians' seventh goal with a scorching 20-yard drive. Two minutes later Gee and Dent combined to set up Compton to score goal number eight.

City completed their tally, to win 9-1, when Dent netted from Compton's pass, to complete a thoroughly miserable afternoon for Aberdare who had been completely outclassed.

On the same day, the City reserves were also enjoying a goal glut, although their margin of victory at Torquay United in the Southern League was not as great, as they won 7-4.

It was all square at half-time as the teams were level at 2-2, but City went on to take control of the second half and run out worthy winners with goals from former Torquay player Harold Andrews (4), Wilf Lievesley (2) and Patrick McDade.

For City's first team, the win over Aberdare was the start of a run in the F.A. Cup, which saw them defeat Ilford and then Rotherham United before meeting Blackburn Rovers in round four. After a 2-2 draw at Exeter, the Grecians lost the replay 3-1 at Ewood Park.

DID YOU KNOW?

Aberdare Athletic were elected to the Football League in 1921. They spent six years in the Third Division South, but in 1926–27 ended in bottom place. They failed to gain re-election and their place was taken by Torquay United.

In 1927–28 they were playing in the Southern League, but their F.A. Cup visit to Exeter City ended disastrously as described above.

There cannot be too many professional footballers who aspire to the position of Town Mayor after their playing careers have ended but former Exeter City centre-forward Percy Varco did just that.

Born in Fowey in Cornwall on 17th April 1904, Varco returned to his place of birth after hanging up his goalscoring boots and took an interest in local politics, eventually reaching the lofty heights of Mayor of Fowey.

Varco, at 5' 10" and 12 stone, was one of the mainstays of an Exeter City team that took the footballing world by storm in 1931 when the Grecians reached the quarter-final of the F.A. Cup.

He played a major part, scoring in the early rounds against Derby County and Bury. He also found the net in the quarter-final replay at St James' Park against Sunderland.

Exeter City were not Varco's first Football League club though, for he had joined the Grecians from Norwich City on 3rd February 1930.

No transfer fee was paid, although after his exploits at Exeter over the subsequent months, Norwich must have wished they had placed a transfer figure on him!

Varco had played for his local side Fowey Town before moving to Southern League Torquay United. He left Plainmoor in 1924 to join Aston Villa for a fee of £200, scoring twice in ten league games for the West Midlands side. He then moved to Queens Park Rangers (four goals in 16 league games), before joining Norwich City in 1927.

He quickly became a hero at Carrow Road, scoring 32 times in his first season, including ten goals in his first seven league games. In 1929, after 37 goals in just 57 league games for Norwich, he moved to Exeter City.

Varco was a legendary figure in Norwich City's history if only for the chant that used to ring around the ground of 'Give it to Varco', whenever he played.

Varco made his league debut for the Grecians two days after he signed, in a 4-0 home win over Clapton Orient, but it was not a happy first match as he injured his thigh and was sidelined for two weeks.

He was to play six league matches for Exeter in his first season at the Park, without a goal to his name. He had to wait until the opening game of the following season – 1930–31 – against his former club, Norwich City, before he registered his first goal for the club.

This proved to be the first of 25 that he scored in the league that season, as not surprisingly he topped the Exeter City goalscoring charts.

Varco was not best pleased with the terms offered to him by the City directors at the end of the 1930–31 season and a few years later was quoted as saying that despite the club having enjoyed such a success in the F.A. Cup and making some money out of it, the directors had the cheek to offer him reduced wages!

The local sports reporter for the *Express & Echo* was full of praise for the manner in which Varco had contributed to the club's success and wrote:

'Percy Varco has in the last season equalled the Club scoring record of 25 league goals. As a perfect a team player as could be found from Lands End to John O' Groats, the big Cornishman's unselfish leadership of the City attack has been a pleasing phase of the past season's work.'

The following season – 1931–32 – saw Varco again amongst the goals, this time he hit 16 of them in the league, the same number of fellow inside-forward Harold Houghton.

Varco was also to register his only hat-trick at the City, when he scored all three goals against Cardiff City at St James' Park in October 1931. City also had a good season in the Third Division South, ending in seventh position.

His last match as an Exeter City player was at Craven Cottage on 7th May 1932, in a game that saw Fulham win 3-1.

Varco was fittingly on target to end his City career on a personal high. Within days he had decided that his future lay elsewhere and he later signed for Brighton and Hove Albion to end his highly successful association with the Grecians.

He played just once for the Seagulls before returning to Cornwall where he played for St Austell and then St Blazey. Varco died in 1982.

Exeter City 1930–31
Back row: Billy McDevitt, Reg Clarke, Richard Baugh, Arthur Davies, Charlie Miller, Stanley Barber.
Front row: William Armfield, George Purcell, Percy Varco, Harold Houghton, Arthur Doncaster, Jack Angus.

Ninety minutes of football would decide whether Exeter City continued their quite amazing run in the F.A. Cup and thus earn a semi-final tie against Birmingham City.

No one would have predicted how successful the Grecians were to be in the 1930–31 season when at the first round stage they defeated Northfleet United 3-0 in Kent.

However, as City got further and further in the competition, could there really be a sensational end to the story? After disposing of Northfleet, they drew 1-1 at home to Coventry City, then beat them 2-1 in the replay at Highfield Road.

Next up in round three were Derby County, who left St James' Park after being beaten 3-2. In the fourth round City achieved a great 2-1 win at Bury.

Onto round five and another notable Cup victory as they defeated Leeds United 3-1 at the Park. Surely the run would come to an end now, as they travelled to Sunderland in the quarter-final, but no, a stunning result – 1-1 – brought the Roker Park club back to St James' Park for a replay on Wednesday 4th March 1931.

Not surprisingly the whole area was buzzing with anticipation and excitement and Exeter City's record attendance of 20,984 (match receipts £2,561) at St James' Park, unlikely to ever be beaten, crammed into the ground hoping for a very famous victory.

Unfortunately the weather was not on its best behaviour as it had rained for almost 24 hours, leaving the playing surface near to being waterlogged in many places.

The *Express & Echo* reported: 'Excursionists from Sunderland put in an appearance in force this morning, from about 9 a.m., after a party numbering about 200 arrived in the city sporting their red and white colours, but also a few rosettes of white, the Wearsiders' colours for today.

'The referee, Mr Fogg of Bolton, was among those who paid a visit to Exeter City's ground this morning. He inspected the pitch and took the opportunity of doing a spell of sprinting to loosen his limbs in readiness for the match.

'There was a regular procession of telegraph messenger boys between the General Post Office and St James' Park with dozens of telegrams of good wishes and good luck being received form all parts of the country and beyond, one coming from Devonians aboard a warship in Montevideo.'

With the replay kicking off in the afternoon, the City players and officials had lunch together at Dellers Cafe in the High Street. The Sunderland team and officials were at the Royal Clarence Hotel and were heard to be making very unkind comments about the Devon weather!

Many businesses closed down for the afternoon to allow employees to see the match and other firms made arrangements so that as many workers as could be spared attended the Park. Some of the schools in Exeter were also closed for the afternoon.

Exeter relied on the same 11 players who had earned a draw at Roker Park, namely: Davies, Baugh, Miller, Clarke, Angus, Barber, Armfield, Purcell, Varco, Houghton, Doncaster.

'Dido's day' was the general comment when the spectators saw the waterlogged playing pitch and pictured the old seagull lucky omen taking his bath in the puddles.

As in the case of the earlier cup tie against Leeds United, youngsters were allowed inside the railings – pitch side – although this time they had to stand rather than sit due to the puddles of water.

As the teams came out, the Exeter City Military Band, under the conductorship of George Newman, played 'There's a Good Time Coming' just as they had done for the earlier rounds.

Sunderland took a 15th-minute lead through Connor and seven minutes later they got another, with Gurney scoring. Despite this setback City fought very hard and reduced the deficit in the 37th minute when Percy Varco was on target.

Sunderland regained their two-goal advantage on the hour mark when Connor got his second of the game to make it 3-1. Still Exeter fought back and with 20 minutes remaining their hopes were raised once more as George Purcell headed home.

Exeter stormed the Sunderland goal in search of an equaliser as the conditions got ever worse, but their hearts were broken in the 78th minute when Sunderland got a fourth, Gurney once more scoring.

Match programme for City vs. Sunderland, 1931.

Exeter City, it was reported, 'went out with their colours nailed firmly to the mast. They fought a very gallant fight against one of the best teams in the country.'

'The vision of a semi-final at Highbury has faded away, but the Grecians have written a glorious chapter in the football history of Exeter.'

THE GRECIANS' F.A. CUP RUN OF 1930–31

29th November 1930: round one:
Northfleet United 0 Exeter City 3
13th December 1930: round two:
Exeter City 1 Coventry City 1
18th December 1930: round two replay:
Coventry City 1 Exeter City 2
10th January 1931: round three:
Exeter City 3 Derby County 2
24th January 1931: round four:
Bury 1 Exeter City 2
14th February 1931: round five:
Exeter City 3 Leeds United 1
28th February 1931: round six:
Sunderland 1 Exeter City 1
4th March 1931: round six replay:
Exeter City 2 Sunderland 4

Attendance figures hold a certain fascination for some of us. One supposes it could be the love of facts and figures, or maybe you just have that certain anorak streak within you that makes them so interesting.

Everyone knows the record attendance at St James' Park was set way back in 1931 when Sunderland visited for an F.A. Cup quarter-final replay.

However, even that figure is disputed, for the official attendance was 20,984, but in the match report that appeared in the *Express & Echo*, was shown as being 21,015!

One thing is certain though, whatever the attendance really was for that particular cup tie, it will never again be beaten at the Park with its much reduced ground capacity.

It must have been pretty packed, as some will recall how crowded it was inside the ground for the cup ties against Manchester United in 1960 and 1969 respectively.

At the former meeting 16,000 were inside St James' Park for the Football League Cup first round tie, and at the latter, an F.A. Cup third round encounter, 18,500 were present.

Going from one extreme to the other, there have been some pretty low turnouts of supporters for the cup competition that has had many names – Freight Rover Trophy, LDV Vans Trophy etc. – a competition that failed to ignite interest until the latter stages.

Less than a thousand City die-hards bothered to go to some of the matches, and then you had to wonder why the competition was still being played, as figures elsewhere were also very, very poor.

However, there was one Football League match that some may recall where the attendance had slumped to just 1,863 for the final game of the 1975–76 season.

Scunthorpe United were the visitors, but those who stayed away were probably wishing they had gone along to the Park, for fans were treated to nine goals, City scoring five of them!

Ten years later, the 1985–86 season was a particularly bad one for the Grecians in terms of attendances and the average for matches at the Park was only 1,972.

The lowest crowd for a league fixture that season

The St James' Road turnstile block.

was just 1,369 – for the goalless draw with Cambridge United.

Having said that, football in Devon appeared to be going through a bad spell, as Torquay United only averaged a miserable 1,240.

While City averaged between 3,000 and 3,500 in the Conference, this is only half of the figure that they achieved in 1959–60 for instance, when the average for the Fourth Division fare on offer was 7,421.

But if you go right back to the every first season as a Football League club, in 1920–21, Exeter City averaged 7,740 for their Third Division home fixtures.

So in the space of 40 years, very little had changed in terms of average attendances. Whilst City were one of the best supported clubs in the Conference (2003–04 to 2007–08), they still have a long way to get back to those figures of yesteryear.

Finally, what sort of crowds were attracted to St James' Park during the club's three promotion seasons in the Football League?

In 1963–64, City averaged 7,291. The next promotion season of 1976–77 averaged 4,624, whilst the Fourth Division championship winning season of 1990 averaged a perhaps disappointing 4,859, in view of City finishing top of the table.

Exeter City may not have the same luxurious away days that the Premier League clubs enjoy, but they are certainly a lot more comfortable and quicker than they were.

The Grecians didn't always go to fixtures by coach. Indeed most teams preferred to use the train, certainly before the days of motorways criss-crossing the country.

Travel to matches didn't always go to plan, even by train, and City have been involved in a number of incidents and mishaps over the years.

In March 1933 for instance, Exeter were on their way to Reading for a Third Division South fixture when the train had to be diverted from its usual route and go via Swindon.

With kick-off time approaching, the players had to change into their kit on the train, and when they got off at Reading station they were taken to the nearby Elm Park ground by taxis. The rush did not appear to have too much effect on the team though, as City drew 2-2.

On another occasion the City team were delayed after their match at Watford on 29th September 1951. Inside-forward Richard Smart had been taken to the local hospital at the end of the game for stitches to a badly cut lip.

Unfortunately by the time Smart had rejoined the rest of his colleagues, it left only 45 minutes to get from Watford to Paddington station to catch the 6.30 p.m. train back to Exeter. The City party quickly made their way across London and arrived at Paddington after the train had left.

So instead of arriving in Exeter late evening, they had to wait for the overnight train and eventually reached Exeter St David's at 4 a.m. Needless to say Smart was not popular amongst his team mates!

The Exeter City reserves team missed their train in London on the way to Kettering for a Southern League fixture in 1956. The 12.18 p.m. St Pancras to Manchester express, which did not stop at Kettering, was halted specially to allow the players to alight.

The Exeter side therefore managed to arrive at Kettering three-quarters of an hour prior to kick off. One cannot imagine a train making a special stop for Exeter City now!

On Boxing Day 1956 the City reserves travelled as far as Gloucester station when they heard that their Southern League fixture at Worcester City had been called off. There were seven inches of snow lying on the Worcester pitch.

The stationmaster obligingly held *The Cornishman* express train for a few minutes to save the Exeter players a long wait for a train back to Devon.

When Exeter City arrived at Walsall station in December 1958, a porter handed Grecians' manager Frank Broome a message stating that the game with Walsall was called off. A telephone call to the Walsall ground from the station confirmed the postponement.

The City party then travelled on to The Hawthorns for the West Bromwich Albion versus Luton Town match instead. It wasn't Exeter City's day though as even the game at The Hawthorns was abandoned after 70 minutes due to the state of the pitch!

In September 1963 Exeter City announced that they would not be travelling to games by train in the future. However, they must have had a change of heart for by the end of that season, they used the train for the final game at Workington.

The decision to stop using trains had been taken by the board of directors on the grounds of cost and reliability. Exeter City F.C. secretary Keith Honey commented:

'As far as we are concerned, British Railways have priced themselves out of the market. Most of our fellow Fourth Division teams are in the north of England, so we face a good deal of travelling. From bitter experience we gave found we cannot trust the railway timetables.'

With Exeter City now making the occasional journey to games by plane, courtesy of Flybe, one wonders what the players from the above teams and incidents would have made of it!

It is not every day that Exeter City reach the final of a cup competition. For apart from numerous appearances in the Devon Professional Bowl, the Grecians last major cup final was way back in 1934.

It proved to be something of a struggle to reach even that one, with two replays needed in the semi-final against Brighton and Hove Albion.

The Third Division South Cup was competed for in the 1933–34 season for the very first time, the Third Division North section playing for a similar trophy.

No one could have been prepared for the game in the first round at St James' Park though, for no fewer than 17 goals were scored!

In a quite amazing match Exeter City defeated Crystal Palace by the incredible scoreline of 11-6!! The 2,000 spectators present on 24th January 1934 could not have believed what they were seeing!

Ace goalscorer Fred Whitlow scored six that day, including one from the penalty spot, whilst Stan Hurst and Frank Wrightson added two each, and a goal from John Scott, made up the Grecians' tally.

The City were drawn at home again in the second round on 21st February 1934, this time Watford being the visitors.

Not such a goal feast on this occasion, although having said that, there were still six of them! The Grecians won 4-2, before an attendance of 3,000, with two goals from Reg Clarke and one each from Hurst and John Barnes.

Surprisingly, despite all those goals the St James' Park crowd dipped to just barely 1,000 for the visit of Coventry City in the third round on 14th March 1934.

The Grecians drew 1-1, with Barnes netting again, and so travelled to the Midlands eight days later for a replay. Barnes again struck the only goal of the match before 4,000 spectators.

So Exeter City had reached the semi-final, and were paired with Brighton and Hove Albion. The match was to be played on the neutral ground of Craven Cottage, home of Fulham, on 12th April 1934. Before 3,221 people the City drew 1-1 with Hurst scoring the all important goal.

The replay took place 11 days later, this time at St James' Park. But despite Exeter having home advantage, still the teams could not be separated, even after extra-time, the scoreline again being 1-1, with Hurst on target again for the Grecians.

The Exeter public had obviously decided by this time that City had a real chance of winning a cup competition, for 5,000 were present at the Park.

Exeter City Third Division South Cup Winners 1933–34
Back row: Walters, S. Barnes, Risdon, Poulter, Barber, Chesters, Lock, Webb, Hughes, J. Barnes.
Middle row: Wrightson, Whitlow, Angus, Ditchburn, Davies, Kenyon, Welsby, Childs.
Front row (sitting): Gray, Scott, Miller, McGahey (Chairman), Clarke, Hurst, Kennedy.

A second replay took place at Brighton's Goldstone Ground on 26th April 1934, with an even better attendance present of 7,000.

In a thrilling contest Exeter just edged through winning 4-3. Henry Poulter got two goals, together with the almost inevitable goal from Hurst and one from Wrightson, making up the Grecians' tally.

There could not have been a better final in prospect even if it had been planned, for Exeter City's opponents were neighbours Torquay United.

The match was staged at the neutral ground of Home Park, Plymouth Argyle, to make the final a real all-Devon affair.

The final, played on 2nd May 1934, did however, draw a slightly disappointing attendance of 6,198, as the City team lined up: Chesters, Gray, Miller, Clarke, Webb, Angus, Scott, Poulter, Wrightson, Barnes.

Exeter had to wait until the 75th minute before they got the only goal of the game through who else but Stan Hurst? Poulter's initial shot had been parried by the Torquay keeper but the ball ran free to Scott who squared it back into the goalmouth for Hurst to tap into the empty net.

The Third Division South Cup was presented to City captain, Reg Clarke, by Mr Louis Bellattie, the chairman of Crystal Palace Football Club, who was representing the Football League.

Each of the Exeter City players, and the trainer, were then presented in turn with a winners' medal. The Grecians had won their first-ever major trophy.

The Exeter City Football and Athletic Co., Ltd.

o—o

**Members of the Football Association,
the Football League Third Division
and Southern.**

Chairman:
Mr. M. J. McGAHEY

Secretary:
Mr. S. H. THOMAS

Players' Manager:
Mr. JACK ENGLISH

ST. JAMES' PARK,
EXETER.

4th May, 1936.

Dear Sir,

My Club is compelled to apply for re-election to the Southern Section, and it is a matter of great regret to us that we are in the position of having to do so.

Exeter City became a professional Club in the year 1908 joining the old Southern League, and from that day to this we have carried out every obligation, both to the Leagues we are Members of, and to the Clubs we are associated with.

Five years ago we went into the draw for the Semi-Final of the F.A. Cup in company with Sunderland, upon whose ground we drew, only, however, to be defeated in the replay at Exeter, and we were fortunate enough to defeat that Season in the Competition, Coventry City at Coventry, Bury at Bury, Leeds United at Exeter, and Derby County at Exeter.

The next Season we fought out the Championship of the Section with Brentford finishing Second to that Club in the League Table.

From that year we have spent considerable sums of money in transfer fees in the hope that promotion might be achieved, and during the past unsuccessful Season paid nearly £1,500 in players' transfers with that object,

not an inconsiderable sum for a Third Division Club. The lesson we have learnt is that money is not a certain road to success in football.

One of the reasons for our non-success has been injuries to players. On the opening match of the Season we lost the services of our First Team centre forward and he has remained unfit to play, and bad luck in this direction has dogged us right through the year.

Exeter with a population of 70,000 is the Capital of the County, with an immediate surrounding population of a much larger number, and with reasonable success we are always able to command gates sufficient to run a good team.

During the Cup year referred to we took the following gates at Exeter:

	£	s.	d.
Derby County	1,669	0	0
Leeds United	2,397	0	0
Sunderland (Mid-Week Replay) ...	2,558	0	0

and in League Matches with Plymouth Argyle, when they were in the Third Division, we have taken gates exceeding £1,000.

With regard to players we shall, of course, place two professional sides in the field, in the Third Division and Southern League, most of these players have already been signed on for next season.

FINANCIALLY we are in a wonderful position for a Third Division Club.

We have no bank overdraft, our directors, therefore, have no need to give any guarantee to the Bank.

The Club owns its own ground valued at £20,000 subject to a mortgage of £8,000 only.

It is sheer misfortune that compels us to seek your assistance and we feel certain that we shall not ask in vain. The Capital City of the West cannot do without its League Football.

Thanking you in anticipation,

Yours faithfully,

M. J. McGahey

Chairman.

Exeter City had to apply for re-election to the Football League on far too many occasions. This is the letter the club sent pleading their case to be re-elected for the 1936–37 season. They were, of course, successful.

With the excitement of reaching the quarter-final of the F.A. Cup just six years earlier, Exeter City were hoping to make the same impact when they travelled to First Division Preston North End in round five on 20th February 1937.

To reach that stage the Grecians had beaten Folkestone 3-0 in the first round at St James' Park, followed by victories over Walthamstow Avenue (3-2 away). Oldham Athletic (3-0 at home) and a creditable performance at the Park when they defeated Leicester City 3-1.

The City team, the chosen 11 players, plus travelling reserve Harry Johnston, left Exeter St David's Station on the Friday before the game, accompanied by club directors, Capt. F.J. Hunter, J. Rigby, S. Thomas, J. Orchard, C. Hill and C. Hoskins, plus club president Mr J. McGahey.

Stopping at the same hotel as the City players was the Arsenal team, who were en route for their game at Burnley. This gave an opportunity for former Grecian Cliff Bastin to wish his old team the very best of luck.

There was quite a lot of cup tie excitement in the streets of Preston early on the morning of the match when the excursion train transporting nearly 700 Exeter City supporters arrived.

The City fans soon made themselves heard and there was considerable comment and amusement from the Preston locals when a stuffed seagull attached to a long post was paraded through the streets.

The playing surface was quite soft following a lot of rain in the area and another shower didn't help matters just prior to kick off.

Nonetheless there was still a very good attendance at Deepdale as 22,936 spectators produced match receipts of £1,671.

The City team lined up: Arthur Chesters, William Brown, Michael Boyle, Reg Clarke, Jack Angus, John Shadwell, Fred Smith, Walt Bussey, Rod Williams, Stan Pope, William Owen.

A stern test was expected for the Grecians, for Preston North End included several notable players,

none more so than Bill Shankly, later to make his name as manager of Liverpool.

The Grecians shocked their hosts by taking a third-minute lead when Owen's shot ballooned into the net off a Preston defender.

Exeter certainly more than held their own and it wasn't until five minutes before the interval that Preston finally conjured up an equaliser when O'Donnell netted.

The goal rocked Exeter back on their heels and three minutes later they conceded another when O'Donnell again scored after an effort had been cleared off the line.

Despite this setback, City came out fighting in the second half and in the 48th minute it was all square again as Smith made the most of a goalkeeping error.

The Deepdale crowd, apart from the travelling City fans, were stunned on the hour mark when Exeter took the lead through Owen, his second goal of the game.

The cup tie then swung from end to end and a free-kick taken by Shankly was nodded into the City net by O'Donnell in the 70th minute to make it 3-3.

Once again Preston made the most of their comeback and were in front when O'Donnell beat City keeper, Chesters to the ball.

City were far from a beaten side though and were desperately unlucky when a 'goal' from Owen was ruled out for offside and the chance of a replay back at St James' Park seemed to have slipped by.

In the final minute Preston broke away and Berresford steered the ball home to make it 5-3 and book his team's passage into the next round.

City were certainly not disgraced against their First Division opponents though, for they had twice taken the lead and more than matched them for long periods of the game.

Although Preston had controlled the game towards the half-time break, there was no real superiority by either of the sides in a gruelling second half until the last 20 minutes when North End got three goals.

Little is ever written about the aborted Football League season of 1939–40 when the Second World War effectively ended competitive football.

Although matches continued to be played, these were either as friendlies or hastily arranged league formats, however, a handful of clubs, including Exeter City simply put up the shutters until normality returned.

It must have been galling for City fans to see the 1939–40 season end as the Grecians had made a marvellous start, being unbeaten in their opening three Division Three South fixtures and lying second in the table behind Reading.

The season began with a local derby at St James' Park against Torquay United on Saturday 26th August 1939. The game attracted an attendance of 7,000 and they watched a hard-fought 2-2 draw, as Dick Ebdon netted twice for Exeter.

Two days later City had travelled to Northampton Town where they won 2-1 with goals netted by Harry Bowl (a penalty) and Harold Riley.

City then played a friendly fixture at the Park on Wednesday 30th August against Plymouth Argyle, but this wasn't between the then present-day teams, but the former professionals of the respective teams.

A good crowd was present to see the Grecians win 7-1, which included a hat-trick from former favourite Harold Blackmore. His team mate, at both Exeter and Bolton Wanderers, Dick Pym, played in goal for the City.

Back to the ill-fated Football League campaign and Exeter City travelled to Port Vale on Saturday 2nd September, for what was to be their last fixture for quite some time.

There has already been some doubt as to whether the game would take place or not, for on the previous Wednesday officials of the Football Association and the Football League had met to discuss the worsening situation in Europe.

Having had no information to decide that the season should be suspended, it was announced that the games would go ahead as planned, but it did seem that the fixtures for that day would be the last.

At this time, Port Vale did not play at Vale Park, Burslem as they do today, but were based at nearby Handley. City started the match in fine form and went ahead five minutes before the break when Riley scored from close range.

This proved to be the only goal of the afternoon as Exeter were generally quicker and more adventurous in attack than the Valiants.

The City team that day was: Charles Thomson, Jack Blood, Fred Speed, Steve Walker, Jack Angus, Bill Fellowes, George Wardle, Harold Riley, Harry Bowl, Dick Ebdon, Charlie Sutherley.

Back at the Park the City reserves entertained Hereford United in a Southern League fixture, a game that ended goalless and drew an attendance of just under 1,000.

As expected the season was brought to a close, although clubs did have the option to continue as best they could, but not in a Football League competition.

It was decided by the board of directors that Exeter City, due to their geographical situation and the distance from the rest of the other main football centres, would close down for the duration of what was described as an 'emergency'.

As in the First World War, a number of regional leagues were organised. The Football League did not restart until August 1946 although the F.A. Cup was played in season 1945–46.

DID YOU KNOW?

At the time the Football League suspended its programme of matches, Blackpool were top of Division One, whilst Luton Town, Accrington Stanley and Reading topped Division Two, Division Three North and Division Three South respectively.

Exeter City Football and Athletic Company Limited was badly hit by the outbreak of the Second World War having had to close the gates for the duration, but in April 1945, the directors made an appeal for £5,000.

The directors said that the sum was required to pay summer wages, engage a first-class manager, renovate St James' Park and do everything that was necessary so that the club could start playing competitive football once more.

There were over 2,000 ordinary shares and 3,000 preference shares available, and all the money raised from the sale of those would be paid into a special fund for purposes stated above.

The report of the directors stated that when war broke out the 1939–40 season had just begun. Considerable success was being achieved in the league matches and a good year was therefore contemplated, but the closing down of the game meant that the whole of the summer wages, an item running to nearly £2,000, was entirely thrown away, entailing heavy losses to the Company.

Since September 1939, when City ceased playing competitive football, St James' Park and the stands had been requisitioned and the income received from that source was just sufficient to cover any expenditure.

The balance sheet showed a very heavy deficit, but the directors were determined to make an effort in conjunction with the shareholders and the 'sport loving public' to pull the club around.

The continued running of Exeter City would be of the greatest importance to the city of Exeter, during the reconstruction period after so much war time bomb damage and destruction.

Regret was expressed at the loss through death of Mr M.J. McGahey, the club's first president, Colonel F.J.C. Hunter, chairman, and Mr A.J. Chamberlain, director. Hunter died as a result of injuries received in the Blitz.

The balance sheet to 30th June 1944 showed that issued capital, less calls in arrears totalled £11,354. There was a mortgage loan of £8,000 on the ground, plus accrued interest of £546.

Directors loans amounted to £1,278 and the bank overdraft stood at £1,839, The amount due to creditors, plus accrued charges was £3,007.

Director Mr S.H. Thomas felt confident that the football public of Exeter and district would respond to the appeal for the £5,000. It was also proposed to hold a big fête at St James' Park in the summer and maybe a public meeting of sportsmen could be called with advantage.

Raising the money would be a collective effort, explained Thomas, and all must lend a hand if first-class football was going to survive in Exeter.

Answering a question from a shareholder, Thomas said that in June 1939 the club's deficit stood at £19,000 and was frankly a millstone that Company could not bear and that the better course may have been to have gone into liquidation.

Such a course, however, would have presented many difficulties. Creditors and shareholders would have lost heavily and therefore the honest way was to carry on and try to put matters right.

The Company's plight was not as bad as it appeared at first glance. There had been no revaluation of assets since the Company was formed in 1908 and they were worth considerably more than the figures shown on the balance sheet.

The following directors were duly appointed: Messrs F.P. Cottey, A.T. Ford, C.W.H. Hill, J. Lake, F.P. Nicholls, J.G.R. Orchard, J. Rigby, S.H. Thomas and J.G. Warne.

Sid Thomas was elected as chairman and Fred Cottey vice-chairman. Both the directors had followed the game from their boyhood and had great administrative experience in football in later years.

Thomas had played for City as an amateur and became secretary of the club when it joined the Southern League in 1908. Cottey had been a referee and served as chairman of the East Devon Football Association.

Exeter City 1945–46

Back row: Edwards, Walker, Murray, Goodfellow, Latham, Jordan, Brown, Lee (Groundsman).
Front row: Challis, Wardle, Ebdon, Kernick, Elliot.

Record books show that Exeter City Football Club ceased to function in all but name between 1939 and 1945. There were of course far more serious matters on everyone's minds just across the English Channel (and even nearer than that), than simply a game of football.

The Grecians played their last match for several months when they travelled to Port Vale on Saturday 2nd September 1939. Harold Riley netted the only goal of the game to give Exeter victory and put the side into second place in the Third Division South table.

But within hours of that game ending, the Football League was suspended for the duration of the Second World War. Although many clubs continued to play in hastily organised regional leagues using guest players, Exeter City did not take part, and in effect the club was mothballed until happier times.

St James' Park was eventually taken over for military use by United States forces who were stationed locally, and various huts appeared around the ground. An assortment of military vehicles were driven across the hallowed Park playing surface.

It was not until August 1945 that Exeter City officially started playing again, in a regionalised form of the old Third Division South, the first match being played at the Park against Swindon Town.

For the 1946–47 season, the Football League competition recommenced from whence it had left off in 1939–40, although, of course, every team started afresh in terms of their respective programme of matches.

However, several games were to be played at the Park during the 1944–45 season that involved Exeter City sides containing guest players, and various representative Service teams.

The matches were in the main used as a fundraising exercise for an assortment of war charities. Not many record books though detail these games, and so the 1944–45 season, as far as Exeter City were concerned, could be described as 'The Season that Time Forgot'.

Perhaps the strangest game to have been played at St James' Park in 1945 occurred on Sunday 7th January. A game of American Football was staged between the Sea Lions and McKee's Maulers – formed of teams of American Servicemen.

The Maulers lost by 13 points to 6, with the Merchant Navy Comforts Fund benefiting financially. Admission was one shilling and an attendance of 1,500 was present. No doubt many Exonians went along only to be thoroughly confused by the 'alien' game.

On the football front, the first to take place in 1945 at the Park was on 13th January. The Services League played an East Devon League XI with the former winning 5-3.

A week later Exeter City played their first match since their visit to Port Vale in 1939. A crowd of 2,720 saw City hold Plymouth Argyle to a 2-2 draw, both teams fielding a number of guest players.

The Grecians side had as their guests Corbett (Manchester City), Ryan (Swindon Town), Hellier (Torquay United), Urquhart (Hearts) and surprisingly, in view of their opponents, both Hodge and Mitcheson of Plymouth Argyle.

Following the match against the 'old rivals' several other games involving Exeter City took place. The Grecians won 6-2 at Yeovil Town on 10th February with Mitcheson again guesting and scoring a hat-trick. Other players included Crossley (Cliftonville), Donoghue (Portsmouth), Hunt (Oldham Athletic) and Jeffries (Sheffield United).

City were back at the Park on 17th February 1945 for a fundraising game against the Royal Marines. All the proceeds went to the Royal Marine Prisoner of War Fund. Exeter City won the game 4-1 before an attendance of 2,000.

The return meeting with Plymouth Argyle took place on 10th March, but the Grecians had great difficulty in raising a side, with many players unable to take part due to Service commitments. Indeed, Argyle very kindly loaned the Grecians four players to make up the numbers. Not surprisingly perhaps, City crashed to a 5-1 defeat.

A week later another return fixture was played by City, this time against Yeovil at St James' Park. The result was a 2-2 draw.

A third match was staged with Plymouth Argyle back at St James' Park on 2nd April – Easter Monday. Exeter gained ample revenge for their defeat at Home Park by reversing the previous scoreline, winning 5-1. The crowd of 3,500 saw City goals from Mitcheson (2), McCartney (an 18-year-old Royal Marine), Ebdon and Rich.

It was to be another three weeks before the City

took to the field again, when they played at Weymouth against the Devonshire Regiment. Receipts were donated to the Merchant Navy Week Appeal.

Once again the Grecian team contained few familiar faces, with only Ebdon being on the club's books. The rest of the team was made up entirely of guests from such teams as Blackpool, Halifax Town, Liverpool, Fulham, Third Lanark, Oldham Athletic and Plymouth Argyle. City won 3-1 before an enthusiastic crowd of 3,000.

The visit to Weymouth was to be the last played by City that season, but there were several representative games staged at St James' Park, including Services HQ versus The Rest of the Services League, and the Great Western Railway against the Southern Railway in aid of the Red Cross Prisoner of War Fund. For the record the Great Western Railway 'steamed' to a 7-1 win!

SEASON 1945–46 – THIRD DIVISION SOUTH – SOUTH OF THE THAMES

	P	W	D	L	F	A	Pts
Crystal Palace	20	13	3	4	55	31	29
Cardiff City	20	13	2	5	69	31	28
Bristol City	20	11	2	7	51	40	24
Brighton & H.A.	20	10	1	9	49	50	21
Bristol Rovers	20	7	6	7	44	44	20
Swindon Town	20	8	3	9	35	47	19
Bournemouth	20	7	3	10	52	50	17
Aldershot	20	6	5	9	38	56	17
EXETER CITY	**20**	**6**	**4**	**10**	**33**	**41**	**16**
Reading	20	5	5	10	43	49	15
Torquay United	20	5	4	11	22	52	14

SEASON 1945–46 – THIRD DIVISION SOUTH – CUP TOURNAMENT

	P	W	D	L	F	A	Pts
Bournemouth	16	8	4	4	37	20	20
Bristol Rovers	16	8	3	5	27	19	19
Reading	16	8	2	6	46	29	18
Crystal Palace	16	7	4	5	37	30	18
Cardiff City	16	8	1	7	39	22	17
Bristol City	16	7	3	6	30	27	17
Torquay United	16	6	4	6	19	30	16
EXETER CITY	**16**	**5**	**4**	**7**	**22**	**28**	**14**
Swindon Town	16	5	4	7	21	35	14
Aldershot	16	3	4	9	23	48	10
Brighton & H.A.	16	1	6	9	23	45	8

Exeter City were out to build a team that would settle for nothing less than promotion. Sound familiar? This was the prophecy made by Sidney Thomas at the start of the 1946–47 season during a meeting held at the Exeter Guildhall.

He added that every director had that goal in view but warned fans that there were 21 other clubs in the Division Three South who had similar ambitions.

The meeting – which had been convened by the Grecians' Association – would later be described as the most enthusiastic gathering of City supporters for years.

With the club about to embark on the first season of league football since before the Second World War, there was even more optimism in the air than usual.

In the year ahead, 1946–47, the City directors had approved a playing budget of approaching £8,000, and to that amount had to be added travel costs, hotel expenses and other commitments, bringing the total to about £12,000.

Thomas added: 'It is evident therefore, that the club needs to average [match receipts from] home gates of about £600 clear to pay their way and provide for next summer's wages.'

Manager George Roughton explained that it would be wrong to spend wildly on bringing in new players, in view of what he described as a hopelessly inflated transfer market.

Admission charges to St James' Park had been fixed. Entry to the Big Bank would cost one shilling and threepence. Boys could enter for sixpence. There was no mention of girls.

To stand on the popular Cowshed side of the ground would set an adult fan back one shilling and sixpence.

A massive amount of work had been undertaken to bring St James' Park up to standard, even though matches had been played there the previous season.

Guest speaker at the meeting was George Harrison, a well-known sports writer of the time, who declared that the ground had been transformed into one as good as any in Division Three outside of London.

The chairman reminded the fans that the situation at Exeter City had looked desperate only two years earlier when the club lost its president, chairman and other directors.

Army huts had covered large areas of the terracing and drainage of the playing pitch had been ruined, as American forces took over the ground as a base to store vehicles and equipment.

But thanks to the hard work of Norman Kendall, the Grecians' Association had been formed to stimulate support and raise finance, not only from the city itself, but also from outlying towns and villages.

For the opening fixture of the Division Three South season on 31st August 1946, Torquay United were the visitors to St James' Park.

The Grecians were sporting their brand new red and white hooped jerseys for the first time and the match was attended by the Mayor and Sheriff of Exeter, as well as Football League secretary Fred Howarth.

And a bumper attendance of 11,468 paid a total of £912 15s 6d to watch the game, way above the break-even figure quoted by the chairman.

Torquay forged into a first-half lead, but City hit back to equalise through Ray Wright, a player who had been signed from Wolverhampton Wanderers.

Dick 'Digger' Ebdon had a excellent opportunity to start the Grecians' season off with a win in the dying minutes, but could only guide the ball past the post with only the Torquay keeper to beat.

Unfortunately the pre-season optimism and hopes slowly disappeared as Exeter eventually finished the campaign in 15th place.

However, the directors must have been pleased with the average attendance figures for league matches at the Park, which reached a phenomenal 8,888.

The first match to be played under floodlights at St James' Park in 1953 against Plymouth Argyle.

Exeter City were among the first senior clubs to install floodlighting for matches in the 1950s.

The Grecians had actually used lights for training purposes as early as October 1946, when on a floodlit pitch, City's part-time professionals and amateurs were able to go through their paces. This innovation was deemed to be a big success at the time.

The first-ever full-scale floodlit match at St James' Park was due to be staged on Tuesday 3rd March 1951 between Exeter City and Plymouth Argyle. The friendly fixture was, however, postponed, when just 45 minutes before the kick off the ground was enveloped in swirling fog.

Argyle's journey to Exeter was not entirely wasted though, for they were entertained by the Exeter City directors at a dinner held at the Queens Hotel. Edgar Dobell, a Plymouth Argyle director, said at the dinner that he thought floodlit football was here to stay, although at that particular time it was still a novelty.

The official switch on of the St James' Park floodlights eventually took place on 9th March 1953, when Plymouth Argyle once again provided the opposition.

The *Express & Echo* report of the game read:

'The lights were brilliant, Plymouth Argyle were dazzled and Exeter City were eclipsed. No fault could be found with the floodlights. Play could be followed from all parts of the ground.'

Despite that glowing report, however, the lights were of a rudimentary design in comparison to what one comes to expect today. Argyle won the game 3-0.

Before the kick off there was a short opening ceremony during which the City board of directors thanked the ever-supportive Grecians' Association for their considerable help in donating funds to meet the cost of the floodlights.

A crowd of 8,130 was present, producing match receipts of £908, as the respective teams lined up as follows:

Exeter City: Singleton, Anderson, Doyle, Booth, Wood, Davey, Mitchell, Knight, McClelland, Murphy, Digby.

Plymouth Argyle: Shortt, Jelly, Jones, Dougall, Chisholm, Robertson, Dobbie, McCrory, Davis, Dews, Govan.

City chairman Sidney Thomas told supporters: 'Professional football demands more than ever that clubs must be progressive. That is why my board were keen to be in the forefront of modern developments and have installed floodlighting at St James' Park.

'Wherever the necessary equipment is available, the story is the same. The public are rallying strongly to soccer under lights and I am confident that our own supporters will do the same.

'While floodlit football is in the experimental stage, the future holds out all manner of intriguing prospects. It is not unlikely for example, that an evening league, on a regional basis will come into being in due course.

'I know that the latest venture at St James' Park will have the unanimous blessing of well wishers of the club.'

The Exeter City 'A' team made history on Tuesday 8th December 1953 when they took part in the first-ever Exeter and District League match to be played under floodlights.

Their opponents at St James' Park were Chelston. The Torbay-based side obviously did not shine on the evening as they crashed to a 5-1 defeat.

Floodlit football was still very much in its infancy in March 1956. Commenting after his team had just lost 6-1 to Exeter City reserves at the Park in a Southern League fixture, the Llanelli manager said that it had been the first time his side had played under floodlights and the dazzle had affected his players!

The Exeter City versus Watford match on 10th November 1956 was the first Saturday afternoon fixture at St James' Park to be played partially under floodlights.

Both clubs had agreed beforehand that the lights could be turned on whenever necessary. The Third

Division South fixture ended in a 2-1 win for the men from Vicarage Road.

Exeter City really were one of the pioneers as far as floodlights were concerned, and were certainly the first club in Devon to have them installed, followed a year later by Plymouth Argyle. It would be the early 1960s before Torquay United had a set at Plainmoor.

DID YOU KNOW?

Members of the City team that faced Argyle for the historic first match under the St James' Park floodlights had been signed from a variety of clubs as follows:

Barney Singleton (Wolverhampton Wanderers); John Anderson (Northampton Town); Les Doyle (Everton); Sammy Booth (Derry City); Francis Wood (Shrewsbury Town); Fred Davey (Crediton); Arnold Mitchell (Notts County); John Knight (Chesterfield); Charlie McClelland (Blackburn Rovers); Eddie Murphy (Barnsley); Derek Digby (Dawlish Town).

Exeter City held a players' reunion in 1995 to mark the 75th birthday of former Grecian Harry Bartholomew. A special party and get-together of players who had appeared alongside Bartholomew during his time at the club between 1947 and 1949 was organised.

The event, held at the British Legion Club in Exeter, attracted great media attention and was attended by the Exeter City F.C. chairman, Ivor Doble, and team manager Terry Cooper.

Bartholomew was born in Motherwell on 16th January 1920 and played for his home town club in the Scottish League, before moving to Exeter City in May 1947.

It was a 'whole different ball game' as regards managers signing players in those days. It was often the case that the City manager would go away for a few days to a particular area and interview a number of prospective players, before making one or more signings.

This was the case with Bartholomew. For the then City manager, George Roughton, had spent a few days in Scotland before announcing that he was about to sign the player.

Roughton had to beat off considerable competition for the player's signature, including a very tempting offer from Irish League outfit, Shelbourne.

Bartholomew actually remained in Scotland for a while and was allowed to miss the first weeks of the pre-season training at Exeter, before eventually joining up with his new team mates.

Bartholomew made his first appearance for the City in the traditional pre-season practice matches that always featured the whole playing staff.

They formed the basis of two teams and played against each other. In this case it was Colours versus the Whites with the Colours winning 4-3. Local newspaper reports described Bartholomew as a 'scheming positional player who looks to be a useful acquisition'.

Bartholomew's first league outing for the Grecians came in unhappy circumstances as the City crashed to a 4-0 defeat at Walsall. It was all smiles four days later, however, for back at the Park, Reading were defeated 1-0.

His first league goal for the club came in a 4-0 victory on 20th March 1948 in a Third Division South encounter against Bristol Rovers. He had, however, scored earlier in the season in an F.A. Cup tie versus Northampton Town.

Earning only a mere fraction of what players can today, many of the City staff had to take summer jobs to make ends meet. In Bartholomew's case, it was in the building trade. His wages with Exeter City were never more than £11 per week, but this was occasionally topped up with bonuses, £1 for a draw and £2 for a win!

Bartholomew went onto make 66 league appearances for Exeter City, many of them as captain, and scored six goals. There were three very contrasting highlights of his time with the Grecians.

He was a member of the Exeter City team on that ill-fated afternoon of 16th October 1948, when Notts County proceeded to run up a 9-0 scoreline!

On a happier note, Bartholomew scored in just six seconds against Barnet in an F.A. Cup tie. He was also in the City side that drew 1-1 with Bournemouth and Boscombe Athletic in the first-ever match to be staged on a Good Friday at St James' Park in March 1948.

Bartholomew was placed on the 'open to transfer' list by the Grecians in May 1949 and at one point it was reported that rivals Plymouth Argyle were among the clubs interested in signing him.

However, Bournemouth and Boscombe Athletic won the race for his signature, but he never made a first-team appearance at Dean Court, and in June 1950 he was on the move again, this time to Newport County. His stay at Somerton Park was a short one though, making just three league appearances.

Bartholomew returned to Devon to play Western League football with Bideford. After one season there, he was appointed player-manager of Ilfracombe Town.

Like so many Exeter City players, he decided to settle down in the area once he had hung up his boots. He did pursue at one time, what was one of the more popular professions of retired footballers, that of pub landlord, when he ran the Lamb Inn, Exwick, Exeter.

The City players meet up in 1946, prior to the start of another season

They are: George Thompson, Glyn Vaughan, Ray Wright, Stan Challis, Richard Ebdon, James Gallagher, Bert Hoyle, William Fellowes, Arthur Hydes, George Wardle, John Long, Arthur Coles, Albert Hammond, Jack Blood, Stan Cutting.

England centre-forward Tommy Lawton was a player who was guaranteed to add several hundred to attendances wherever he played, and some times more.

When his club, Notts County, was due to visit Exeter City for a Third Division South fixture on 14th February 1948, such was the interest that a new record of £1,312 5s was set for gate receipts at St James' Park.

Lawton had played for Burnley, Everton (where he won the first of his England caps) and Chelsea, before making a £20,000 move to Notts County in 1947. It proved to be good move as he rattled in 103 goals in 166 appearances over the course of five seasons.

The Exeter City directors felt that at least 5,000 who wished to watch Lawton play could be added to the usual attendance, so imagine their complete and utter disappointment when it was learned that the player would not appear after all!

There were 16,942 inside St James' Park (the highest crowd figure of the season at the Park), many of whom had no idea that Lawton would not be in the Notts County side.

City had been informed the night before the game that an attack of gastric influenza was reportedly the reason he did not play, despite travelling to Exeter with the rest of his team.

When it became known that Lawton would not appear, the City directors and club officials decided to place notices outside the entrances to the ground.

Fred Cottey, the Exeter City vice-chairman, issued a statement that read:

'We acted in good faith with our supporters when we passed the details of the Notts County team to the press for publication. Had Exeter City known in time that Lawton was a non-starter we would certainly have acquainted the press. We share in the disappointment which must be felt by all the club's following at being unable to see the England centre-forward.'

Despite the absence of their star player, Notts County still proved to be too a good a side for the Grecians as they won 1-0, a goal netted by Lawton's replacement, Albert Parks.

The City team lined up: Barney Singleton, George Thompson, Cyril Johnstone, Harry Bartholomew, Reg Gibson, Steve Walker, Dennis Hutchings, Angus Mackay, Charlie Sutherland, Trevor Granville, Doug Regan.

The *Express & Echo* reported that City's performance against County had been inexcusable. The goal-shy Exeter forwards had played without a plan, and their approach work was shoddy.

It proved to be sad day all round for Exeter City supporters, bitterly disappointed at the absence of Lawton, as they witnessed an inept display from the Grecians.

The *Echo* summed the afternoon up by stating: 'Disillusioned and disgruntled, the vast concourse totalling 16,942 left the ground with unhappy memories.'

What had made matters worse was undoubtedly the reports in the local press two days prior to the game that Lawton would definitely appear.

Some City fans felt that the club had known for a while that Lawton was not going to play, but in order that the attendance figure was not to be affected, decided to stay quiet on the subject.

Notts County went on to finish 6th in the Third Division South, whilst Exeter had to settle for an 11th place finish.

BRITISH RAILWAYS
SOUTHERN REGION

FOOTBALL

At EXETER
(EXETER FOOTBALL CLUB AND EXETER RUGBY FOOTBALL CLUB)

EVERY SATURDAY
MARCH 27th to MAY 1st inclusive

DAY EXCURSIONS
BY ALL TRAINS

To EXETER
AS UNDER :—

FROM	Return Fares, Third Class	FROM	Return Fares, Third Class
	s. d.		s. d.
AXMINSTER (A)	5 / 7	NEWTON POPPLEFORD (A)	3 / 11
BARNSTAPLE JUNCTION	8 / 2	NEWTON ST. CYRES	– / 11
BARNSTAPLE TOWN	8 / 2	NORTH TAWTON	3 / 9
BOW	3 / 3	OKEHAMPTON	5 / 2
BROAD CLYST (A)	1 / –	OTTERY ST. MARY (A)	3 / 3
BUDLEIGH SALTERTON (A)	3 / 3	PINHOE (A)	– / 8
CHAPELTON	7 / 3	PORTSMOUTH ARMS	5 / 10
COLYFORD (A)	5 / 5	SAMPFORD COURTENAY	4 / 6
COLYTON (A)	5 / 4	SEATON (A)	5 / 8
COPPLESTONE	2 / 10	SEATON JUNCTION (A)	4 / 11
CREDITON	1 / 5	SIDMOUTH (A)	4 / 3
EAST BUDLEIGH (A)	3 / 7	SIDMOUTH JUNCTION (A)	2 / 7
EGGESFORD	4 / 6	SOUTH MOLTON ROAD	5 / 4
EXMOUTH (A)	2 / 4	TIPTON ST. JOHNS (A)	3 / 7
HONITON (A)	3 / 6	TOPSHAM (A)	1 / 2
LAPFORD	3 / 7	UMBERLEIGH	6 / 7
LITTLEHAM (A)	2 / 7	WHIMPLE (A)	1 / 10
LYMPSTONE (A)	1 / 10	WOODBURY ROAD (A)	1 / 5
MORCHARD ROAD	3 / 3	YEOFORD	2 / 4

→ RETURN BY ANY TRAIN SAME DAY ←

A—Tickets available to alight at and return from St. James Park Halt.

CHILDREN 3 AND UNDER 14 YEARS, HALF-FARE.

TICKETS MAY BE OBTAINED IN ADVANCE AT STATIONS AND AGENCIES.

NOTICE AS TO CONDITIONS.—These tickets are issued at less than the ordinary fares, and are subject to the Conditions published in the Notices and Publications of the Railway Executive, or the Southern Railway Company.

Waterloo Station, S.E.1,
March, 1948.

JOHN ELLIOT,
Chief Regional Officer.

C.X.24/6/17348.

Printed in Great Britain.
Waterlow & Sons Limited, London and Dunstable.

Exeter City 1948–49
Back row: Cyril Johnstone, Fred Davey, Ray Goddard, Ken Powell, Barney Singleton, Bill Harrower, Jim Clark, Steve Walker, James Gallagher (Trainer).
Front row: Peter Fallon, Richard Smart, Archie Smith, John Greenwood, Doug Regan.

Exeter City 1948–49 prior to their first practice match of the season.

What could be worse than spending a week in Cleethorpes, laid low with the trots? Two weeks in Cleethorpes perhaps? Could the situation be any worse?

For Exeter City's players, it most certainly was, for they were staying in the town preparing for their F.A. Cup third round tie against Grimsby Town.

Having beaten Barnet 6-2 away in the first round, and then Hereford United 2-1 at St James' Park in round two, the Grecians were looking forward to continuing their F.A. Cup adventure in the 1948–49 season, with a trip to Grimsby, who were then a Second Division team.

It wasn't the ideal draw for City, in view of the distance involved in travelling, but they were able to pit their skills against a team from a higher division.

Although City were not exactly making a great impact in the Third Division South, the club's directors decided that as the team were due at Norwich City for a league fixture a week before the cup tie, the players should then travel onto Cleethorpes and stay there preparing for the Grimsby game.

Thirteen players set out for Norwich, but the first part of their two-match 'tour' ended in a New Year's Day defeat as the Canaries won 3-0.

It was seemingly a Devonian bug that caused the gastro-enteritis discomfort that swept through the City playing squad, and by the time they had arrived at their hotel in Cleethorpes, several players were reportedly feeling the effects.

With only a small playing squad, it was hoped that the players would recover sufficiently in time to take their place in the team to face Grimsby at the end of the week.

City were also hoping that winger Doug Regan, who had been left behind in Exeter recovering from the stomach bug, would be fit enough to travel and join his team mates.

Grimsby had put their Blundell Park pitch at the disposal of the City squad, where they enjoyed some light training sessions.

The Grecians also had the use of the Wonderland Amusement Centre in Cleethorpes which consisted of an area of 20,000 square feet of undercover basketball and netball courts.

This proved to be very useful indeed, for it was not only the illness that was hampering City's plans, but the weather too, which turned for the worse as snow fell and thus outdoor training proved to be very difficult in the circumstances.

As the week progressed, slowly but surely, the City players reported that they were beginning to feel better, and there was further good news in that Regan was on his way from Exeter to join up with the party.

The day of the third round cup tie arrived – 8th January 1949 – and City eventually took to the field with the following team: Bert Hoyle, Cyril Johnstone, Jim Clark, Harry Bartholomew, Steve Walker, Peter Fallon, Bill Dymond, Richard Smart, Archie Smith, Bill Harrower, Doug Regan.

Despite their week of disrupted preparation due to the illness, City more than matched their higher league opponents for a large part of the match, but eventually went out of the competition, losing 2-1.

Grimsby took a fifth minute lead, but the early setback did not rock the City boat and five minutes before the interval the Grecians equalised through Regan – his late call-up being justified.

Unfortunately Exeter were unable to hold on until the half-time break and Grimsby hit back almost immediately to take the lead once more, with a goal that proved to be the winning one.

City had made a good impression and it was reported in the press that the Exeter team were 100 per cent triers, whose midfield surpassed anything their Second Division opposition could produce. It was in attack where Grimsby held the upperhand.

Grimsby went on to play their Humberside rivals, Hull City, at Blundell Park in the next round, but their cup run ended as the Tigers won 3-2.

The Exeter City squad, who stayed at the Kingsway Hotel in Cleethorpes, prior to their third round F.A. Cup tie at Grimsby Town in 1949
Back row: Not known, James Gallagher (Trainer), George Roughton (Manager), Jim Clark,
Bert Hoyle, Bill Harrower, Steve Walker, Reg Gibson.
Front row: James Rigby (Director), Bill Dymond, Archie Smith, Richard Smart, Angus Mackay,
Peter Fallon, Cyril Johnstone.

The English are well known for their eccentrics. They are found in all walks of life. Football clubs have their own versions of eccentrics and they are generally referred to as 'characters'.

We probably all know of at least one person who might fit the category of a football character. Even Exeter City has had them. None more so than the now departed 'Gilbert', who many of you will no doubt recall.

Gilbert Whyte helped groundsman Sonny Clark prepare the playing surface in the 1950s and 60s, and supported the Grecians from the St James' Park terraces.

He first watched City play in 1949, making the journey to Exeter from his home in Okehampton.

He offered words of encouragement to the City players, although not many supporters (or players for that matter) could understand a word of what he was trying to get across.

Who could forget how he reacted when City were on the attack and within shooting distance of the goal? 'Hup, hup, hup', he would shout.

The fact that people mimicked his actions on the terraces speaks volumes for him and how he was not just noticed, but also how he had become part of the 'fixtures and fittings' at St James' Park.

Nobody knew too much about Gilbert though, and not many even knew what he actually did on matchdays, other than making encouraging noises with sudden jerk-like movements whilst stood on the terraces.

But there was certainly no denying his devotion to Exeter City Football Club as he supported them every match, no matter what the result.

It was not just at Exeter games that Gilbert could be found though, for although he was a Grecian through and through, there were many occasions when he was seen walking to and from matches at Torquay United.

He always had a transistor radio with him, which he held aloft to his ear, as if it were almost stuck to it.

This was especially so after a match, as he listened to all the results on the BBC as he walked back into the town centre from Plainmoor.

No matter who you were, as you walked alongside or by him, he always repeated the results as if it was specially aimed at you!

It wasn't just football that grabbed Gilbert's attention, for he obviously loved sport in general and could be seen following the fortunes of the Exeter Falcons Speedway team, or Exeter Cricket Club.

Nor did Gilbert restrict his football watching to the City first team. He watched the reserves in the Southern League in the 1950s and 60s.

Sadly Gilbert is no longer with us, having died in 1985, but such was his popularity that many of the Exeter City staff attended his funeral to pay their last respects.

Gilbert Whyte was a real character, a loveable one, and part of Exeter City folklore. We really do love eccentrics and characters.

Two very different recent Exeter City mascots:
Alex the Greek (on the left) and current mascot Grecian the Lion (on the right).

The Grecians had reached the fourth round of the F.A. Cup for the first time since 1937 and they were going to make the most of their trip to First Division Liverpool.

To reach this stage of the competition, the tie being played at Anfield on 28th January 1950, City had started off by winning an eight-goal thriller at Millwall, where they won 5-3.

In round two, first-time visitors to St James' Park, Chester, were sent packing as they lost 2-0 and this earned City another home tie against non-league Nuneaton Borough, who they beat 3-0.

It seemed a bit of a daunting prospect having to travel to Anfield to face a Liverpool side that was top of the First Division and contained such well-known players such as Joe Fagan, Bob Paisley and the legendary Billy Liddell.

City warmed up for their trip north by winning 2-1 at Aldershot in a Third Division South fixture a week earlier, as Richard Smart and Steve Walker got the goals.

Immediately after that match the attention turned to the cup tie and it was decided that the City team should have plenty of time in which to prepare for it.

As a result the team left for Liverpool by train on the Tuesday preceding the match, a squad of 13 players, plus directors travelling north to their base at the Grand Hotel, New Brighton.

There had been one possible absentee, that of winger Doug Regan, who had what was thought to be an appendix problem the previous week, however, he was pronounced fit and also made the journey.

The team were met at Liverpool Lime Street station by former City player, Harold Houghton, a stalwart of the 1930–31 cup team who had netted the equalising goal when Sunderland were held to a draw at Roker Park. Houghton now had a flourishing fish merchants business in Liverpool.

Houghton was not the only former City player to meet the team, for Harry Gee, a half-back who was in the 1928 cup team that drew with Blackburn Rovers before losing the replay in extra-time, also called into the Grand Hotel. Gee was a newsagent and tobacconist on the Wirral and was a Wallasey Borough councillor.

Yet another visitor was half-back Jimmy Gray, who played in the City team that finished runners-up in the Third Division South in 1932–33. Gray was working in a Liverpool telephone exchange.

The big day arrived and a massive crowd of 45,209 was inside Anfield to greet the teams, as City lined up: Barney Singleton, Cyril Johnstone, Jim Clark, Peter Fallon, Ray Goddard, Fred Davey, Dennis Hutchings, Richard Smart, Steve Walker, John Greenwood, Doug Regan.

The *Express & Echo* reported: 'If courage could have been rewarded then the shock result of the fourth round would have gone to Exeter City. The team's fighting spirit was magnificent.

'Against Liverpool, the proud leaders of the First Division, gallant Exeter City, lowly placed in the Third Division, were the equals of their foe in all save penetrative thrust.'

Exeter were in with a chance until the 80th minute, when Liverpool went 2-0 up, but even then the Grecians fought their way back.

City had a 'goal' disallowed in the first half when Smart charged goalkeeper Sidlow over the line after gathering a header from Walker, but the referee ruled it out, which didn't please the estimated 2,000 Exeter supporters in the ground.

They also voiced their displeasure following another incident when Smart appeared to be tripped from behind in the area, but the appeals for penalty were waved away.

Seconds before the half-time whistle, Barron put Liverpool in front, but they couldn't find a way through the City defence again until ten minutes from time when Fagan added a second.

Despite this setback, the City players immediately fought their way back into the game and two minutes later were rewarded when Smart scored.

Five minutes from time, it was all over for the Grecians as Payne made sure that Liverpool were in the hat for the draw for the next round.

The match report stated: 'It was a tremendous performance from Exeter, that will be remembered for a long time.'

Liverpool went on to reach the final at Wembley, beating Stockport County, Blackpool and Everton on the way, but they were to lose at the 'twin towers', 2-0, to Arsenal.

There were several notable off-the-field occurrences in the life of Exeter City during the 1950–51 season, the first of which concerned alarm at the 'poor' attendances that the team was attracting to St James' Park.

Although the average for the season was 9,771, this was down on the previous two seasons, a point made by director Leslie Seward at a meeting of the Grecians' Association in September 1950.

He said that the City were not getting the support that they deserved and to run the club on an economic basis, attendances of between 12,000 and 14,000 were needed at home matches.

It seems amazing that an average attendance of nearly 10,000 was not enough to satisfy the club directors. Exeter City would dearly love an average attendance of those proportions these days.

Seward added that the City directors were trying to give the people a good team, the Grecians' Association was playing its part by raising money for ground improvements, but their joint efforts were not being appreciated as they should be.

The very next home Third Division South fixture immediately after the meeting saw Reading visit St James' Park, and an attendance of 11,116 was present to watch the visitors take the points in a 3-1 win.

Number one priority in the list of proposed improvements to St James' Park was the provision of a new entrance to the ground leading from Old Tiverton Road to the Big Bank.

The work for this was estimated to cost £613 and was to be undertaken during the season. The cost of the job was to be met by the Grecians' Association.

It was hoped to be completed in time for the visit of Plymouth Argyle in February 1951 when a full house was anticipated. The new entrance was to be called the Norman Kendall Gate, the president and founder of the Grecians' Association and someone who did so much to sponsor the election of Exeter City to the Southern League in 1908.

The new entrance was in fact used before the Argyle game, as 18,177 spectators watched Exeter City's 4-2 home win over Grimsby Town in the F.A. Cup third round, which earned them a home game against Chelsea.

Mr S.H. Thomas, the chairman of the City directors, praised the Association for undertaking the decision to raise the money for the scheme

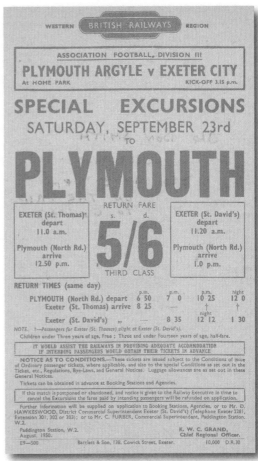

It was not unusual for special excursion trains to be run to City's matches. This poster advertises the Grecians' fixture at Plymouth Argyle in September 1950.

and appealed to all supporters to become members so that the necessary finance would be available.

The club had announced a trading loss of £5,241 on the year, mainly attributable to transfer fees, having spent £9,000 as opposed to receiving £200.

The total match receipts were £23,349, whilst season ticket sales totalled over £5,000, then a club record.

Nearly half the club's income went in wages. In 1908 the club expenditure budgeted for £2,312, but in 1950 this had increased to £34,000 per year.

There was a mortgage loan outstanding of £12,000 and another on players' housing amounted to £6,867. The total liabilities were £20,650.

As far as assets were concerned, a conservative value of St James' Park put it at £25,000 (including stands and equipment), whilst housing for players was valued at £9,800. The value of players was stated to be £15,000, giving the club a total asset value of £49,800.

Mr Thomas reiterated the previous comments of Mr Seward by stating that whilst Exeter City had to rely on attendances of 10,000, they wouldn't possibly be able to spend lavishly on players.

A very muddy St James' Park. Action from a match in the late 1940s.
City were at that time playing in red and white hooped shirts.

In the week (December 2004) that Exeter City drew the third round F.A. Cup tie everyone else wanted – a trip to Manchester United, it was oh so easy to forget that the Grecians had a less than impressive record in the competition.

Nevertheless, it was no surprise to see City fans jumping with joy when the club were paired with Manchester United. After all, such games do not occur too often as far as Exeter City is concerned, and certainly not one as big as the trip to Old Trafford, which would wipe the clubs debts out in one fell swoop.

Who could forget the F.A. Cup run of 1981 to the quarter-finals, and also the matches against the likes of Manchester United, Wolverhampton Wanderers, Aston Villa and Everton?

Those ties provided a welcome relief after the ignominy of losing to supposedly inferior opposition all too often in the F.A. Cup.

This time it would be different however, with City being far and away the underdogs and the team that the football world would have their eye on when they travelled to the Theatre of Dreams.

It was a real David and Goliath tie. It is what the F.A. Cup is all about and why it retains its unique position in the game of football.

There haven't been too many occasions when we have seen a scramble for tickets to watch Exeter City play. But when it has happened, it has usually been for an F.A. Cup tie.

It happened in 1951, when the Grecians had reached the fourth round and were drawn at home to First Division Chelsea.

Having already beaten Glastonbury, Swindon Town and Grimsby Town, all hell broke loose when Exeter were drawn at home to the Stamford Bridge side.

Despite the fact that St James' Park was full to bursting, with a 20,000 capacity crowd inside, there were still hundreds who wanted tickets for the game, but, for one reason or another, were not successful.

Tickets went on sale prior to the game at the Park and queues stretched back along Well Street long before the ticket office opened.

Unfortunately demand far outstripped supply, to prove not for the first time that there never really is a 100 per cent satisfactory system devised to sell or distribute tickets for big matches at the Park.

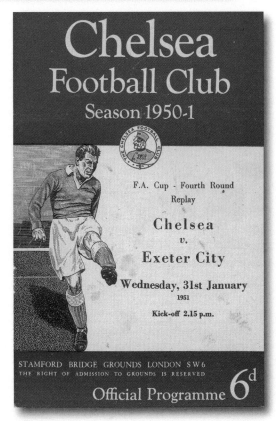

Chelsea Football Club
Season 1950-1

F.A. Cup - Fourth Round Replay

Chelsea
v.
Exeter City

Wednesday, 31st January 1951
Kick-off 2.15 p.m.

STAMFORD BRIDGE GROUNDS LONDON SW6
THE RIGHT OF ADMISSION TO GROUNDS IS RESERVED

Official Programme 6d

There is always someone with a hard-luck story who doesn't get a ticket. On this particular occasion, 27th January 1951, those fortunate enough to watch the tie, saw City put up a magnificent display to draw 1-1.

Exeter's scorer, who earned the Grecians a second crack against Chelsea, was winger Doug Regan. Unfortunately, City sustained a few injuries that meant enforced changes for the replay.

Despite that though, before an attendance of 40,000 in south-west London, the Grecians belied their Third Division South status and only went down by a creditable 0-2.

It was to be Exeter City manager George Roughton's last big cup tie at the club, for the following season he left to take over as boss of Southampton.

Amazingly, the very next game at St James' Park following the Chelsea cup tie also drew a capacity crowd of 20,000.

The visitors were Plymouth Argyle, with City bouncing back from their cup defeat to win 3-2 with goals from Angus Mackay, Archie Smith and Charlie McClelland.

The trip to Manchester United in January 2005, would surely erase those painful memories and F.A. Cup defeats at the hands of Bath City, Dartford, Gravesend and Northfleet, Bedford Town, Alvechurch, Walton and Hersham, and Bognor Regis Town etc.

Exeter City's Angus Mackay (far left, in the hooped shirt) watches the Chelsea goalkeeper gather the ball in the first match at a packed St James' Park.

27th January 1951: F.A. Cup round four
Exeter City 1 Chelsea 1
City team: Barney Singleton, Derek Warren, Jim Clark, Bill Harrower, Ray Goddard, Fred Davey, Charlie McClelland, Joe Lynn, Archie Smith, Angus Mackay, Doug Regan.
City scorer: Regan.
Attendance: 20,000

31st January 1951: F.A. Cup round four replay
Chelsea 2 Exeter City 0
City team: Barney Singleton, Derek Warren, Stan Rowe, Peter Fallon, Ray Goddard, Fred Davey, Charlie McClelland, Bill Harrower, Reg Dare, Joe Lynn, Doug Regan.
Attendance: 40,000

A party of Exeter City directors, officials and players left for a four-match tour of Holland on 17th May 1951.

The players in the City party consisted of goalkeeper Barney Singleton; full-backs Cyril Johnstone, Derek Warren and Jim Clark; half-backs Peter Fallon, Ray Goddard (captain) and Fred Davey; forwards Bill Harrower, Charlie McClelland, Dick Smart, Angus Mackay, Doug Regan and Derek Digby.

Amateur goalkeeper Graham Lear was to join the City squad in Amsterdam a day later as he was involved in a match for Exmouth Town on the day that City were due to leave for their much awaited tour.

The son of the Exeter City secretary George Gilbert lived in Amsterdam and had acted as liaison officer for the tour. Ajax F.C. were to be Exeter City's hosts and the club president and various officials met the Grecians at Amsterdam railway station.

A band played 'God Save the King' and the Dutch officials welcomed everyone from Exeter City Football Club to Holland.

The first game was to be against DOS Utrecht on 20th May 1951. Both teams lined up in front of the main grandstand for the respective playing of the national anthems.

Photographs and pennants were exchanged and the City captain, Ray Goddard, was presented with an inscribed plaque to mark the occasion.

City took a sixth-minute lead through Angus Mackay, and although Utrecht attacked strongly they found the Grecians defence in fine form.

Mackay added a second goal in the 35th minute and shortly after Charlie McClelland beat three men in a dazzling run to score from 12 yards.

Although neither side found the net in the second half, Exeter should have scored a fourth goal from the penalty spot, but Peter Fallon fired over the bar.

A useful start had been made to the tour by the Grecians, having given a very good account of themselves in winning 3-0.

Three days later Exeter City faced a stiff task against Haarlem Eftal, who included no fewer than seven full internationals in their side.

The Grecians, however, made a sensational start and swept into a 3-0 lead. Charlie McClelland (4th and 35th mins) and Richard Smart (36th) being the Exeter scorers. De Vetter reduced the arrears shortly before half-time.

Haarlem scored again at the start of the second half through Roozen. Play then swept from end to end before Smart increased City's lead.

McClelland completed his hat-trick, but Haarlem never gave up and following a scramble in the Exeter goal area, Greenevald scored from close in,

The players of Exeter City (dark shirts) and Haarlem Eftal line up prior to the match in 1951.

to make the final score 5-3 in favour of the Grecians.

On Sunday 27th May, Exeter City suffered their first and only defeat in Holland, when they lost 4-2 at BVV Hertogenbosch.

Charlie McClleland did fire City into an eighth-minute lead and Angus Mackay added a second 21 minutes later as the Grecians completely outplayed their opponents. Exeter were to pay dearly for not taking further chances though.

When the team returned to the pitch for the start of the second half the band was still playing and were determined to finish their piece. The conductor asked the referee for permission to play an encore. He agreed and the interval was extended to 20 minutes.

When the game did eventually restart, BVV staged a remarkable comeback and in the final ten minutes netted three times, much to the delight of their fans, and thus snatched victory away from Exeter.

The final game in Holland took place on 30th May, when Exeter City took on a Combined Hague XI. Once again City scored an early goal, McClelland netting direct from a free-kick via the underside of the crossbar after 15 minutes of play.

The standard of refereeing left a lot to be desired and some bad feeling crept into the game. Richard Smart had what looked like a perfectly good goal disallowed for offside, which incensed the city team.

The Grecians kept plugging away and were rewarded for their efforts when with two minutes of the game remaining, Doug Regan made it 2-0.

An enjoyable tour had come to an end, and Exeter had won three and lost one of the four games played, scoring 14 goals and conceding seven. The tour had been a personal triumph for Charlie McClelland, who found the net in all four games, scoring six goals in all.

City's hosts, Ajax F.C. presented souvenir clogs to the Exeter directors, officials and players, as mementoes of their visit to Holland.

The president of Ajax F.C. paid tribute to the Exeter City team and hoped that they would make a return visit at some time in the future.

As well as playing football, the City party had also found time to visit many other attractions, including a tour around a diamond factory and a trip to the famous bulb fields.

GRECIANS' TOUR OF HOLLAND

Sunday 20th May 1951
DOS Utrecht 0 Exeter City 3
City team: Singleton, Warren, Clark, Fallon, Goddard, Davey, McClelland, Smart, Smith, Mackay, Regan.
City scorers: Mackay (2), McClelland.

Wednesday 23rd May 1951
Haarlem 3 Exeter City 5
City team: Lear, Warren, Clark, Fallon, Goddard, Davey (Digby), Harrower, Smart, McClelland, Mackay, Regan.
City scorers: McClelland (3), Smart (2).

Sunday 27th May 1951
BVV Hertogenbosch 4 Exeter City 2
City team: Singleton, Warren, Clark, Johnstone, Goddard, Fallon, Harrower, Smyth, McClelland, Mackay, Regan.
City scorers: McClelland, Mackay.

Wednesday 30th May 1951
Combined Hague XI 0 Exeter City 2
City team: Lear, Warren, Clark, Fallon, Goddard, Harrower, McClelland, Smart, Smith, Mackay, Regan.
City scorers: McClelland, Regan.

The name of Ivan Armes will forever appear in the Exeter City F.C. record books, for it is unlikely that his 'achievement' will be equalled, let alone surpassed.

Who is Ivan Armes? He was a right-half who was signed by the Grecians from Norwich City in December 1951.

So what is so special about our Ivan that he entered the St James' Park record books? Well, he was the last Exeter City player who was to make his Football League debut for the club in a Christmas Day fixture.

As it seems pretty improbable that the Grecians will ever play again on a Christmas Day, Armes' record is therefore almost unbreakable.

Having been recruited by long-serving City boss, George Roughton, the defender went straight into the team that faced local rivals Torquay United at St James' Park on 25th December 1951.

The Exeter team that day lined up:

Barney Singleton, Derek Warren, Stan Rowe, Ivan Armes, Ray Goddard, Fred Davey, Derek Digby, Richard Smart, Dick Walton, Angus Mackay, Charlie McClelland.

Armes had actually been signed on the Saturday, three days before the Third Division South fixture against Torquay, so he had little time to get to know his new team mates.

It was reported that the Grecians had paid a four-figure fee for the services of Armes, who had lost his first-team place at Norwich, despite having featured in 61 league matches for the Canaries.

What made his Exeter City debut even more remarkable was the fact that, until moving to St James' Park, he had only ever scored one league goal.

Yes, you've guessed it, he capped his first match

in an Exeter City shirt by scoring as the side romped to a 4-0 win in front of a crowd of 8,429.

The *Express & Echo* reported: 'Ivan Armes made a dream debut and scored a gem goal to highlight a performance unbettered by any City wing-half since the war.

'Solid in defence and magnificent in the constructive arts, he demonstrated over and over that the first-time, low, accurate cross is one of the effective moves in football.

'The crowd rose to the newcomer at the end of the match, for City fans were appreciative of a great display.'

Armes netted what was the third goal of the match, with a flashing drive from just outside the penalty area. The other City goalscorers were Smart, Mackay and makeshift centre-forward Dick Walton, who was more accustomed to playing as a full-back.

The return meeting took place at Plainmoor the following day (!) and euphoria of City's triumph was soon forgotten as Torquay gained handsome revenge with a 5-1 thrashing of the Grecians.

Despite all the plaudits that Armes had earned on his debut, he was obviously unable to consistently produce that sort of display, for he had lost his place in the City team by the end of the season, having made a total of 13 appearances.

He did, however, find the back of the net again in a 6-1 home win over Leyton Orient, once more at the Park, and just three days after the 5-1 beating at Plainmoor, such was the topsy-turvy form of Exeter City.

Armes was completely out of the picture the following season. He was to make just one more senior appearance for the Grecians, in a 1-1 draw at home to Watford on 15th November 1952. It was no surprise that he was released at the end of his contract, with City being his last professional club.

In the summer of 1952 Exeter City manager Norman Kirkman announced that he had signed a young right-winger from Notts County. It was a signing that proved to be one of shrewdest ever to be made in the history of the club.

The player was 23-year-old Arnold Mitchell, who had started his career with Derby County as a professional in February 1948. Mitchell moved on to Nottingham Forest in March 1950 and then to neighbours Notts County in May 1951.

It was with County that Mitchell finally made his Football League debut, playing just the one game. Not a great start to his career, but the best was yet to come!

The Rotherham-born player was to embark on a career with Exeter City that spanned 14 years and 495 league appearances.

He was to become one of the most willing and enthusiastic footballers ever to wear the red and white striped Grecians' shirt, and was able to play in every position asked of him, including that of goalkeeper when he took over from the injured Geoff Morton in a match at Southend United in September 1954. He even managed to keep a clean sheet!

Mitchell's sheer enthusiasm and drive for the game he so loved was an inspiration to all who played alongside him, and to all who were privileged to watch him from the terraces.

He made his debut for the City in a 2-0 home win over Northampton Town on 27th August 1952 and went on to score ten goals in 38 league appearances.

Mitchell was switched to a regular and more familiar half-back position for the 1954–55 season, and from then on it was strange not to see his name in a City team line up.

Mitchell went on and on, amassing appearance after appearance – full-back, half-back, centre-forward, winger – he played equally as well whatever shirt he wore.

Exeter City almost made a tragic mistake at one time in Mitchell's career by putting him on the transfer list at the end of his first season with the club! Fortunately he was quickly re-engaged and was to stay for another 13 years.

His greatest triumph was when he skippered, at the age of 34, the first-ever Exeter City team to win promotion. During the 1963–64 season Mitchell

Arnold Mitchell.

featured in 38 matches and scored three vital goals as the Grecians gained promotion to the Third Division.

He was a member of a City defensive line up that even today rolls off the tongue of all those who witnessed one of the Grecians' finest hours. They were: Alan Barnett, Cecil Smyth, Les MacDonald, Arnold Mitchell, Keith Harvey, Des Anderson.

They formed the backbone of City's success, whilst Alan Banks was knocking in the goals at the other end, and the cultured play of Dermot Curtis earned international recognition for the Republic of Ireland.

Third Division football beckoned, but still Mitchell played on. In fact he only missed three league matches the following season, and whilst he may not by then have been displaying his best football in what was the twilight of his career, it was his pure drive that kept him and his colleagues around him going.

Finally the club were to give Mitchell a free transfer at the end of the 1965–66 season – a season when he played in just 19 league matches.

His last league outing at St James' Park was in happy circumstances as the City won 2-0 against Brighton and Hove Albion on 3rd May 1966.

His very last league appearance came in a 4-1 defeat at Reading on 18th May 1966. By then, Exeter City had all but suffered relegation back to Division Four.

By the time he had left the Grecians, not only had Mitchell made a club record-breaking 495 league appearances, but he had also played in a further 17 F.A. Cup ties and four Football League Cup matches, to take his grand total to 516 competitive appearances for the club, with a total of 46 goals. They are figures that are unlikely to be broken for some time, if ever, by any other Exeter City player.

An era was over. Mitchell had been a legend in his own time as far as any City supporter was concerned. A fine servant and ambassador to the club, who surely deserved greater recognition when he eventually did leave St James' Park.

Not even a testimonial game was staged for a man who devoted a large chunk of his life to the Grecians.

He did actually play on for a further season at Western League Taunton Town, but his career was finally brought an end when he was unfortunate enough to sustain the only serious injury of his career – a broken leg.

Some may say it could only happen at Exeter City! Certainly the situation with Tim Ward in March 1953 was bizarre to say the least.

Player-manager Norman Kirkman had departed to take over at Bradford Park Avenue, enticed by a four-figure salary, after a year in charge at St James' Park.

Favourite to replace Kirkham was former England and Derby County wing-half Tim Ward, who was on the books at Barnsley as a player and their chief coach.

Ward had played for England against Wales in 1949 and toured Canada with the Football Association. He had been transferred from Derby to Barnsley in March 1951, but had taken over in a coaching capacity for the start of the 1952–53 season.

Born in Cheltenham, Ward had played for his home club, prior to signing for Derby in April 1937 for a transfer fee of £100.

He travelled to Exeter for talks with the City directors on Thursday 5th March 1953, and later that evening, following a board meeting his appointment was announced.

Twenty-four hours after Ward's appointment as manager of Exeter City, he set off, along with the team, for the Grecians' game at Ipswich Town.

Ward could not have wished for a happier start as City won the Third Division South fixture 1-0, with John Knight netting the all-important goal.

However, the situation with regards to Ward and Exeter City then became farcical, for just eight days after his appointment, he was on the overnight train from Exeter back to Barnsley.

There were rumours that he had a disagreement with the City directors because they had interfered with the selection of the team, but that was quickly denied as events progressed and proved otherwise.

Mr S.H. Thomas, the Exeter City F.C. chairman strenuously denied that there was any truth in the rumours and went on to say that when Exeter City were seeking a manager to succeed Norman Kirkman, Ward had applied for the post at St James' Park and he said he had the consent of the Barnsley F.C. board of directors to do so.

The first inkling of a possible problem emerged on the Tuesday after the victory at Ipswich, when the Barnsley club chairman contacted the Exeter City chairman informing him that the final decision had not been reached, but promising that the subject of Ward's release would be considered in due course.

As a signed player, Ward naturally was bound by his Barnsley contract and he had no alternative but to go back. His registration still belonged to Barnsley and it would remain the case until his release was granted.

Thomas, clearly concerned by the sudden turn of events, said all the club could do was to wait and see what further developments may occur and should it happen that Ward ceased to be with Exeter City, then the club would have to try and get someone else in to take charge of the team.

The story took another twist when the Barnsley directors held a meeting to discuss a managerial replacement at their club for Angus Seed.

The meeting was held on Wednesday 18th March and they were keen to speak to Ward who was also amongst the applicants for the vacancy.

The Grecians had to wait until Wednesday 30th March, when it was formally announced that Ward had been appointed manager at Barnsley, thus it was back to square one in their hunt for a successor to Kirkman.

The whole situation had been a complete debacle, and very embarrassing for Exeter City, who had seen Ward take charge of one game and in name only had been manager for just eight days!

Eventually Exeter turned to Norman Dodgin as their next player-manager, the former Northampton Town half-back taking charge in April 1953.

So what of Ward? He remained in charge at Barnsley until February 1960. He was then manager of Grimsby Town, Derby County and Carlisle United, being appointed as a scout at Nottingham Forest in August 1969. He died aged 75 in 1993.

Many players go through their entire playing career without sustaining an injury other than minor knocks and bruises, but for some, like Frank Houghton, his career seemed to be blighted with one setback after another.

The Preston-born player first hit the football headlines in Northern Ireland, whilst playing for Ballymena United. In 1947 he was described as one of the finest wing-halves in the whole of Ireland.

By January 1948 he was on the books at Newcastle United, who had paid a fee of £6,000 for his services. On 17th April 1948 United hosted Sheffield Wednesday and it proved to be an eventful match for Houghton.

He collided with a goal post with just three minutes of the match remaining and knocked himself out whilst scoring. He came around and almost in the final minute added a further goal, again crashing into an upright. This time though he was not so fortunate and he broke an arm.

In season 1950–51 Houghton suffered a serious respiratory illness and Newcastle sent him to Switzerland to recover. He spent two years in a sanatorium and with typical spirit and determination worked his way back to fitness. He returned to Tyneside anxious to break back into the Newcastle United first team.

At the start of the 1953–54 season, Houghton was transferred to another St James' Park, home of Exeter City, but by then doctors had told him his playing career was over due to his illness, so he had been appointed as assistant trainer by the Grecians.

However, Houghton had other ideas, and he took part in the pre-season matches for the City, itching to get back into action. He managed to persuade the Exeter directors that he was fit enough to turn out for the Grecians' reserve team in the Southern League.

He crowned his comeback success when he was selected to play centre-forward against Crystal Palace on the opening day of the 1954–55 season, and celebrated the occasion by scoring a goal in the 2-0 win.

He went on to feature in 18 Third Division South matches for City, notching six goals, but his career was about to take another unfortunate turn.

In August 1955, Houghton was playing in one of the pre-season games when he sustained a broken leg, but having overcome illness, he didn't let this get him down and by the following February he had not only made a great recovery but was back in the City team for the game at St James' Park against Swindon Town, a fixture that Exeter lost 2-1 – and yes, Houghton scored!

Tragedy struck again the following season when Houghton was in the City side that made the short journey to Home Park. It was bad day all round, not just for Houghton who was sadly stretchered off the field with yet another broken leg, but for the Grecians, who crashed to a 5-0 defeat against their arch rivals, Plymouth Argyle.

This proved to be the last game that Houghton ever played for Exeter City, for the break was a particularly bad one and took a very long time to heal properly. This time he did take the advice of the doctors and he reluctantly hung up his boots as far as competitive games were concerned.

Moving into the bookmaking business, Houghton then started to play in the Exeter Wednesday League, alongside some of his former Grecian team mates, such as George Willis, Angus Mackay, Bill Dunlop and Roger King.

Houghton described the team as being 'all chaps who frequent my betting shop!'

Dunlop and King were also in the bookmaking business, whist at the time, Mackay ran a pub in Exeter and Willis was a publican in Torquay, not far from Plainmoor.

Frank Calvert Houghton had played a total of 55 league matches for Newcastle United, scoring ten goals. He also scored ten times for Exeter City in 27 league outings. He died in 1994, aged 68.

As mentioned in Chapter 47, you should never say never, but it seems pretty unlikely that Exeter City will ever again fulfil a fixture on Christmas Day.

Yet at one time the games played on 25th December would draw some of the best crowds of the season.

Perhaps what makes it even more amazing that games used to be played on the 25th was because there wasn't the same access to cars that there is today. However, there was public transport on Christmas Day – something that is virtually unheard of now.

There will be some Grecian supporters who will probably recall first-team Christmas Day matches at St James' Park, the last of which was played in 1954.

Swindon Town were the visitors for the Third Division South fixture and 6,527 spectators were present. City won the game 2-1, with goals from Ray John and Ed Murphy.

It was a welcome win and one that must have brought the proverbial Christmas cheer to Grecians' fans, for they hadn't seen a City victory for a couple of months. They probably celebrated with a drink or two!

It must have been a massive improvement on previous performances for the match report stated: 'No finer football has been played by City this season than in the first half of this game.'

The City team was: Hugh Kelly, Brian Doyle, Norman Douglass, Maurice Setters, Fred Davey, Arnold Mitchell, Peter Thomas, Angus Mackay, Ray John, Ed Murphy, Charlie McClelland.

On the same afternoon, the City reserves team made a Christmas Day journey to Bath City in the Southern League and lost 3-0.

It was the reserves who played what proved to be the very last Christmas Day fixture to be staged at the Park, in 1957. This time they did taste festive success, as they defeated Weymouth 2-0 with goals from Ted Calland and Dilwyn Hill.

The first team were also in action that Christmas Day, though it was down the road at Torquay United in another Division Three South encounter.

This was to be the last time the Grecians fulfilled a Football league fixture on 25th December, but they celebrated in style winning 3-1 at Plainmoor.

The attendance of 6,774 saw Peter Rapley put Exeter into a 50th-minute lead from a Gordon Dale pass, Arnold Mitchell scored number two in the 70th minute and Johnny Nicholls netted his first goal for the club with ten minutes to go.

That was it for Christmas Day fixtures for Exeter City. It ended a tradition that had started in the club's very first season as a professional team, when Millwall travelled by train to Devon on Christmas Day 1908.

No chance of train travel on the 'big' day now, but it was quite common then with regular services operating throughout the country.

City's highest crowd of the season – 11,500 – had plenty to cheer as goals from James 'Daisy' Bell and Andy McGuigan gave Exeter a 2-1 victory.

The following season, City played their first away fixture on Christmas Day, making the trip to Plymouth Argyle. Exeter lost 1-0 in front of 14,000 people.

One hates to think what the police bill would be now, if City were to meet Argyle on Christmas Day! Can you imagine the game even being staged? No, neither can I!

DID YOU KNOW?

Whilst Exeter City last played in a Christmas Day fixture in 1957, the very last Football League fixture on 25th December occurred two years later when Blackburn Rovers defeated Blackpool 1-0 in the First Division. And on the same day in the Third Division, Coventry City won 5-3 at home to Wrexham.

Football continued to be played on Christmas Day in the Scottish League until 1976, when Clydebank drew 2-2 with St Mirren, and Alloa Athletic beat Cowdenbeath 2-1 at home.

Maurice Setters was born in Honiton on 16th December 1936 and turned professional with Exeter City in January 1954.

At that time he played an outside-right and it was in that position that Setters got his first-team chance to add to the England Schoolboy honours that had come his way.

He lined up in a City team that played against Southend United at St James' Park on 6th March 1954, when the side was as follows: Hugh Kelly, Jim Storey, Norman Douglass, John Owens, Fred Davey, Norman Dodgin, Maurice Setters, Bill Ellaway, Andy Donaldson, Angus Mackay, Charlie McClelland.

The Grecians drew 1-1, with the equalising goal for Exeter having come from the penalty spot courtesy of McClelland.

Southend had taken the lead in the 50th minute, but City were quickly back on terms in an otherwise poor game.

The *Express & Echo* report mentioned Setters being 'overawed in the early stages, but he settled down after the interval and a range of accurate crosses made him a prominent forward when City were crowding on the pressure midway through the second half.'

It was to be the one and only first-team outing that Setters got that season, and the following week he was back in the reserve team as he lined up for them in a Southern League fixture at the Park against Headington United.

Player-manager Norman Dodgin felt that Setters would make a more than useful right-half and moved him back into that position. What an inspired decision that proved to be!

It was in the number 4 shirt that Setters got his next first-team opportunity, but he had to wait until November 1954, another Division Three South fixture.

He must have got a rude awakening when playing in that Exeter team who crashed to one of their heaviest ever home defeats, going down 1-7 to Leyton Orient.

However, Setters had obviously done enough to retain his place, as he featured in the next eight games, during which time City's form improved markedly, losing just once.

The form of young Setters caught the eye of West Bromwich Albion and his meteoric rise through the ranks continued when a £3,000 fee took him to The Hawthorns in January 1955.

Three years later his value had increased tenfold, as Manchester United, still rebuilding their squad after the tragic events of Munich, parted with £30,000 for his signature.

Setters also added an England Under-23 cap to the Schoolboy ones he had won earlier, and was selected to play for The Football Association XI at Old Trafford.

He became an important first-team member at United and played in their F.A. Cup winning team of 1963.

His next club was Stoke City, who also paid a £30,000 fee, and then Setters completed his playing career with spells at Coventry City and Charlton Athletic.

He made a total of 434 league outings during his career, including the ten that he had made with the Grecians.

After hanging up his boots, Setters turned to managing and coaching and he became boss of Doncaster Rovers.

He then had coaching appointments with Sheffield Wednesday and Rotherham United before becoming a scout for Newcastle United.

His name was thrust into the national media spotlight between 1986 and 1995 when he became assistant manager to Jack Charlton as the duo led the Republic of Ireland international side through their most successful period and reached the World Cup Finals.

The excitement of the World Cup was a far cry from those embryonic days when playing for the City reserves against the likes of Llanelli, Margate and Gloucester City!

'A house without books is a house without soul.' This will ring true for many who avidly read and digest the printed word.

There is something very satisfying about seeing a shelf (or shelves) of books. It adds that homely feel to the place and also gives a good insight into the person who owns or lives in the property.

There are those who are never without a book, and some who always have two or three books in various stages of reading, and others waiting to be read on all manner of subjects.

There have been reports in the media about people who buy books, the bestsellers, only to never actually finish reading them, something I can't identify with!

For Exeter City fans, some would say that when they first watched the Grecians at St James' Park, their own favourite 'bestseller' was that written by Maurice Golesworthy.

For many years in the 1950s and 60s, Golesworthy was the Grecians' match programme editor, in addition to being an author of football-related and other sports books.

We would eagerly look forward to the opening home fixture of each season in order to see the very first programme, a bit like someone today queuing up to buy the latest Harry Potter book.

In the 1960s the programmes used to cost the princely sum of four pence, a far cry from the cover price of £2.80 in 2007–08, although the product has changed both in terms of the way it is produced and the content.

Supporters avidly read the City programme from front to back cover, taking in the latest news and opinion and the all-important details of the visiting team.

It was a means of learning about the game and the way that Golesworthy imparted this for many years was a joy to someone eager to expand their footballing knowledge, as well as enjoying a good, informative read.

It was a completely different style and format to modern-day programmes. No articles on individual players, no words of wisdom from the manager.

There were no contributors other than Golesworthy himself and each page had adverts across the top and bottom of the text, which was really one long article from the first page until the last.

Commercialism of football was unheard of and

you wouldn't find anything resembling marketing speak within the pages of the City programme. Supporters were just that, supporters, not customers.

Times have changed of course and you must move with them, even if from your own viewpoint the changes are not for the better.

Now Exeter City as a club has changed as well. Supporter-led, community-based and enjoying a highly important thriving relationship with the local business community.

In the early 1960s there were advertisements in the City programme for the Clock Tower Café in Exeter, and the County Steam Laundry in Exwick – now you are more likely to have adverts for well-known national and even international companies, who show their support for the Grecians.

However, there are still many local companies who do likewise and play their part in the well being and advancement of Exeter City Football Club.

Many supporters collect and keep their City match programmes. Like books, they form a valuable resource and record, as well as for the football historian alike.

They also form a social history of the area, if only by looking at the various advertisements.

Unlike more recent times, the front cover of each City programme was a pretty standard, aerial photograph of St James' Park. So when a change was made, either for a cup tie or perhaps a benefit or testimonial game, then they proved to be extra special.

Like books, Exeter City programmes are fascinating to look back at through each season. So many memories of City as you flick through each page, no matter who the editor might have been at that particular time, for they have helped preserve a little bit of Exeter City history in words and photographs through the medium of the match programme.

MEMORIES OF THE COWSHED AND THE BIG BANK

At the Annual General Meeting of Exeter City Football Club, held on Tuesday 1st November 1955, club chairman Mr S.H. Thomas reported that the £36,561 income the previous year was satisfactory for a city the size of Exeter, but that it was not enough.

The expense of running a football club was terrific. The company had in fact to find £700 per week throughout the year. Without the generous support of the Grecians' Association and the Exmouth (Exeter City) Supporters Club he doubted if the Grecians could survive.

At the start of the 1954–55 season the Grecians' Association had provided the sum of £1,700 for the purchase of new club houses and without those new players would not come to Exeter.

Exeter City F.C. had made a profit of £272 in the year ending 30th June 1955, but they still faced a total deficiency of £18,605. There was a credit balance of £1,200 on the transfer of players.

Income for the year was nearly £4,000 down on the previous 12 months. It had been necessary to depreciate certain company assets and the final figure showed an increased deficit of £70.

Entertainment tax totalled £4,609, wages, bonuses and pension scheme cost £17,906, travel, hotel and removal expenses were £3,951 and transfer fees paid for players totalled £2,259.

On the income side, match ground receipts totalled £22,711, season tickets £5,456 and there was a profit made on the programme of £603. Transfer fees received for players was £3,750.

Thomas added that he felt that the present team was the best the club had seen since the war. He praised the work of manager Norman Dodgin and secretary George Gilbert.

The shareholders were reminded that the club had successfully argued against the Inland Revenue who had wanted the Grecians to pay more rates because a 'good samaritan' had painted the roof of the grandstand.

They had proposed that an increase of rateable assessing from £234 to £247 be applied. The original assessment had been agreed back in 1935 and had remained unchanged ever since.

The proposal for the increase was because of an advertisement on the roof of the grandstand. However, this was rejected by the valuation panel for Exeter, East and North Devon.

The Inland Revenue had argued that the structure

EXMOUTH (EXETER CITY)

SUPPORTERS. CLUB

Formed to support Exeter City F.C.

Members of the National Federation of Football Supporters Clubs

SEASON 1955-56

MEMBERSHIP CARD

Nº 0487

This Card must be produced when application is made for a ticket for an "all ticket" game

was worth more with the large advertisement, but Mr J. Scott, solicitor for Exeter City F.C. said that no rent was payable to the club.

In 1952 the roof of the stand had been in such a bad state that the club could not afford to pay £300 to have it repainted. However, a keen supporter, who was connected with an oil company, agreed that they would pay for the cost of the repainting providing they could advertise on the roof.

The report and accounts were adopted, whilst retiring directors, Messrs G.W.H. Hill, A.T. Ford and L.J. Seward were re-elected. Mr W.J.R. Heath's election to the board was confirmed.

The annual meeting had been preceded by an extraordinary meeting when it was formally agreed to increase the club's share capital by £8,000 to £25,000.

This was achieved by the creation of 8,000 ordinary £1 shares, thus the overall share capital of the club would consist of 18,000 £1 ordinary shares and £7,000 non-cumulative 5 per cent preference £1 shares.

Following the conclusion of the Annual General Meeting at the Imperial Hotel, Exeter, directors, staff and players were entertained to dinner by new City director, Mr W.J.R. Heath.

There was much discussion amongst supporters, some of whom were unhappy with regards to the voucher system introduced by Exeter City for tickets for their F.A. Cup first round tie at home to Plymouth Argyle on 17th November 1956.

Supporters had complained to the club about the voucher system and also about the sixpence increase in the cost of admission to the tie.

Why the voucher system? And why the increase? These were the two questions being asked.

Followers from outside of Exeter pointed out that with the increased price, the stamps, postal order poundage and the fare to the game, it would be an expensive 90 minutes. Others didn't think Argyle were a big enough attraction to introduce such a voucher system for tickets.

City chairman Sid Thomas said: 'We found in the past that our own people have been unable to get in a decent position in the ground. It was often the case of first come, first served, for a big game.

'We issued vouchers for that very reason, to protect our regular supporters and ensure them of a ticket. No matter what their position is in the league, the Argyle are always capable of drawing a large crowd.

'Applications came in from all over Devon and some parts of Cornwall. This would not have happened, for instance, if we had been drawn against Torquay United.

'I have recollections of an old Argyle game on a public holiday when the Park was literally besieged. People swarmed in from everywhere – even over the fences – some paid, some didn't.

'The increase in price was an all round agreement between Plymouth Argyle and Exeter City. It was also an attempt to keep the attendance figure down to a reasonable figure – again giving the regulars a chance.'

On the subject of the admission price increase, Thomas was unrepentant, adding:

'Sixpence was a small amount to part with, and if people though that City were going to make a large profit from the game, they were sadly mistaken. There is not much left for the club after all the expenses have been taken out. Anyway, is half a crown so dear for an hour and a half's entertainment?'

It proved to be a real derby atmosphere on the day of the cup tie with tickets going steadily outside the ground and at the Sidwell Street blitzed site.

Argyle's five-man band – a concertina, rattle, cymbals and two drums – invaded the St James' Park pitch before the kick off and they marched around the perimeter, followed by a lone City fan with a sign reading: 'Up Exeter.'

The tie ended in defeat for the Grecians as they lost 2-0, but still questions were asked about the attendance figure which was officially given as 13,855, well short of capacity for the Park. Receipts totalled £2,103.

Questions were posed as to why there were still 6,000 spaces inside the ground, yet only 3,000 tickets were available?

It was explained that on the morning of the match Plymouth Argyle returned nearly 2,000 and the rest were returned from various agencies.

There was also a rumour doing the rounds that day that the City players were involved in a 'pep pill' controversy!

City director, Bob Heath, a hotelier at Plymouth, was given a sample of pills by a salesman staying at his establishment.

Heath passed them onto manager Norman Dodgin, who left them in the City dressing room. The City player reaction? They treated it as a huge joke!

DID YOU KNOW?

After defeating Exeter City 2-0 in the first round of the F.A. Cup in November 1956, Plymouth Argyle played Torquay United at the next stage and lost 1-0 at Plainmoor! Torquay had beaten Ely City 6-2, away, in round one, but then lost 2-1 at New Brighton in the third round.

A new broom swept the corridor of power at Exeter City on 1st April 1957. The club announced the appointment of a new chairman and the release of team manager Norman Dodgin.

The new chair was Albert Stanley Line, a 46-year-old Londoner who had big timber interests in the Midlands and Exeter. He had joined the City board 12 months earlier.

Line succeeded the long-serving Sidney Thomas, who became the club's first-ever president. Thomas had been associated with the City since the club's formation in 1904.

The biggest shock though concerned manager Dodgin, after the directors decided to release him from his contract having spent four years in charge at Exeter City.

The release of Dodgin did not meet with the approval of the City players who decided unanimously to protest to the board of directors against the decision.

All the players present at a training session at St James' Park decided to let the directors and the public know of their displeasure and that they backed Dodgin 100 per cent.

The following day, City's new chairman called the Exeter players to a meeting in the boardroom. This followed receiving a letter, signed by 14 of the players against the release of the manager Dodgin.

Line said that he appreciated their support of Dodgin, but the club could not continue any longer without the support of the public. Attendances had dropped to 5,000 showing the club had not got the required support and therefore changes had to be made.

The boardroom meeting lasted half an hour with Line promising to listen to any City players' grievances at any time. The players gave the chairman their full support following the meeting but it was reported that there was still a feeling of 'wait and see what happens'.

Line said he was to announce a reconstruction of the board of directors, which would consist of six or seven men who had financial ability and the will to help further the interests of Exeter City Football Club.

The start of the City reconstruction plan would be a public appeal for support and funds with the following three aims:

1) To re-engage a band (possibly the Southern Railway band) appearing at matches as the crowds wanted to be entertained.

2) To develop social facilities by establishing a club, as at Torquay United F.C.

3) To see that those supporters in hospital are kept in touch with the game by broadcast system.

4) When sufficient money is available after team rebuilding, to start ground improvements at St James' Park to make it a ground to be proud of.

The newly appointed chairman had earlier visualised the day when supporters at St James' Park were entirely under cover.

Line added that the team was the public of Exeter's team, and it was for them to support it. The directors would do all that they could, but it was up to the public to do the rest.

The Appeal Fund was officially launched by the club on 3rd April 1957, when Line issued the following statement:

'We must obviously rekindle the enthusiasm where it has fallen off and give some of the ardent supporters a return for their continued support.

'Unfortunately our finances have become very strained and in order to carry on it is necessary for me to make an appeal to all sportsmen in the city for financial contributions.'

Within two days the fund stood at £200, and at a board meeting this was added to when Sidney Thomas and Mr Line, along with four directors each donated £50.

To help the appeal for funds, Mr Arthur Ford, a City director, agreed to waive interest charges for 12 months on the £12,000 mortgage he held on St James' Park.

Unfortunately the Appeal Fund had made little progress seven months later when in November 1957, it was announced that the total stood at just £700.

One of the City directors was reported as saying that he was dismayed at the lack of help given by former directors in comparison to the many hundreds of ordinary City supporters.

Apart from Tim Ward and more recently Neil McNab and Gary Peters, this particular Exeter City manager endured one of the shortest ever reigns in the St James' Park hot seat.

Bill Thompson had the task of taking over from Norman Dodgin, who had managed City for the previous four years.

Thompson was appointed in May 1957 – a surprise choice due to his lack of any Football League management experience, although he had played for Portsmouth between 1948 and 1950, before moving along the south coast to join Bournemouth and Boscombe Athletic.

The Glaswegian had been recruited by Grecians' club chairman Albert Line after an impressive spell in charge of Southern League Guildford City, which included winning the league title in 1955–56.

He didn't arrive at the Park at a particularly good time, however, as there had just been a major upheaval off the field, especially in the boardroom.

Line declared that Thompson would 'manage with a completely free hand', adding that he was sure he was the type of character who would fit in well at St James' Park.

However, only 24 hours later, Thompson's task was made more difficult when it was announced that the players would have to face severe wage cuts.

This was partly due to the fact that the club was keen to cut costs and it was expected that several of the 24 players on the books would make a rapid getaway.

Thompson's first game in charge ended in disaster, as the Grecians slumped to an embarrassing 5-0 defeat at Southend United, and it wasn't until the sixth match of the campaign that City recorded their first win in the Third Division South.

The poor run continued, including an ignominious 2-1 defeat in the first round of the F.A. Cup at Southern League Bath City.

Up until Christmas, the Grecians managed to win just four matches, but they then strung together a run of three successive victories over Torquay United (twice) and Brighton and Hove Albion.

However, all was not well, and the team succumbed to a 5-1 hiding at Swindon Town, before suffering a 6-0 thrashing a week later at Southampton.

The day before the Southampton debacle it was announced that Thompson's tenure was to end. His contract was terminated by mutual consent after just eight months in the job.

Line appeared to have changed his views how the club was to be run in the short space of time that Thompson was manager.

Line said: 'I feel the position of manager has become obsolete in modern football. Time which should be spent with the team is being spent in the office and I now intend to appoint a coach rather than a manager.'

The Grecians moved quickly to find a replacement, appointing former England international Frank Broome immediately after the Southampton catastrophe.

Indeed it was reported that initial talks between Line and Broome had taken place in the corridor outside the dressing rooms at The Dell.

Exeter eventually ended the 1957–58 season, perhaps not surprisingly in view of the dreadful first half of the campaign, in bottom place and had to successfully apply for re-election to the Football League.

As for Bill Thompson, within two weeks he had found another job in football, returning to whence he came, to the Southern League, by accepting the role of secretary/manger at Worcester City.

They say that you should never return to a job that you have had before, but in Frank Broome's case, he did just that, by managing Exeter City Football Club in two separate spells.

The former England international (with seven full caps), was born in Berkhampstead, Hertfordshire in June 1915. After playing for local sides, Boxmoor United and Berkhampstead Town, his playing career really took off when signing for Aston Villa in November 1934.

He topped the scoring charts for Villa during his 12 years with the club, playing mainly as a winger. As well as being selected for his country, he also appeared in one war time international and went on to represent the Football Association during their tour of Australia in 1951.

After leaving Villa, Broome joined Derby County in September 1946, and then moved on to Notts County (October 1949), Brentford (July 1953), Crewe Alexandra (October 1953) and finally Shelbourne of the Irish League in February 1955.

During his playing career, as well as winning international honours, Broome also won a Division Two Championship medal in 1938; Division Three South Championship medal in 1950; Football League North Cup winners' medal in 1944; and Football League Cup winners' medal in 1942.

Turning his attention to coaching and managing, his first post was with Notts County as their assistant trainer in 1955, and he had a spell as their caretaker boss between January and May 1957.

He was approached by Exeter City to take over as their manager in January 1958, and although he must have realised what a huge task lay in front of him as he watched the Grecians lose 6-0 at Southampton, Broome still agreed to become manager.

He, along with the help of City chairman Albert Line, virtually rebuilt the squad, so much so, that the playing fortunes were remarkably transformed as City only just missed out on promotion for the first time in their history in 1958–59.

Unfortunately all was not well behind the scenes at St James' Park, and despite the best efforts of the players to persuade him to change his mind, Broome left the City to become manager of Southend United in May 1960 – a post he held for just seven months.

Broome then moved to Australia where he was

The Grecians were relegated at the end of the 1957–58 season to the newly formed Fourth Division
Back row: Harry Hanford (Trainer), Dennis Churms, Ray John, George Hunter, Ken Oliver, Theo Foley.
Front row: Johnny Nicholls, Graham Rees, Ted Calland, Arnold Mitchell, Gordon Dale, Les MacDonald.

manager-coach to Bankstown F.C. (New South Wales) between July 1961 and October 1962.

His next appointment was to become manager-coach of Corinthians (Sydney) and it was whilst he was there that City chairman Les Kerslake made contact and invited him to return to take charge of Exeter in May 1967 for a second time.

Once again Broome arrived at a struggling club, more so than the first time he became manager, and he had very little money to spend on players and therefore had to make do with mainly free transfer signings and a very small squad.

In his first season – 1967–68 – with wafer thin resources, it was perhaps not surprising that Exeter faced a battle towards the foot of the Fourth Division and they eventually ended in 20th place.

It wasn't a lot better the following season as City found themselves one off the bottom, and it almost inevitably led to a parting of the ways between Exeter City and Frank Broome.

This was not, however, before he had guided the

Grecians to the third round of the F.A. Cup and earning a home tie against Manchester United, a game that City lost 3-1.

Broome was to spend much of the 1970s coaching in the Middle East, before returning to live in Ottery St Mary, where he died in 1994.

SEASON 1958–59 – CITY JUST MISS OUT ON PROMOTION

The Grecians' Fourth Division results

Aug 23	Walsall	H	3-0
Aug 28	Barrow	H	4-0
Aug 30	Darlington	A	1-1
Sep 1	Barrow	A	0-1
Sep 6	Shrewsbury Town	H	1-0
Sep 10	Oldham Athletic	H	3-2
Sep 13	Coventry City	A	0-2
Sep 15	Oldham Athletic	A	1-2
Sep 20	Torquay United	H	2-2
Sep 27	Gillingham	H	3-0
Oct 4	Carlisle United	A	2-1
Oct 8	Aldershot	H	2-0
Oct 11	Northampton Town	A	1-1
Oct 18	Workington	H	1-0
Oct 25	York City	A	2-0
Oct 27	Gateshead	A	2-1
Nov 1	Bradford P.A.	H	4-0
Nov 8	Port Vale	A	3-5
Nov 22	Chester	A	2-4
Nov 29	Watford	H	3-0
Dec 13	Southport	H	3-2
Dec 27	Crewe Alexandra	H	3-0
Jan 3	Darlington	H	2-2
Jan 24	Hartlepools United	A	3-3
Jan 31	Coventry City	H	2-1
Feb 7	Torquay United	A	4-3
Feb 14	Gillingham	A	2-0
Feb 21	Carlisle United	H	2-1
Feb 28	Northampton Town	A	3-4
Mar 5	Crewe Alexandra	A	0-0
Mar 7	Workington	A	2-2
Mar 14	York City	H	0-2
Mar 17	Walsall	A	0-3
Mar 21	Bradford P.A.	A	3-0
Mar 27	Millwall	A	1-1
Mar 28	Port Vale	H	3-4
Mar 30	Millwall	H	3-1
Apr 4	Crystal Palace	A	1-1
Apr 6	Gateshead	H	1-1
Apr 11	Chester	H	1-1
Apr 15	Crystal Palace	H	3-1
Apr 18	Watford	A	1-2
Apr 22	Aldershot	A	0-1
Apr 25	Hartlepools United	H	3-0
Apr 28	Southport	A	1-0
Apr 30	Shrewsbury Town	A	0-3

FOURTH DIVISION – FINAL LEAGUE TABLE 1958–59

(Top ten places)

	P	W	D	L	F	A	Pts
Port Vale	46	26	12	8	110	58	64
Coventry City	46	24	12	10	84	47	60
York City	46	21	18	7	73	52	60
Shrewsbury Town	46	24	10	12	101	63	58
EXETER CITY	**46**	**23**	**11**	**12**	**87**	**61**	**57**
Walsall	46	21	10	15	95	64	52
Crystal Palace	46	20	12	14	90	71	52
Northampton Town	46	21	9	16	85	78	51
Millwall	46	20	10	16	76	69	50
Carlisle United	46	19	12	15	62	65	50

City Fourth Division appearances 1958–59:
Theo Foley 46; Arnold Mitchell 46; Ken Oliver 46; Ted Calland 44; Nelson Stiffle 44; Graham Rees 43; Gordon Dale 41; Johnny Nicholls 39; Les MacDonald 39; George Hunter 36; Jim Thompson 26; Keith Harvey 13; John Lobbett 10; David Butterworth 8; Brian Birch 7; Brian Whitnall 7; Ray John 6; Dilwyn Hill 2; Norman Packer 2; Robinson 1.

City Fourth Division goalscorers 1958–59:
Ted Calland 27; Graham Rees 22; Johnny Nicholls 15; Nelson Stiffle 8; Arnold Mitchell 7; Keith Harvey 3; Gordon Dale 2; Brian Birch 1; Dilwyn Hill 1; Jim Thompson 1.

It is doubtful if all but a mere handful of Exeter City fans can recall the silky skills of left-winger Antonio Cruz who joined the Grecians in March 1958.

'Spaniard Winger in City Reserves' roared the headline in the *Express & Echo* – well, perhaps not, but it did warrant a mention at the foot of a column.

The player had been brought to the attention of Exeter City by *Echo* football reporter, Clive Toye. But three weeks had elapsed before he was initially mentioned to City, and by then Cruz had signed for Western League side, Bridgwater Town.

All was not lost though, as Cruz accepted the chance of a trial with Exeter City and a game with the reserve team in the Southern League.

Not Real Madrid or Barcelona for Cruz then? No, this time it was Barry in South Wales. Forget the Nou Camp, City and Cruz were playing in the more modest surrounds of Jenner Park, scrapping for Southern League points.

The City team lined up: Bell, Bowkett, Palmer, Butterworth, Rapley, Waterman, Wilson, Hill, Beer, Atkinson, Cruz.

It proved to be a rude awakening to Southern League football for Cruz and co. as they were shot down by Jesse James. Actually it was Billy James, although Jesse sounds better, as he fired five shots into the back of the City net helping Barry Town to a resounding 8-2 victory.

The Grecians were obviously worried about filling the wing positions, and Cruz must have got the message when, just six days after he had signed for City, another 'wide-man' arrived at St James' Park.

Nelson Stiffle, who was to prove to be a terrific signing for Exeter was snapped up from Bournemouth and Boscombe Athletic. Stiffle on one wing, Gordon Dale on the other – a joy to watch.

For Cruz it was time for another opportunity to shine for the reserves, his next game being at the Park against Hereford United.

It is difficult to say whether City and Cruz played any better. Certainly they didn't concede as many goals as they had done at Barry, only five this time, with Tom Wilson replying for Exeter.

So was the chance gone for Cruz to make it in the English game? Would he be off back to Spain to perhaps pursue a new career after hanging up his boots? Not quite.

He was to feature in a 3-1 win over Merthyr Tydfil at St James' Park, and what's more, he scored one of the goals.

Cruz also took his place in a 0-3 home defeat at the hands of Hastings United and then played his part in a 1-0 success in the return meeting with Hereford at Edgar Street.

But there was one further and final outing for Cruz – in the Devon Professional Cup tie at home to Barnstaple Town, played on 9th April 1958.

Cruz was in the big time now and an attendance of 1,597 saw two goals from David Robinson and one from Ted Calland give City a narrow and hard-fought 3-2 victory.

The match report stated that 'Cruz looked City's most dangerous forward' but sadly this proved to be his last match for the Grecians. No one knows what happened to the player after that.

DID YOU KNOW?

During season 1957–58, City supporters had the opportunity to watch the following South Western League teams play against the Grecians' 'A' side at St James' Park: Bodmin Town, Bugle, Camelford, Falmouth Town, Helston, Launceston, Newquay, Penzance, Plymouth Argyle 'A', St Austell, St Blazey, Saltash United, Tavistock, Truro City, Wadebridge etc. This was in addition to City's reserve team fixtures being played at the Park in the Southern League.

When the Football League was reorganised for the start of the 1958–59 season, Exeter City found themselves playing in the newly formed Fourth Division, but they were to enjoy a successful season, which almost ended in winning promotion for the first time in the club's history.

The Grecians eventually missed out by just one point, finishing in fifth place, behind promoted clubs, Port Vale, Coventry City, York City and Shrewsbury Town.

By a strange coincidence it was a trip to Shrewsbury for the final game of the season that ended City's promotion hopes. They had to win to deny the Shrews promotion, and thus gain a place in Division Three themselves, but it was not to be. A magnificent attendance of 15,318 squeezed into Shrewsbury's Gay Meadow ground, but Exeter lost 3-0.

Exeter City's team was fairly settled throughout the season and this was one of the prime reasons why the team did so well. The words 'squad rotation system' had never been thought of back in 1958–59.

Talented goalkeeper George Hunter made 36 appearances between the posts before unluckily sustaining a broken leg at St James' Park in a 4-3 defeat against Port Vale. His place was taken by John Lobbett for the final ten matches of the season.

Right-back Theo Foley was an ever-present, whilst the left-back position was the domain of Les MacDonald, apart from a handful of outings made by Brian Whitnall.

Right-half Arnold Mitchell was his usual tower of strength in the side, and he too played in every game, as did centre-half Ken Oliver. Young Kirtonian Keith Harvey commenced the season in the number 6 shirt, before Jimmy Thompson was signed from Oldham Athletic and took over the position.

Calcutta-born right-winger Nelson Stiffle only missed two matches, whilst the other forward positions were in the main filled by big Ted Calland, Graham Rees, Johnny Nicholls and Gordon Dale.

The wing play of Stiffle and Dale was a joy to watch, and the sight of two skilful, fast-raiding widemen caused many a visiting team to St James' Park more than a few problems.

Calland formed a lethal partnership with Rees, the pair netting 27 and 22 goals respectively.

Calland was a big favourite with the crowd, possessing a cannonball shot, and this proved to be by far his most successful season with City.

With former West Bromwich Albion inside-forward Johnny Nicholls also weighing in with a further 15 goals, it really was no surprise that the Grecians had a promotion-chasing team.

Nicholls provided the guile and skilful touches for the front runners, and was a player who really should have been playing at a higher level.

Ray John, Brian Birch, Norman Packer, David Butterworth, Dilwyn Hill and David Robinson all contributed to City's promotion push with a handful of appearances between them.

Hill had been a prolific scorer in the City reserve team, but sadly after leaving the club to play for Salisbury City, he was to take his own life.

Packer, too, was a good servant to the club, playing most of his football, like Hill, in the reserves, but he did come into the first team on several occasions and never let his colleagues down despite combining playing with a teaching career.

Exeter's best win of the season was a 4-0 victory in what was the second league fixture of the season, against Barrow. Indeed the Grecians were to only lose three matches all season at the Park, against Northampton Town (3-4), York City (0-2) and Port Vale (3-4).

Despite the goals regularly flowing into the opposition net, only one City player actually claimed a hat-trick – Graham Rees netting three times in an exciting 5-3 defeat at Port Vale.

Not surprisingly, attendances boomed – with the opening game of the season at the Park against Walsall being watched by 8,750, but this had climbed to 13,102 for the local derby against Torquay United a month later.

Attendances of 10,000 and over were also recorded for the visits of Bradford Park Avenue, Carlisle United, Coventry City, Crewe Alexandra and Port Vale.

Exeter had no luck in the F.A. Cup though, being defeated in the first round at Brentford, going down 2-3.

Unfortunately the City team was broken up after this successful season in the Fourth Division and although they did manage to finish in ninth spot the following season, Grecians' supporters had to wait until 1964 before they finally witnessed a promotion-winning side.

It was the day the fixtures were released and the annual ritual of seeing who the Grecians were playing, where and when, was eagerly looked forward to by the City faithful.

Their hearts sank in disappointment as not only were the 'A' team away in the opening match of the season, but they were also sent on their travels for a Boxing Day encounter.

Two trips to deepest Cornwall. Could this be right? Indeed it was and there were a lot more away days to come in the Duchy.

It was shortly before the 1958–59 season and the Exeter City board of directors had taken the bold decision of running three teams.

The first team were in the Football League Fourth Division; the reserves played in the Southern League; and a new 'A' team would compete in the Cornish-dominated South Western League.

And so it was – an opening day journey to Bodmin Town at their Priory Park ground. There was no festive cheer either for the City fans or the 'A' team players, as they were being sent to Truro City for their Boxing Day treat.

All three of the City sides used St James' Park for their home fixtures, so if you were a season ticket holder, you certainly got value for money! Although the groundsman was probably not so keen at the number of times his pitch was used.

The first day of the new season arrived and off went the City 'A' team into the unknown of Bodmin.

The same afternoon saw the first team open their Fourth Division campaign in some style as they defeated Walsall 3-0 before an attendance of 8,750, with goals from Keith Harvey, Ted Calland and Graham Rees.

The senior side lined up: George Hunter, Theo Foley, Les MacDonald, Arnold Mitchell, Ken Oliver, Harvey, Nelson Stiffle, Ray John, Ted Calland, Graham Rees, Gordon Dale.

City reserves had to make the long trek to Hastings. The good folk of the coastal town saw honours even, as they drew 1-1 with the Grecians' second string.

The City, who scored through Robinson, lined up: John Lobbett, Charlie Rutter, Brian Whitnall, David Butterworth, Norman Packer, Bert Carberry, Trevor Atkins, Dilwyn Hill, Peter Rapley, Ian Grinney, David Robinson.

So what of City's newly formed South Western League side? It wasn't to be a happy start as they lost 3-0 much to the delight of the Bodmin supporters.

The St James' Park regulars could now look forward to visits to the Park from the likes of Helston, Newquay, Penzance, Falmouth Town, Tavistock and Camelford as the season unfolded.

The Boxing Day encounter at Truro City also ended in defeat as the Grecians went down 2-4, the Exeter goals coming from Newell and Williams.

Despite ever-increasing costs, City continued to operate with three teams for the following 1959–60 season, but that was to be the final one as far as the South Western League side were concerned.

The reserve team was also pulled out of the Southern League at the end of the same season as a dramatic cutback in the club's outgoings was made.

The final match played in the South Western League involved the longest trip of the season as City visited Penzance on 5th May 1960.

They ended their association with the league in style, however, as Calland netted a hat-trick and Hill added another one in a 4-0 romp.

A week earlier St Blazey had been the last visitors to St James' Park for a South Western League fixture.

They fared a little better than Penzance were to do, but only just, as the Grecians won 3-0 with Atkins, Emery and Burnett on the score sheet.

With Exeter City having become founder members of the Football League Fourth Division, following the scrapping of the Third Division North and South sections, club chairman Albert Line explained that although the club were in debt, they were feeling the benefits.

At the Annual General Meeting of the Grecians in December 1958, Line explained that the club had put themselves in debt by spending about £13,000 on players, but were still relegated to the Fourth Division.

However, he added that the benefits were then being felt and he thought that Second Division football was nearer than many people believed.

With the team doing well in 1958–59 and looking to get promoted (they just missed out by finishing in fifth place), and with attendances higher, the club would not only have capital, but also be able to carry out ground improvements.

Line said that he was sorry for the 'dilapidations and inconveniences that exist at present at St James' Park'.

Three months earlier the City chairman had said: 'Even if we only have the slightest chance, we will do everything possible to get out of the Fourth Division. We want to make it this year if possible.

'Don't think that cash will be an obstacle, for manager Frank Broome has the instructions of the board that when he finds the right players, he can buy.

'I had been warned that the northern teams in this division are really very tough. So we want to get every position in the team strongly duplicated and triplicated if possible.

'It is obvious that the Third South based teams are going to finish in front of the Third North sides.

'There is every chance that northern teams will be relegated to the Fourth Division at the end of the season in place of four from the South. That would mean far more travelling for Exeter City next season if we are still in the Fourth.'

The lack of investment in St James' Park as far as ground developments were concerned, were also mentioned in October 1958, only that time it was specifically the floodlights that needed an upgrade.

The system was the latest one available when installed in 1953, but it was generally agreed that the lights were poor and left large dark patches in each goalmouth.

A new system, one pylon in each corner of the ground, would cost £15,000 to install, but although City had not got that kind of money available, it still prompted Line to add that it would be possible to raise it.

'There are 5,000 floating supporters at Exeter', he said. 'If they were to turn up every game that would put another £300 to £400 on the gate receipts, providing the money to update the lights.

'I know supporters have in the past been promised so many things, but they have never materialised, but I can assure them that we really are anxious to make improvements like this and bring more and better football to Exeter. The lights are simply not good enough.'

Certainly the directors did back the manager with regards to signing players, and as a result by December 1958 the Exeter City board decided to call a halt on further dips into the transfer market that season.

The signing of wing-half Jimmy Thompson from Oldham Athletic for £2,500, plus Ray John from Barnsley had left no money in the kitty for further arrivals.

'We have scraped the bottom of the barrel', explained Line. 'And if we do go into the transfer market again, it will only be through an absolute necessity. Otherwise we have had our last fling of the season.'

With the signings of Ken Oliver (£1,250 from Derby County); Nelson Stiffle (Bournemouth and Boscombe Athletic), Gordon Dale (for a club record fee of £7,000 from Portsmouth), Johnny Nicholls (Cardiff City), Charlie Rutter (Cardiff City), Brian Birch (Barrow), the City directors had spent a reported £20,000 on players in less than 12 months.

It was admitted that whilst players had been signed for fees, the ground had been neglected as there was nothing left to be spent on improving it.

In October 1959, Exeter City director and former chairman Mr A.S. Line called for another reconstruction of the City board. He said he wanted younger members of the board to take over and that he would not be attending any more meetings until something was done. He added that there was an unhappy atmosphere on the board of directors and felt that this lack of harmony had spread to the players' dressing room and was affecting results.

Since Mr Line's return to attend meetings following an illness, he had noticed the absence of enthusiastic ambition on the faces of supporters and it was quite obvious to him that something was lacking.

He felt there was not a complete understanding in the boardroom and in view of the circumstances he would not be attending meetings until something was done to modernise the attitude of the current directors. Line added that the directors had to show ambition towards progress.

A day later the Exeter Clty F.C. chairman, George Gillin and his fellow directors presented a solid front to Mr Line's appeal for a reconstituted board and they issued the following statement:

'With regard to Mr Line's statements, the board wish to emphasise that there is complete harmony and understanding in the boardroom and between the board, managers and players. Mr Line has only attended one meeting since June and the board consider that if he carried out his duties to shareholders by attending these meetings he would have been in a much better position to discuss the activities of his fellow directors.'

Three days later, however, there did indeed seem to be a rift between the board and City manager Frank Broome, as the directors issued another statement.

'At a special meeting held at St James' Park on Monday 5th October 1959, manager Frank Broome asked to be released from his contract with full compensation. This request was considered and all the directors were unanimous in their decision that the request of Mr Broome could not be granted. The board are anxious to assist the manager in his efforts to obtain promotion and had previously promised Mr Broome a bonus of £750 should this be achieved. As a further incentive it was agreed unanimously by the board that the players should be put on a sliding scale of wages to reach the maximum of £20 per week by March 1960 if the team is in the first four places in the League table.'

Less than a week later the situation changed once again as following a lengthy board meeting, not only was Mr Line appointed vice-chairman, but Broome had also withdrawn his resignation offer.

Such was the uncertainty surrounding St James' Park, that incredibly, four days later, Line was removed from the position of vice-chairman! This followed statements made by him to national Sunday newspapers.

A special meeting of the board of directors was called on 12th October 1959, and the following statement was duly issued:

'Mr Line was unanimously deposed from the vice-chairman's position of the club in view of the contradiction of his pledge to keep all reports within the framework of the boardroom. By his action he had lost the support of every member of the board. Mr Line was not invited to the chair, each director stating that he was not prepared to serve under him because of previous experiences.

'Mr Line also stated that he and the chair would carry all the financial responsibility, but some individual directors have more financial interest in the club than Mr Line, and it must be stated that Mr Line has very little financial interest in the club. The chairman has a bank guarantee of £3,000 and loans of approximately £3,000 free of interest, and has recently made a further guarantee to the bank.

'It was essential during the summer that £2,000 be found and Mr Line refused to increase his guarantee. In the circumstances Mr Gillin was unanimously invited to take the chair and he provided the money in cash. Mr Line conveyed by his wording to the press that he agreed to share the whole of Mr Gillin's bank guarantee and cash loans. This was not so. What Mr Line agreed to do was to share only the bank guarantee of £3,000, the interest of which is being paid by the club.

'Under Mr Line's chairmanship Exeter City F.C. has spent nearly £20,000 on players in two seasons. This has caused the serious financial problems that the club now finds itself in. Despite this the club has recently paid £3,000 to sundry creditors and the sum of £2,000 has been expended on ground improvements which supporters well know have been well overdue.

'The policy of the present board is to strive to a more solvent position. Under Mr Line the club retained this season 27 full-time professionals as against the average number in the League of 17. This left little room for expansion, owing to the size of weekly expenses.'

Mr Line commented on the board's decision that he was disgusted in view of the many inaccuracies in their statement. He felt he could say much, but to do so would only harm the club.

FOURTH DIVISION FINAL LEAGUE TABLE 1959–60

	P	W	D	L	F	A	Pts
Walsall	46	28	9	9	102	50	65
Notts County	46	26	8	12	107	69	60
Torquay United	46	26	8	12	84	58	60
Watford	46	24	9	13	92	67	57
Millwall	46	18	17	11	84	61	53
Northampton Town	46	22	9	15	85	63	53
Gillingham	46	21	10	15	74	69	52
Crystal Palace	46	19	12	15	84	64	50
EXETER CITY	**46**	**19**	**11**	**16**	**80**	**70**	**49**
Stockport County	46	19	11	16	58	54	49
Bradford P.A.	46	17	15	14	70	68	49
Rochdale	46	18	10	18	65	50	46
Aldershot	46	18	9	19	77	74	45
Crewe Alexandra	46	18	9	19	79	88	45
Darlington	46	17	9	20	63	73	43
Workington	46	14	14	18	68	60	42
Doncaster Rovers	46	16	10	20	69	76	42
Barrow	46	15	11	20	77	87	41
Carlisle United	46	15	11	20	51	66	41
Chester	46	14	12	20	59	77	40
Southport	46	10	14	22	48	92	34
Gateshead	46	12	9	25	58	86	33
Oldham Athletic	46	8	12	26	41	83	28
Hartlepools United	46	10	7	25	59	109	27

SOUTHERN LEAGUE FIRST DIVISION FINAL LEAGUE TABLE 1959–60

	P	W	D	L	F	A	Pts
Clacton Town	42	27	5	10	106	69	59
Romford	42	21	11	10	65	40	53
Folkestone Town	42	23	5	14	93	71	51
EXETER CITY RESERVES	**42**	**23**	**3**	**16**	**85**	**62**	**49**
Guildford City	42	19	9	14	79	56	47
Sittingbourne	42	20	7	15	66	55	47
Margate	42	20	6	16	88	77	46
Trowbridge Town	42	18	9	15	90	78	45
Cambridge United	42	18	9	15	71	72	45
Yiewsley	42	17	10	15	83	69	44
Bexleyheath & Welling	42	16	11	15	85	77	43
Merthyr Tydfil	42	16	10	16	63	65	42
Ramsgate Athletic	42	16	8	18	83	84	40
Ashford Town	42	14	12	16	61	70	40
Tnbridge Wells Utd	42	17	5	20	77	73	39
Hinckley Athletic	42	14	8	20	62	75	36
Gloucester City	42	13	9	20	56	84	35
Dover	42	14	6	22	59	85	34
Kidderminster Harr	42	14	6	22	59	97	34
Corby Town	42	15	3	24	75	91	33
Burton Albion	42	11	10	21	52	79	32
Rugby Town	42	10	11	21	67	91	31

EXETER CITY 1959–60

Fourth Division appearances:
Theo Foley 45; Jim Thompson 44; Arnold Mitchell 42; Graham Rees 42; Nelson Stiffle 41; Les MacDonald 40; Allan Jones 32; Ken Oliver 30; Ted Calland 29; Jack Wilkinson 29; Gordon Dale 26; Keith Harvey 23; Andy Micklewright 18; John Lobbett 14; Brian Birch 12; Brian Whitnall 6; Peter Bennett 5; Eric Welsh 4; Trevor Atkins 2; Dilwyn Hill 2; David Butterworth 1; Peter Rapley 1.

Fourth Division goalscorers:
Graham Rees 17; Jack Wilkinson 16; Andy Micklewright 11; Nelson Stiffle 9; Ted Calland 7; Jim Thompson 6; Peter Bennett 5; Gordon Dale 5; Trevor Atkins 2.

EXETER CITY IN THE F.A. CUP 1959–60

14th November 1959: round one:
Exeter City 4 Barnstaple Town 0
City scorers: Rees (2), Wilkinson, Stiffle.
Attendance: 9,200

5th December 1959: round two:
Exeter City 3 Brentford 1
City scorers: Dale, Rees, Stiffle.
Attendance: 13,000

9th January 1960: round three:
Exeter City 1 Luton Town 2
City scorer: Daniel (own goal).
Attendance: 20,000

Following the changes on the Exeter City F.C. board of directors, which had seen Albert Line leave the club and George Gillin take over as chairman, a number of alterations were made.

Line's vision of Second Division football being nearer than one may think, and having recruited several players for transfer fees, seemed to have been forgotten, as alarm bells started to ring at the club and rumours emanated as regards the financial situation at St James' Park.

A shock announcement at the end of December 1959 only added to supporters' concerns as the club decided that as from the following season the teams operating in both the Southern League and the South Western League would be scrapped.

Whilst the Grecians' association with the South Western League had been a relatively short one, links with the Southern League went back to 1908 when the Exeter first team played in that competition, right up until being elected as a founder members of the Football League Third Division in 1920, and even then the City reserves had continued to play Southern League football.

A statement was issued by the City directors that read:

'At a meeting of the board held on 3rd December, it was agreed by all the directors present that the club should withdraw from the Southern and South Western Leagues and that application should be made to enter the Western League.

'In the last annual balance sheet it was clearly shown that the club was facing tremendous difficulties in hotel and travelling expenses. The attendances at Southern League games have shown a serious decline over the past three seasons.

'The board agreed that the above mentioned changes would help meet today's additional expenses and by slightly reducing the personnel at the club at the end of the season, it will enable them to pay increased wages to the retained men. It is the intention of the club to bring Third Division football to Exeter as soon as possible.'

Mr Gillin said that City took an average of £40 from home gate receipts and that the reserves cost approximately £200 per week to run.

The City chairman reckoned that the move would save about £5,000 per season. The cost of running the South Western League side alone was roughly £1,250 for the season.

With wages, hotel and travelling expenses balanced against gate receipts, the club was reportedly losing £2,000 a week before a ball was kicked.

Gillin added that the club could obviously not continue to keep 30 players on the staff as they had done that season, but they would have sufficient good men to always have a good first-team strength.

Later it emerged that City were to retain just 12 players out of their current staff in readiness for the 1960–61 season.

As regards the last match in the Southern League, this took place on Wednesday 4th May 1960 when the Grecians travelled to Rugby Town and drew 1-1, courtesy of a goal from Bob Rackley.

The City team lined up: Alan Jones, Theo Foley, Brian Whitnall, Peter Rapley, Keith Harvey, Mike Cleverley, Nelson Stiffle, Barry Pulman, Peter Bennett, Jack Wilkinson, Bob Rackley.

DID YOU KNOW?

The last goal scored by an Exeter City player in the Southern League was netted by Bob Rackley. The Teignmouth-born player never made the Grecians' first team and was to join Bristol Rovers in July 1960. Three months later he linked up with Oldham Athletic and finally made his Football League debut, playing 19 matches for the Latics, scoring five goals.

A national newspaper journalist joined the Exeter City team for their long trip to Carlisle in January 1960 and his account of the weekend-long journey makes fascinating reading. City won the game 4-0 with goals from Nelson Stiffle, Jack Wilkinson, Ted Calland and Graham Rees.

'Sunday 24th January 1959 – Exeter St David's.

'The ticket collector on the station here this morning mistook me for a player, prodded the peak of his cap and said: "Well done m'dear."

'I modestly admitted I had never kicked anything more than the neighbours cat and that I had merely gone along to experience the agony of a long weekend in the work horse of football's Fourth Division.

'"You must be mad", he muttered, which said a great deal for the perception of Devon railwaymen.

'Mad or not, my sporting education has been extensively widened in the past 60 hours. So much so, that I want to hear no more of the anguish of Arsenal, the woes of West Ham United, or the tax tribulations of our Football League bosses.

'Just count your blessings gentlemen, while we of Exeter City recover our land legs and quietly tell you a story.

'We have just rumbled 722 miles up and down the backbone of England on hard second-class seats, and in cramped second-class sleepers.

'We have just seen the last two-thirds of the final feature film from the cheaper seats of a Carlisle cinema, and mooched around the wet, murky streets in Manchester while waiting for a connection.

'We have played poker until we are red in the eyes, discussed politics, religion and Diana Dors until we are blue in the face.

'We could fill a courtroom with witnesses willing to swear under oath that the football we played at Carlisle ranks with the finest ever seen in the Fourth Division.

'We scored four goals. And as you will see from our balance sheet, we have lost precisely £349 and a penny for our pains.

'We even remembered to bow low in obeisance as we passed through Preston, the headquarters of the Football League on our long haul home.

They haven't yet, we remembered, moved into luxuriously built quarters in socially superior Lytham St Anne's.

'I recalled that fact with some satisfaction this morning as we tumbled, tousled, a little short tempered out of our mobile cells onto the damp, desolate platforms at Exeter St David's station.

'Economy measures – now as vital an aspect of Fourth Division management as soccer tactics themselves – were beginning to take their accumulative toll.

'The reception committee of one ticket collector and a few weary cattle patiently waiting their turn to see Britain by rail did little to help.

'The players waited numbly for their taxis and breakfast. But they have done it before and will do it again. Whenever a fatuous fixture list decrees they must lose still more money at Workington, Darlington, Barrow, Gateshead and Hartlepool.

'But how long can it last? Even 60 hours in the Fourth Division have been sufficient to confirm that the brave new world, built two years ago for football's lower classes, would crash tomorrow if its members were left to rely on their meagre resources.

'The players were aware of the fact of the new £100 minimum rule brought in this season to assure visiting clubs of at least some financial return had nearly paid for their lodgings.

'Under the old system their share of the gate would have been less than £64. Their bigger disappointment, however, was that so few turned out to watch them on the day (4,304) when they hit their finest form.

'Their resentment was not even forgotten over two rounds of free drinks – an extravagance permitted by their employers to commemorate outstanding performances.

'City received their £100 guarantee, but on the expenditure side of things they had spent £96 10s on rail fares; £15 for sleepers on the return journey; £27 11s 1d on meals on trains; £35 19s on hotels; £14 on incidentals including taxis; players' wages at £17 per player, including reserve equalled £204; bonuses – £4 each for 12 players, manager and trainer £56; overall loss on the trip £349 0s 1d.'

Every season we hear a whinge from a manager that the players are worn out as they are playing far too much football.

This more often than not occurs when a team is playing twice a week, and it always seems to be sides at the top level of the game – poor devils!

These supremely fit, highly paid individuals are not capable of performing for three hours per week, or at least that is what certain managers say.

As for playing twice over the Easter Holidays, well, it seems that they cannot cope. Yet Exeter City supporters will recall when teams, including the Grecians, would play on Good Friday, Easter Saturday and then Easter Monday. Not so today.

Take Easter 1960 for instance. It started, as far as Exeter City were concerned, on 15th April, with the Good Friday visit to Crystal Palace for a Fourth Division fixture.

Palace were riding high in the table, and were eventually promoted a couple of weeks later. Not surprisingly interest in the game at Selhurst Park was high as 15,731 were at the game.

It remained goalless until 14 minutes from time when former City player Gerry Priestley swung over a cross that right-winger John Roche nodded home.

A 1-0 defeat and the Grecians were heading straight back to Exeter after the game to face Rochdale at St James' Park 24 hours later.

This time City made no mistake and ran out fairly easy winners 4-1, with goals from Graham Rees (2), Andy Micklewright and Jack Wilkinson.

Amazingly City hadn't found the back of the net at all in their previous four games, but with the return of Nelson Stiffle and Gordon Dale to the side it seemed to revitalise them.

City's team against Rochdale was: Alan Jones, Theo Foley, Les MacDonald, Arnold Mitchell, Keith Harvey, Jimmy Thompson, Nelson Stiffle, Graham Rees, Jack Wilkinson, Andy Micklewright, Gordon Dale.

Exeter could hardly have got away to a better start, which had the Easter crowd of 6,699 expecting great things. Rees opened the scoring in the fourth minute, and followed that up with another goal three minutes later.

Two quick-fire goals followed in the space of four minutes in the second half as Wilkinson made it 3-0 in the 68th and Micklewright added number four in the 72nd.

Rochdale did manage a consolation goal ten minutes from time, when Cairns took advantage of some sloppy play in the City defence.

Two Easter fixtures played, won one, lost one. Next up, the return meeting back at the Park on the Monday against Crystal Palace.

Another good attendance present (6,661) and they were to witness four goals being shared.

City made one change from the side that had beaten Rochdale – no such thing as a squad rotation policy, thankfully – with young Eric Welsh stepping in for the injured Stiffle.

Wilkinson opened the scoring in the 33rd minute and Micklewright made it 2-0 three minutes later.

An upset looked to be on the cards with Exeter struggling towards the foot of the Fourth Division table and in need of two points.

Alas, it wasn't to be. Palace fought their way back with Gavin reducing the arrears in the 54th minute, and then equalising with another goal not long after.

It must be mentioned that in addition to the three Easter fixtures in the space of 72 hours, the previous Saturday the Grecians had travelled all the way to the north-east and lost 1-0 at Gateshead.

Add to that another lengthy trip to Workington the Saturday after Easter – and a 2-1 defeat – it showed what a hectic time it was for footballers in the 1960s, unlike today, despite what modern-day managers and players might otherwise think.

EASTER 1960 WITH THE GRECIANS

Good Friday: 15th April 1960: Crystal Palace 1 Exeter City 0: Attendance 15,731
Easter Saturday: 16th April 1960: Exeter City 4 Rochdale 1: Attendance 6,669
Easter Monday: 18th April 1960: Exeter City 2 Crystal Palace 2: Attendance 6,661

Reginald James Rose, an Axminster landowner and retired industrialist from the North Midlands was elected to the Exeter City board of directors on 13th October 1960.

He quickly set about looking at the club's finances and planning how to improve them on behalf of his fellow board members.

Rose had lived in the West Country for the previous ten years and was an Axminster Rural District Councillor, and although he had never been connected with a football club before he had an interest in the Grecians for the past two years.

On being elected to the board, Rose felt that Exeter City was a club with potential, but it was a pity that more support was not attracted.

Three months after his appointment the City board had considered various issues raised by Rose to improve the club's financial position.

Having secured the mortgage on St James' Park they then sent a letter to the Exeter City Council asking them to buy the ground from them for £60,000.

The board felt that this would have safeguarded a valuable amenity for all time and resulted in Exeter City F.C. raising a substantial sum of money so urgently required.

There would be certain conditions attached to the sale, for the football club would want to rent or lease the ground in perpetuity at a nominal rent.

Vice-chairman Rose said that in spite of the fact that Exeter City had secured the mortgage of St James' Park, the club still needed a lot of money and he revealed that he was working out plans to raise it.

For some time the club had been struggling and just making ends meet, but Rose was attempting to get the club on a sound financial base.

Securing the mortgage had cost Rose the sum of £17,000. However, this now meant that no outside body could force the club into selling St James' Park.

Rose emphasised that there was no danger of former Exeter City director Tom Ford putting the Grecians in that position. Ford was interested in the well being of the club.

However, unforeseen things could have occurred and because of that it was felt the club should secure the mortgage from Ford, which they did so.

Rose had also put a further £1,000 into the club to pay off accrued shares of benefit owed to five players who had joined the Grecians the previous summer.

The burning ambition of Rose was to help turn Exeter City into a Second Division club and for a team at the bottom of the Fourth Division, that seemed a very far-reaching plan.

By March 1961, the *Express & Echo* reported that admission prices to the ground would increase and the reserve team would be scrapped, thus keeping a playing staff of only 15 or 16 professionals was the basis of another part of Rose's plan for prosperity for Exeter City F.C.

For the 1961–62 season City fans would have to pay three shillings for ground admission, raised from two shillings and sixpence. Grandstand seats would be increased in price from six shillings to seven shillings and sixpence.

A club statement read: 'Whilst the board regret this step, they feel that if the club is to function, supporters must be asked to pay economic rates.

'The board feel that in common with many other clubs, the time has now come when the club should cease to run a reserve side and concentrate on putting out one good side.

'At the present time the reserve side costs £7,000 a year to run, whilst net gate receipts total £500. The board will still encourage local talent and with this in mind will continue to run a side in the Exeter and District League playing home matches at St James' Park.

'The board realises that some of these decisions will cause considerable controversy among supporters, but they feel that football is now at a crossroad and many of the smaller clubs such as ours will not be able to function as in the past, and if they are to continue, bold decisions, even if sometimes unpopular will have to be taken.'

Unfortunately one aspect of the plan unveiled by Rose, the selling of St James' Park to the City Council would not go ahead.

After considering the matter in March 1961, a Council committee report stated that 'the proposal not be entertained'.

On hearing the decision, City chairman, George Gillin said that he had requested a meeting with the Council. He added that everyone must realise that football at Exeter was at the crossroads.

If anyone ever needed proof that football is a passionate game that produces emotions like no other, then you only had to look at the reaction to the news that Exeter City were to play Manchester United in the third round of the F.A. Cup in January 2005.

Supporters were seen leaping into the air, not just because the Grecians were to play arguably the most famous football club in the world, but also because it would go a very long way to solving City's pressing financial commitments.

It immediately brought back memories of the very first time in 1960 that Manchester United played the Grecians, not at Old Trafford, but at St James' Park in the first round of the Football League Cup.

Not every team entered it at that time, the competition being the dream of its instigator, the late Alan Hardaker, of the Football League.

United were, of course, still in the midst of rebuilding their team following the tragic events of Munich in 1958, but nevertheless, there were many household names in their side, such as a young Nobby Stiles and the return of former Grecian, Maurice Setters.

The Park was packed for the visit of United, including kids sat on the wall behind the terrace at the St James' Road end. It is pretty unlikely that would be possible today with much more stringent ground safety regulations in place.

The big day, 19th October 1960, arrived. Surprisingly it wasn't a full house though, with an attendance of 16,494, but even so, it still is the biggest crowd that City have ever played in front of at home in the competition.

It is interesting to note in view of the fact that City banked in excess of £500,000 from their visit to Old Trafford in 2005, that back in October 1960, the gate receipts were £2,993 3s 6d!

The teams lined up as follows:

Exeter City: John Lobbett, Brian Whitnall, Les MacDonald, Glen Wilson, Keith Harvey, Jimmy Thompson, Eric Welsh, Peter Gordon, Fred Donaldson, Graham Rees, Bernard Harrison.

Manchester United: Harry Gregg, Maurice Setters, Shay Brennan, Nobby Stiles, Bill Foulkes, James Nicholson, Albert Quixall, John Giles, Dennis Violet, Mark Pearson, Albert Scanlon.

Like all the 'big' games that City have played in, the occasion seems to zip by for most who are

Graham Rees.

present, such is the atmosphere generated within the ground.

The *Express & Echo* reported: 'A City side that came out fighting from the start turned on a soccer display that amazed everyone in the St James' Park ground.'

It certainly was amazing as City took the lead against their First Division opponents when Graham Rees netted after 15 minutes.

Rees had a goal disallowed three minutes earlier for a foul on United goalkeeper, Gregg, and he had the ball in the net again five minutes into the second half, only for that effort to be ruled out as well, for offside.

As City tired, United took control, the inevitable equaliser coming with 13 minutes of the match remaining.

Shay Brennan's free-kick was deflected into the path of Mark Pearson and he fired in from 18 yards to crush the Grecians' hopes.

City had, however, earned the right to a replay at Old Trafford, but this time the task proved to be too much for them, despite another gallant effort, as they lost 1-4.

Surprisingly the crowd for the replay was lower than at St James' Park. Can you imagine that happening now? Only 15,662 fans were there at Old Trafford. Exeter's goal came from a Jimmy Thompson penalty in the 13th minute, whilst Albert Quixall (2), John Giles and Mark Pearson were on target for the hosts.

Although Swindells and Hudson sound more like a firm of defence lawyers, they were in fact the scourge of the Fourth Division defences, and that included Exeter City's.

The deadly goalscoring duo were Accrington Stanley's strike force in 1960–61, and they bagged a total of 52 goals between them in the league that season as the Peel Park side finished in 18th place in the table.

Jackie Swindells, later to play for Torquay United, was signed by Stanley for what now seems the bargain fee of £1,500 from neighbouring Blackburn Rovers.

His partner, Hudson, who had also been signed from Blackburn, hit an incredible 35 goals in 44 league outings, whilst Swindells managed 17 in 43 starts.

And the Grecians felt the full force of the twin strikers when they met Accrington Stanley for the first time ever in a Division Four encounter at St James' Park on 19th November 1960.

Although City managed to score twice, through Graham Bond and Gordon Dale, Stanley replied with a brace apiece from their dynamic duo.

The 4-2 home reverse prompted Grecian's player-manager Glen Wilson to complain: 'Either my players are not giving me 100 per cent effort, or they have not got the talent.'

When City travelled to Peel Park for the return fixture on 6th April 1961, things did improve from an Exeter point of view. However, they left it late to clinch a victory with a goal seven minutes from time by Fred Donaldson.

It was to be the only time that the Grecians graced the Peel Park turf, as the following season Accrington Stanley Football Club were forced to fold with mounting debts.

City did get the chance to entertain Stanley at St James' Park before the club's collapse, winning 3-0 with goals from Ray Carter, Brian Jenkins and Archie Blue, but by the time the team were due to travel to East Lancashire, alarm bells were sounding for Accrington.

After fulfilling a fixture at Crewe Alexandra on 2nd March 1962, which Stanley lost 4-0, later that week it was announced the club would cease to trade.

When you read of clubs being millions of pounds in debt today, it seems ludicrous that a deficit of less than £60,000 forced Stanley's closure.

By this time both Swindells and Hudson had moved to pastures new, being transferred to Barnsley and Peterborough United respectively.

Exeter City were due to visit Stanley the week after the Crewe fixture, but of course they never did.

There was little compassion shown by Exeter City towards the plight of Accrington, with the Grecians' club secretary quoted as saying that it would save at least £160 in travelling expenses now the team didn't have to go there.

With Stanley out of business, there were one or two other clubs who were anxiously watching their own perilous financial situation, Exeter City being one of them.

But City vice-chairman George Gillin gave an assurance that the club would not follow suit, just 24 hours after the demise of Stanley.

Gillin admitted though that it was only the cash being pumped into the club by himself and chairman Reg Rose that was preventing the club from going under.

While the Grecians continued to stumble from one financial crisis to another, Accrington Stanley were to reform and today have climbed back to the Football League, although they now play at the Crown Ground, rather than Peel Park, which is nothing more than an open space, with a very eerie feel to it, with so many footballing memories from the past.

19th November 1960
Exeter City 2 Accrington Stanley 4
City team: John Lobbett, Theo Foley, Les MacDonald, Peter Grant, Keith Harvey, Jim Thompson, Eric Welsh, Graham Bond, Jack Wilkinson, Ray Carter, Gordon Dale.
City scorers: Bond, Dale.
Attendance: 6,000.

There are two letters in football parlance that can make players, especially defenders, break into a cold sweat. The dreaded O.G. or own goal.

It is also a subject that can bring much discussion as to what exactly constitutes an own goal. Does a deflected shot count as an O.G., even though on target and it might have gone in anyway?

There are some own goals of course where the poor unfortunate player couldn't get out of the way of the ball and turned it into his own net.

Whatever, an own goal is embarrassing at the best of times, and when your side concedes two of them in the same match, then you just want to go and hide!

This happened on a particularly black day as far as Exeter City were concerned when they visited then Football League newcomers Peterborough United on 11th February 1961.

The Posh had been knocking on the door of the Football League for a couple of seasons as they were a successful Midland League club.

Eventually, at the expense of Gateshead, Peterborough gained election to the Football League at the start of the 1960–61 season.

They were to romp away with the Fourth Division title at the first attempt, and on the way they defeated Exeter City twice.

They visited St James' Park on 24th September 1960, against a Grecians team that had only won two of their opening 11 league matches.

But the 9,146-strong crowd was treated to a seven-goal thriller as the Posh edged the match, winning 4-3.

Jack Wilkinson netted a couple of goals for City, to take his tally to four for the season, and player-manager Glen Wilson got the other goal, his first and what proved to be his only one for the club.

With Peterborough in such rampant goalscoring form, it must have been with a little trepidation that

Exeter travelled to London Road for the return meeting on 11th February 1961.

However, City were putting together a good run of results, and prior to the Peterborough visit, had won their three previous matches against Mansfield Town, Stockport County and Bradford Park Avenue respectively.

Any hopes of extending that run were brought down to earth with a resounding crash as Peterborough won 7-1!

What made matters worse was that two of the hosts' goals were netted by City players – the dreaded own goals!

Peterborough had led 3-0 at half-time with two goals from the prolific Terry Bly and one from Billy Hails.

At the start of the second half Bly added another, and then scored yet again, his fourth and his side's fifth after 52 minutes.

City were in disarray even though Graham Rees had managed to reduce the arrears in between the two Bly goals.

The last two Peterborough goals were courtesy of City players, although there was a dispute as to who should get the credit for one of them, and the record books show Hails as the name on the score sheet.

The first O.G. came from Theo Foley, who had otherwise been one of the few shining lights in an overrun City team. The second and disputed O.G. came as a result of a deflection off centre-half Alvin Williams.

The own goal will always be a contentious issue as to whether it really is one or not. Ask Ray Pratt who is credited with a hat-trick in City's opening fixture of the 1984–85 season in a 5-0 home win over Northampton Town.

However, in publications such as the 'City Bible' – Breedon Books' complete record (see the Recommended Bibliography) – it is shown as only two goals for Pratt and his 'third' recorded as an own goal by Northampton's Neil Brough.

DID YOU KNOW?

The first opposition player to net an own goal in a Football League match played against Exeter City was Albert Weston of Swindon Town. He scored in the 'wrong net' as Swindon went on to defeat the Grecians 2-1 on 27th January 1923.

Whilst the football on offer may not have been of the highest quality, the players in this particular Exeter City team are still well remembered, perhaps for all the wrong reasons.

The 1961–62 season opened with a 3-1 defeat at Mansfield Town, followed by two successive home wins over Chesterfield (4-1) and Barrow (3-0).

But then apart from the odd victory here and there, the season proved to be less than memorable as far as the results were concerned.

Defeat in the first round of the Football League Cup at Mansfield Town, and all too familiar humiliation in the F.A. Cup at the hands of non-leaguers Dartford after a 3-3 draw at the Park.

So what of the players in that City team of 1961–62?

Goalkeeping duties were shared by Alan Jones and Colin Tinsley. Jones, it has to be said was a good keeper, and went on to play for Norwich City.

He had plenty to do that season in a less than impressive City defence and Tinsley stepped in towards the end of the campaign and was to win a regular keeping spot the following season.

The two full-backs were of the 'old school' of player, win the ball and get rid of it up field.

George Hudson filled the right-back position, a short, stocky, well-built defender, with much experience in the lower divisions, whilst the left-back position was the domain of City's long-serving Les MacDonald, who gave marvellous service to the club making nearly 300 league appearances.

The half-back line of 1961–62 comprised of any of the following players: Arnold Mitchell, Keith Harvey, Derrick Sullivan, player-manager Glen Wilson and Mike Hughes.

Mitchell was of course yet another loyal servant to the City totalling 495 league appearances, as was Harvey, both players being members of the club's first-ever promotion-winning side of 1963–64.

Sullivan came from Cardiff City, but only had one season at the Park before returning to Wales to link up with Newport County.

Wilson had been appointed player-manager after a long playing career with Brighton and Hove Albion and managed to fill the hot seat at St James' Park for 22 months.

Wilson was sacked by the club the day after City had recorded their best win of the season – a 5-0 win over Chester in April 1962!

Like managers before and after him, Wilson had

little or no money to spend in the transfer market and had to make do with a collection of free transfer signings.

Hughes was another Welshman who never really held a regular first-team place at the Park, but went on to play for Chesterfield, before returning to the West Country to manage Yeovil Town.

The Exeter City forward line was Ray Carter! For in 1961–62 he scored 18 goals in 40 matches. Without him the City were lost, for no one else in the team reached double figures as far as goalscoring was concerned.

Carter scored a lot of goals for City, but then surprisingly gave up playing league football to go into business in 1963, although he did continue to turn out for Crawley Town (his home town club) in the Southern League.

A player of Carter's goalscoring calibre would command a lot of money in today's transfer market, especially in view of the fact he continued to hit the back of the net, though playing in a team that struggled in the league.

Eric Welsh was still making his way in the game in the 1961–62 season, going on to win inter-national honours for Northern Ireland after he had been transferred to Carlisle United.

The ginger-haired and long-serving Graham Rees could be relied upon to give 100 per cent and was used in a number of forward positions.

And then there was Archie Blue. The Scotsman never really won over the St James' Park crowd. The former Hearts striker nevertheless still managed to play in 34 matches that season, scoring six goals. Blue was another to make the move from City to Carlisle.

Blue was actually replaced midway through the season for a handful of games. City had parted with £5,000 for centre-forward Alan Brown from player-manager Wilson's former club, Brighton and Hove Albion.

Brown lasted just 11 league matches, before disappearing from the St James' Park scene and proved to be an expensive acquisition, with the fee being not inconsiderable for City in those days.

Of the other players to wear the City colours that season, there was winger or inside-forward Peter Gordon, and another little Welshman – winger Brian Jenkins.

The latter was an in and out sort of a player, but certainly found his level when he joined Southern

League Merthyr Tydfil after leaving the City, where he was an outstanding success scoring a lot of goals.

The wing positions were something of a problem, for Scotsman John McMillan, bought from Cardiff City, made a handful of appearances on the right wing without success.

The only other face to feature in the Exeter side was full-back Brian Whitnall. Like Rees, he was a little short of hair on his head, and he only made four league outings in 1961–62.

The attendance figures show what sort of season the City had. For in the opening home match 5,944 saw the Grecians beat Chesterfield, whilst for the last game the figure had slumped to 3,310 for the visit of Chester.

Although there was not a lot to shout about, there appeared to be a lot more characters in the City squad then.

They are fondly recalled, good, bad or indifferent, like every player who has worn the red and white stripes of Exeter City.

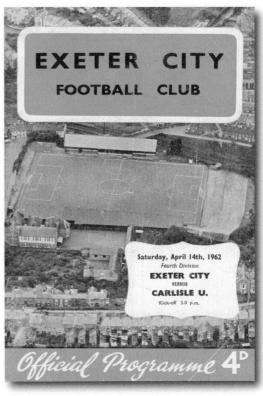

The programme from Exeter City's Fourth Division fixture against Carlisle United at St James' Park on 14th April 1962. It proved to be a good afternoon for the Grecians as goals from Eric Welsh, Keith Harvey (penalty) and Brian Jenkins (2) gave them a 4-0 win over the Cumbrians.

EXETER CITY 1961–62

Fourth Division appearances

Keith Harvey 44; Derrick Sullivan 44;
Peter Gordon 43; Les MacDonald 43;
Geoff Hudson 41; Ray Carter 40;
Brian Jenkins 39; Archie Blue 34;
Alan Jones 32; Graham Rees 25;
Eric Welsh 20; Mike Hughes 17;
Arnold Mitchell 16; Colin Tinsley 12;
Alan Brown 11; Glen Wilson 11;
John McMillan 8; Brian Whitnall 4.

Fourth Division goalscorers

Ray Carter 18; Peter Gordon 9;
Brian Jenkins 8; Archie Blue 6;
Graham Rees 6; Eric Welsh 6;
Alan Brown 3; Keith Harvey 2;
John McMillan 1; Glen Wilson 1.

It's not that often that Exeter City entertain a team from a far-flung country at St James' Park, but there have been a handful of occasions when that has happened.

Whilst City had played a couple of Austrian clubs in the 1950s, the Grecians really did have some unusual visitors to the Park on 26th October 1961.

It was quite a coup to attract any overseas team to Exeter, but to get one from South America was a bit special.

The visitors, CAR La Paz were from Bolivia – not a country that too many City fans could have known much about, let alone their football teams. The CAR part of their name stood for 'Club Always Ready'.

It was the first time that Exeter City had faced a South American side since their famous tour of Brazil and Argentina in 1914.

La Paz had been on a European tour that began in Hungary. They went on to play Aberdeen two nights before they arrived in Exeter.

One abiding memory was not of the game itself, but an incident that occurred during it, involving a Bolivian player.

Requiring treatment after sustaining an injury, the player was administered by not one person, but three – one of whom was a carrying a hot water bottle. Maybe the cold October Exeter night air was a bit too much for the team from La Paz?

Having said that, one interesting fact in the match programme was that La Paz is actually 8,000 feet above sea level, whilst St James' Park is 200 feet above sea level.

So what of the game itself? Well, it attracted an attendance of 5,004 and was probably a welcome relief for City fans as their team hadn't enjoyed the best of times in the Fourth Division that season, with only five wins in their opening 16 matches.

The Exeter City team lined up: Allan Jones, Geoff Hudson, Les MacDonald, Mike Hughes (Peter Rutley), Keith Harvey, Derrick Sullivan, John McMillan, Peter Gordon, Archie Blue, Ray Carter (Arnold Mitchell), Brian Jenkins.

Three goals in 11 minutes during the first half ensured that City beat their Bolivian visitors, whose side contained several internationals.

La Paz put together a series of classy moves and

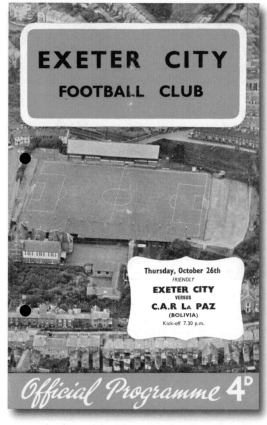

EXETER CITY

FOOTBALL CLUB

Thursday, October 26th
FRIENDLY
EXETER CITY
VERSUS
C.A.R La PAZ
(BOLIVIA)
Kick-off 7.30 p.m.

Official Programme 4ᴰ

seemed a lot quicker than the Grecians, but City had the upper hand when it came to putting away chances in front of goal.

In an entertaining friendly fixture the visitors were denied a goal early on before Archie Blue opened the scoring for Exeter.

Brian Jenkins added the second and Blue scored again to put City well in control.

In the second half the Bolivians were rewarded with a goal, but City claimed a 3-1 win.

One notable moment came in the 75th minute when Grecians' apprentice professional Peter Rutley, aged just 15 years and five months, was introduced as a substitute.

It had been quite strange to have played a team like CAR La Paz – the friendly being 'sandwiched' between league matches with Accrington Stanley and Oldham Athletic. A dose of reality perhaps!

Exeter City chairman Reg Rose made a public appeal in January 1962, mainly to traders and businessmen of the city, to raise money for the club through an issue of £5 loan receipts. The issue of the receipts was announced when 500 letters were delivered to local businesses. It was hoped that a further 500 letters would be sent out the following week.

Rose said he was not setting any target, but the board did think that the traders would benefit from having a Football League club in their city because of the business it could bring.

The letter read:

'We desperately need money not only to carry on, but to enable us to plan for better football, for better attendances and so sustain and prosper our club. With this in mind we have decided to issue a series of loan receipts in multiples of £5 in anticipation that all interested parties, in particular business houses, will take up at least one loan receipt. Commencing September 1963, it is also proposed to have an annual draw for the purposes of repaying such numbers of loan receipts as the directors may decide, but all to be repaid within ten years. We feel it is a fair comment to ask that all such loans could be reasonably be assessed as trading investments as the attraction of a successful soccer team must bring incalculable business to the city. This appeal has not been lightly undertaken and the need is urgent. The time is now. Support your club and invest for the future.'

Like a lot of small clubs, Exeter City were losing money steadily and they could not go on much longer without reaching the same stage as Accrington Stanley who shortly after pulled out of the Football League altogether.

Rose added: 'Our position is particularly aggravated by the millstone of old debts and commitments, lack of credit and the exhaustion of club assets.'

It was reported that City needed a minimum attendance of 7,000 to work economically, and from an estimated population of 85,000 from Exeter and district, it was felt that was a very modest figure.

'If football is to continue at Exeter, the responsibility of its future must rest with the whole community, who must be prepared to share some of the financial burden', explained Rose.

Three weeks later, on 23rd February 1962, it was announced that three Exeter City directors, Mr J.G. Warne, Mr A.W. Crawshaw and Mr J.R. Cowley resigned from the board and as an economy measure the reserve team trainer and club scout, David Pryde, had been dismissed.

Warne, who joined the club in 1951, was the longest serving board member. Crawshaw joined in 1953 after a long association through his playing days and as an official of the Grecians' Association. Cowley joined the board in 1959.

A statement issued by the cub read:

'At a meeting of the board of directors it was felt that the finances of the club must be strengthened and with this in mind and in the best interests of the club, Messrs Warne, Crawshaw and Cowley, voluntarily resigned from the board with the hope that this step would enable the chairman to encourage prominent citizens to join the board and share his confidence in the future of the club.'

This left just chairman Reg Rose and vice-chairman George Gillin on the board. The chairman had already bought the £17,000 mortgage on St James' Park.

Including the mortgage, the club had total debts of almost £40,000 and without the substantial help of the Red and White Draw and the Supporters' Club, City would still lose money on the difference between income and expenditure of around £250 per week.

One of three City directors who had resigned, Billy Crawshaw said the overriding factor was to keep the club operating. It would be a terrible blow to the prestige of the city should the football club cease to trade.

He added: 'The ever increasing need for money due to the lack of success of the team has created circumstances which have been far from enjoyable for the members of the board.

'Too many people are inclined to think that being a football director involves receiving a lot of perks. I would like to assure them that it is not so, and that my association with Exeter City has cost me several thousand pounds.'

The ever worsening financial position of Exeter City Football Club was made public in February 1962 and it was suggested that the future of the club was in grave doubt.

An appeal had been made a month earlier to local businesses and trades people for any assistance they could give to help the Grecians through the crisis and until the results of this were known, it was impossible for the club to plan for the future, if there was one.

'It is a very grave situation that we are facing at the moment', admitted club chairman Reg Rose, who had recently taken over from George Gillin.

'The club's total commitments add up to quite a gigantic figure and I should only be guessing if I outlined any future policy at this stage.

'It is true we have not been getting good results lately and some people have sad that the appeal for help was not well timed. In fact we have had this idea for some time and we were hoping to spring it when things were going a little better, but finance does not wait for anyone. It has had to be now.'

The club had just two directors, a lot of debt and their remaining 4,000 supporters were left wondering whether it would be another Accrington Stanley – in other words, be forced to close up shop completely.

Exeter City were knocked out of the F.A. Cup in the first round by Southern League Dartford and had won only three of their previous 20 matches.

Not surprisingly attendances dipped as a result and the loan appeal raised a paltry £60. Directors, former directors and leading citizens of Exeter met to discuss how the club could be saved.

Three directors had resigned from the board in the middle of February 1962, namely Jack Warne, Billy Crawshaw and Jack Cowley, but it seemed that it was proving to be a hard task to encourage anyone to replace them.

It was reported that Exeter City had the Football League's costliest travelling bill – around £6,000 per season – the nearest opposition being Aldershot, 140 miles away. A financial millstone hung around Exeter City's neck, and they were losing £250 per week.

The *Express & Echo* reported: 'City fans are now quite rightly wondering if the economies have come fast enough to save Exeter City from another re-election application to the Football League and from the close down talk surrounding fellow Fourth Division outfit Accrington Stanley.'

City didn't have the best of records when it came to applying for re-election. In fact they had the worse joint record of any of the then Football League clubs as they had applied no fewer than seven times!

The City chairman, added: 'The fact that three directors have left the board of Exeter City Football Club does not mean that it is the beginning of the end. Everyone has a limit of what money they can invest in a club.'

Indeed, three weeks later City did appoint a new director as Jack Rodgers, a Paignton-based businessman with a furniture business in Totnes, was welcomed to St James' Park to join Reg Rose and George Gillin on the board.

The apathy toward the club continued though, for at the extraordinary meeting of shareholders on 7th April 1962, only 11 turned up, when City had over 500 listed.

The *Echo* commented: 'Is it little wonder that the club can be fairly described as being at rock bottom and that the few men who do show some interest are beginning to wonder if they will ever get any help?'

After the meeting was thrown open to any questions, topics raised included: 'Why don't we have a band playing before matches?' 'Was it really necessary to spend £6,000 on signing player-manager Glen Wilson?'

George Gillin pointed out that Wilson did not cost anything like the figure mentioned, but rightly or wrongly, at least the shareholders who did bother to attend had something to say. And in most cases they tried to be constructive and not just critical.

The final comment on the meeting came from the *Echo* which reported: 'You would have thought that every shareholder who could possibly have attended would have been there, if only to protect their own interests?'

The name of Jack Edwards will forever be associated with Exeter City's first-ever promotion team: a team that he managed, transforming the fortunes of a previously struggling club to one that reached the Third Division of the Football League.

Edwards hailed from Risca in Monmouthshire, being born there in July 1929. A full-back, he joined Cardiff City as an amateur and then played for Lovell's Athletic.

However, his playing career took off when signing for Crystal Palace in September 1949, having starred whilst playing in the 1948 Army Cup Final at Aldershot appearing for The Royal Armoured Corps (Bovington) against No. 121 Training Regiment of the Royal Artillery (Oswestry) in which two players tragically died after being struck by lightning.

Jack Edwards.

He became captain of the Selhurst Park club and made 299 appearances during his ten years with the Palace, before moving to Rochdale in June 1959.

Edwards stayed at Spotland for a couple of seasons, making 68 league outings, then moving back south to link up with Southern League club, Ashford Town, where he was player-coach during 1961–62.

In the summer of 1962 his association with Exeter City began as he was appointed the club trainer, ironically brought to the club by manager Cyril Spiers, whom he later replaced as boss in February 1963.

This was the time of the 'big freeze' when very few matches were played anywhere in the country for over two months, and in some cases longer.

The break proved to be beneficial for the Grecians in two respects, for Edwards took over as temporary manager and whereas the team had struggled prior to the 'freeze', all of a sudden he managed to guide the side to a great run of results that ultimately enabled the Grecians to climb out of the re-election to the Football League places, to end the season in 17th place.

The following season, with Edwards having been named as full-time manager in May 1963, proved to be remarkable, as City fans had been deprived of virtually any league success since the club had entered the Third Division in 1920.

Edwards was to make one inspired signing, that of Alan Banks, from Cambridge City, and his goals

were to be a big feature, along with a very mean defence (only Gillingham conceded fewer goals) that saw Exeter end in fourth place and therefore gain promotion.

Much was expected of City as they adapted to life in the Third Division with Edwards at the helm, but not for the first time in their history, the club 'shot themselves in the foot' when appointing Ellis Stuttard as chief scout without the prior knowledge of Edwards.

This proved to be the final straw for Edwards, who had also had to overcome 'internal squabbling' in the boardroom, and he resigned, much to the dismay of the City fans in January 1965.

He didn't move far though as he became trainer to Torquay United between 1965 and 1968, caretaker manager between December 1968 and Janaury 1969, and then finally manager of the Plainmoor club between October 1971 and January 1973. Edwards, to date, is one of just two men who have managed both Exeter City and Torquay United, the other being John Cornforth.

Edwards was persuaded to return to St James' Park by manager John Newman who wanted him as his trainer, rejoining City in January 1973.

He didn't stay too long though and by the end of that year Edwards had been appointed assistant manager to Bobby Saxton at Plymouth Argyle.

In his later years Edwards did some scouting for Leeds United and continued to live in the Torbay area.

Ireland proved to be a rich source of players for Exeter City in the early 1960s, when several young players tried their luck at St James' Park with varying degrees of success.

One of the first to make a breakthrough was wing-half Des Anderson. He had been signed by the Grecians from Irish League side Glenavon and proved to be a more than useful member of the City first team.

Anderson made his league debut for City in a 3-0 home defeat against Torquay United in August 1962, but was to go on to win a regular place in the first team.

He was a member of the promotion-winning team of 1964 and eventually made nearly 150 appearances for the Grecians, before signing for Chesterfield on a free transfer in 1966. He was later to have a spell at non-leaguers Matlock Town.

The most successful of City's Irish imports at this time was undoubtedly full-back Cecil Smyth. His speed in the tackle and ability of recovery were his trademarks.

Smyth was signed from Distillery and made his first-team debut in a 3-1 defeat at Brentford in September 1962. Like Anderson, Smyth was to play a major part in the promotion team of 1964.

He became a permanent fixture at right-back and made 273 league appearances for the Grecians before making the short move to Torquay United for a small fee in 1969.

Smyth returned to the Park and played for the City reserve side to add experience to what was then a young team. He made Exeter his home on retiring from playing and gained employment in the Prison Service.

Other players to make the journey across the Irish Sea to St James' Park included Belfast-born Irish Amateur International goalkeeper, Jimmy Parkhill, who was signed from Cliftonville in the close season of 1963.

Parkhill had one season at the Park as an understudy to Alan Barnett, and managed just one league outing in a 3-1 home win over Newport County. He moved on at the end the season to play for Taunton Town.

Not quite so successful were Irish imports Tommy Sweetman, Brian Symington, Pat Cavanan and Ray Gough.

Sweetman was a centre-forward who came from the Home Farm club in December 1965, but although he made a few appearances for City's Western League team, he couldn't settle in Devon and was released from his contract two months later.

Another Belfast-born player, Symington, had won international honours for Ireland at Schools and Youth levels, and Exeter City gave him his first professional contract in September 1963.

Symington, a winger, was released by the Grecians, however, after just one season without making the first team.

Cavanan was another not able to gain senior recognition at St James' Park, after being signed at the same time as Sweetman from Home Farm.

He was allowed to join Weymouth on October 1966, and later returned to Exeter to play for Heavitree United.

Gough also hailed from Belfast and arrived at Exeter City in October 1963 from Linfield as an Irish Youth International, and having played for the Irish League XI.

Although not a success with the Grecians, he did go on to make several appearances for Millwall when he joined in October 1964.

Winger Eric Welsh also played a key part in City's fortunes in the early 1960s, although he had joined the club slightly earlier than those players previously mentioned, making the move from Distillery in 1959.

Welsh made 105 league appearances for Exeter, then being transferred to Carlisle United in 1965, where he was extremely successful winning full international honours for Northern Ireland.

Faced with a £1,400 demand from Brighton and Hove Albion Football Club and a breakdown in relations with the Grecians' Association, Exeter City chairman Reg Rose and vice-chairman George Gillin both denied that the club was in a financial crisis. Indeed, Gillin said that Exeter City were far from being broke and they were about to pay out some money for new players.

Rose made a special visit to St James' Park on the morning of 30th October 1962 to speak to the playing staff. He and Gillin were preparing a general statement for the supporters and the City chairman had arranged to meet the Grecians' Association to answer a letter of 'no confidence in the directors' management of the club'. He stressed that the club's financial position was not nearly as bad as it had been painted.

At the Annual General Meeting held the previous evening, the club's total deficiency up to 31st May 1962 was stated to be £42,635. This had been reduced by £3,000 and the majority of the remaining money was in fact owed within the club to the directors themselves. Rose held the £17,000 freehold of St James' Park. Very little of the club's debt was to outside creditors.

Brighton had reported Exeter City to the Football League for non-payment of the last part of the £5,500 fee for former player-manager Glen Wilson. Brighton maintained that they should have received that when Exeter sold goalkeeper Alan Jones to Norwich City for £3,000. Exeter owed Brighton £1,400 and chairman, Rose, said the club would pay it.

The Grecians' Association, who by their weekly efforts through tombola and competitions, had brought in approximately £75 per week to the club over the past playing season. They now said they were withholding the current season's funds until they had assurances from the board of directors.

Rose felt that this was a misunderstanding and the matter could have been resolved had the Grecians' Association come to the board first.

In the first week of November 1962 an emergency meeting was held between the club and the Grecians' Association and the 15-strong committee of the latter organisation decided to release the funds that they had been holding back all season as a protest in support of their letter of 'no confidence'.

Rose met the Grecians' Association at St James' Park with director Mr Rodgers, and with City vice-chairman, Gillin, on holiday in Honolulu, this comprised of the entire City board!

They reached agreement and Grecians' Association chairman Les Kerslake told the press: 'We have had a very full and frank discussion with the board and all our differences have been resolved.'

Three weeks later on 30th November 1962, it was announced that Kerslake had been appointed to the Exeter City board of directors.

Rose said that the board had been unanimous in inviting Kerslake to join them as he had always worked hard for the club and there was no doubt that he would be a valuable acquisition to the boardroom.

It was in 1945 that Kerslake joined the Grecians' Association. In the 1959–60 season he gave up the position of secretary to the Association to become a director.

At that time he found he could not serve on the board whilst still being an official of the Red and White Club – a weekly fundraising venture.

Since then the rule had been changed and Kerslake would therefore have been able to continue to act as secretary of the Red and White Club, of which he was a founder member and which it was estimated had contributed £100,000 to Exeter City F.C. in its nine years of existence.

DID YOU KNOW?

Exeter City player-manager Glen Wilson had arrived at the club after a long playing career with Brighton and Hove Albion where he had appeared in 433 league and cup matches for the club. He was appointed boss at St James' Park in June 1960 and was in charge until April 1962. He then became a publican in Brighton.

Those of us old enough to have lived through the winter of 1963 will recall how miserable a time it was if you were a football supporter. We went several weeks without being able to get to a game at St James' Park.

Little did Grecians' fans know as they left the Park on Boxing Day 1962, moaning about the latest defeat at the hands of Stockport County, that it would be nearly two months before they saw City at the Park again.

It did seem strange that Stockport had been sent all the way to Devon for a Boxing Day fixture, none-theless they made the most of it and won 1-0.

Three days later – 29th December – Exeter travelled to Stockport for the return meeting and were involved in a seven-goal thriller.

Sadly, County netted four of the goals, whilst Arnold Mitchell, Graham Rees and Eric Welsh were on target for the Grecians.

This was in fact the last time that the team played until the visit of Oldham Athletic to the Park on 23rd February 1963.

The big freeze set in and football pretty well shut down, as did most of the country, with snow drifts and arctic-like conditions taking hold.

The year 1963 was the only time during that century that there were two consecutive months with temperatures averaging below zero. Before that it was the winter of 1878–79, and before that, the even more severe winter of 1740.

A blizzard over south-west England on 29th and 30th December brought snowdrifts 18-feet deep in places.

But for the players of Exeter City, the freeze came a bit too soon as they experienced a nightmare journey back from the game at Stockport.

The players left on the midnight (Saturday) train from Manchester, but they didn't arrive back in Exeter until early Sunday evening.

The train was the first of the day to reach Exeter and to get through the snow drifts.

Thankfully it was warm on board and there were plentiful supplies of tea, however, none of the players had eaten since 6pm after the game the previous day.

The journey didn't end there for City centre-half Keith Harvey, for he had to try to reach his Crediton home.

He managed to get a taxi that took him as far as possible, before the conditions meant there was no alternative but to walk through the deep snow for the final four miles.

City manager Cyril Spiers had offered to arrange for Harvey to stay at an Exeter hotel for the night, but the player preferred to make sure that his family were safe, and so he set off for Crediton.

The Stockport games were to be the last in charge for Spiers. The team hadn't enjoyed a great first half of the season and he was eventually replaced as manager by Jack Edwards.

What a remarkable transformation! Under Edwards, once the season got underway again, the team had a great run of results and at the end of the following 1963–64 season, Exeter City had won promotion for the first time in their history.

Whilst many clubs had suffered due to the enforced winter break, the Grecians started again as if it were a new season.

The first game saw them defeat Oldham Athletic 2-1, with goals from Arnold Mitchell and John Henderson.

They then went on to win six of their next eight Fourth Division fixtures against Barrow (2-0), Hartlepools United (3-1), Darlington (1-0), Southport (2-1), Oxford United (3-0) and Newport County (1-0).

The other two matches were both drawn against York City (3-3) and Doncaster Rovers (1-1). The team eventually finished the season in 17th place.

How many current Exeter City supporters can recall the Grecian kids of 1962–63? That was the first time that the club enjoyed a run of any note in the F.A. Youth Cup, and few could have envisaged after dispatching Newton Abbot Spurs (9-0) in the preliminary round that the City youngsters would go on to play against Arsenal at Highbury.

Five of the City youth team made such good progress in the Youth Cup that season that they were given a first-team opportunity. Peter Rutley, Derek Grace, Bruce Stuckey, Alan Riding and Barry Redwood were to make the grade.

But none of them, apart from Stuckey, was to make more than a handful of appearances. Stuckey was eventually transferred by Exeter City to Sunderland, and he went on to appear for AFC Bournemouth and Torquay United.

Redwood, later to be involved in the running of the City youth teams (his son Toby played first-team football for the Grecians), made his senior debut for Exeter in a Football League Cup tie at Hull City in September 1963.

Unfortunately, Redwood's career came to an end after sustaining a head injury in a Third Division fixture at Brentford the following season. A benefit match was arranged for him against a Swindon Town side.

The one surprise was that Alan Riding never really got a chance in the City first team, despite his prolific goalscoring record at both reserve and youth team level. His one and only league outing for the Grecians came in a 2-1 defeat at Scunthorpe United.

The Youth Cup run began at St James' Park in September 1962 when Riding netted four times, Barry Redwood hit a hat-trick and Colin Reed scored two goals in the 9-0 win over Newton Abbot Spurs.

The Grecians had to travel to Bath City for the second preliminary round and triumphed 4-0. The scorers this time were again Redwood (2), Riding and Reed.

It was back to the Park for the first round proper visit of Newport County, the Welsh team being beaten 4-2. That man Redwood was again on the score sheet with a hat-trick, with the tally being completed by Bryn Jones.

More goals flowed in the second round as Bristol City were crushed 5-1. This time it was the turn of Riding to get a hat-trick.

The next round against Bexleyheath was delayed due to the arctic weather that was gripping the country, but when the tie was eventually played, City ran out 3-1 winners.

Round four saw Exeter City drawn away to Arsenal. Highbury must have seemed a vast stadium to play in for the City youngsters.

The Gunners included such players as Peter Storey, John Radford, Jon Sammels and Peter Simpson, all of whom were to make their mark in First Division football.

Despite this, the City youngsters put up a great display before eventually going down 3-0 before an attendance of 1,136.

City keeper Barry Sidey had injured his arm in a collision with Radford, but it was not until after the game that it was discovered he had suffered a break.

Although out of the Youth Cup, it had been the best run by any Exeter City team in the competition, and remains so today.

How many players can you recall in that City squad? Goalkeeper was Barry Sidey; full-backs Peter Quarrington and Peter Arbury; half-backs Peter Rutley, Derek Grace and Chris Gillard; forwards Bruce Stuckey, Barry Redwood, Alan Riding, Bryn Jones and Brian Wills.

Jones had come into the team replacing Reed for the first round proper match against Newport County and was to hold his place for the remainder of the games.

DID YOU KNOW?

After retiring from playing, former Exeter City winger Bruce Stuckey became a child care officer back in his native Devon.

The first-ever Exeter City player to be chosen for his country at full international level was Dermot Curtis. He won one cap for Eire, as they were more commonly known at the time, whilst on the books at St James' Park.

Curtis lined up for his native country in a goalless draw in Vienna against Austria in September 1963. This was in fact also his last appearance for Eire, having previously been capped 16 times.

It was a great honour, not only for Curtis, but for Exeter City as well, for it was very rare for a Fourth Division player and club, as the Grecians were at the time, to have someone selected to play at full international level.

Exeter were chasing a coveted promotion place from the Fourth Division, something they eventually achieved later in the season, and the form of Curtis played a big part in City's success.

Born in Dublin on 26th August 1932, Curtis commenced his senior playing career for Irish side Shelbourne. He won his first full cap for Eire in 1957 against Denmark, and then added another by playing against West Germany.

Bristol City gave Curtis his chance in English league football when he was signed by the Ashton Gate club in December 1956. He was then transferred to Ipswich Town in September 1958 and made 41 league appearances for them, scoring 17 goals.

Curtis had been a squad member of the Ipswich side that won the Football League Championship in 1961–62. The Irishman had continued to attract international recognition whilst playing for Bristol City and Ipswich, appearing against England (twice), Denmark, Poland (twice), Austria (twice) Sweden (twice), Chile, West Germany, Norway, Scotland and Iceland.

Curtis had been persuaded to join the Grecians by then City chairman, Les Kerslake, who had flown to see the player in Ireland, and the signing, for a small fee, proved to be a master stroke. He moved to the south-west in August 1963.

The on-the-ball skills and visionary passing of Curtis, who had played fairly regularly in the First Division with Ipswich, was another important piece in what was the promotion jigsaw.

He formed a memorable partnership with ace goalscorer Alan Banks, the duo proving to be the thorn in many an opposition's defence, with Curtis the provider, Banks the scorer.

Dermot Curtis: The first City player to be capped at full international level.

Curtis scored 23 goals in 91 league outings for City, and was rather surprisingly allowed to join Torquay United on a free transfer in August 1966.

He spent just the one season at Plainmoor with limited success, before making a popular return to Exeter City in June 1967.

Curtis never really settled at Torquay, but was more than welcomed back at St James' Park, where many felt he shouldn't have been allowed to leave in the first place.

Curtis, then approaching 35 years old, was still a more than useful acquisition, although he did play many of his matches in a deeper role than City supporters had been used to seeing him in during his first spell with the club.

A further ten goals in 66 league matches

followed, before Curtis was finally released on a free transfer at the end of the 1968–69 season.

Curtis continued to play locally however, including spells with Bideford and Elmore, and often lining up with the Exeter City Ex-Professionals XI in charity matches.

The name of Dermot Curtis will forever remain in the club record books as being the first to gain a full international cap whilst an Exeter City player, and it was to be many years before another Grecians' player gained similar recognition.

Exeter City 1963–64: The club's first-ever promotion-winning team
Back row: Jack Edwards (Manager), Keith Harvey, Cecil Smyth, Alan Barnett, Dave Hancock, Les MacDonald, Des Anderson.
Front row: Dermot Curtis, Arnold Mitchell, Adrian Thorne, Graham Rees, Derek Grace, Alan Banks.

Whatever happened to those days when players were transferred from club to club for sensible fees? Now if you are an aspiring Premiership player, the bidding starts at several million pounds and rises to astronomical levels.

Gone are the days when Exeter City made their supporters sit up with disbelief when they parted with £8,000 for Alan Banks in 1963!

It did prove to be a superb investment, but £8,000 was a lot of money for the Grecians, and shattered their transfer fee record at the time.

Inflation, progress, call it what you will, but the cost of buying players has risen sharply since then. There are relatively few 'bargains' now. There are no such things as free transfers as players want signing on fees, relocation expenses etc.

Whatever happened to those simple things in life? Whatever happened to the half-time scoreboards that used to be a feature at every Football League ground?

You stood on the terraces at St James' Park during the half-time interval, clutching match programme in hand, and looking at the list of other games being played that day.

Out ran a couple of lads to affix the half-time scores against the appropriate letters on the board, at both the Big Bank and St James' Road ends of the ground.

Letter 'A' – Accrington Stanley 2 Darlington 0; Letter 'B' – Halifax Town 0 Newport County 1. And so it went on.

Now of course, the scoreboards have vanished. instead we have the scores announced over the public address system. The suspense of checking the scores against the list that appeared in the programme has gone.

Whatever happened to those fourpenny Exeter City programmes that we eagerly snapped up at every match? Now it is £2.80 per copy. Frightening really when you consider in the early 1960s you could assemble a complete season's home collection of City programmes for a similar amount!

The one consolation, however, is that the printing and production techniques of the humble football programme, along with the content, has improved beyond recognition, thus justifying the higher price.

Whatever happened to those balmy summer breaks between football seasons? No football, only cricket to watch. No football on the television either.

Now if you are a telly football addict, the season never ends. It is possible to watch the game being played all the year round. Internationals, friendlies, played in some far-flung corner of the world.

Clubs jet off around the globe at the drop of a hat (or should it be a cheque?) to fulfil games, that is, unless you are Exeter City, then the furthest you possibly go is into deepest Cornwall.

Whatever happened to that strong smell of liniment oil that players always used to rub into their legs? Anyone who attended a midweek Exeter City match in the 1950s and 60s would be familiar with the smell. It always seemed to be stronger for evening matches under the floodlights!

Whatever happened to the characters in the game? There seemed to be a whole lot more that visited St James' Park in years gone by than there are now.

Goalkeepers in particular were seen chatting to City fans behind their goal. Plenty of good natured banter. Keepers such as John Burridge of Workington and Charlie Wright of Grimsby Town in particular always had something to say to the Exeter supporters.

Now if they are seen talking to the crowd, they would more than likely be accused of inciting the home support, yet at one time it was all friendly chatter, with the players and City fans trading comments.

There are so many aspects of the game long disappeared at Exeter City and St James' Park. Whether it is a good or bad thing is a moot point and for those who never experienced these days, they cannot obviously relate to just how different things really were and how much more friendly it all was, even though it was just as competitive on the field.

Within days of winning an historic first-ever promotion, Exeter City were announcing plans for life in the Third Division for season 1964–65. This included the formation of an Exeter City Supporters' Club.

Unfortunately along with the higher grade of football, came higher admission prices. However, there was also news of a new contract for manager Jack Edwards.

The board of directors decided that there would be an all-round increase in admission prices. Ground season tickets would go up from £7 to £8 and on the day adult prices would be increased by sixpence to four shillings. Junior prices would be two shillings, and increase of threepence.

By implementing the increases, City chairman, Reg Rose, said that the whilst the club was not crying poverty, it was trying to bring better football and conditions to those who support Exeter City.

'Everyone knows that Third Division football will be harder', he explained. 'New players will have to be bought in the close season. And a new set of floodlights are needed which will cost between £8,000 and £10,000.'

The board had also offered manager Jack Edwards a new contract which he readily accepted and signed immediately. Rose added that the board appreciated that Mr Edwards had been very fair in his approach to them, so they were quite willing to agree his terms.

An overwhelming majority show of hands sparked the formation of a new Exeter City Supporters' Club, when more than 400 City fans packed the ballroom of the Rougemont Hotel, Exeter at a special meeting called jointly by the Exeter City board of directors and the Grecians' Association.

'We cannot stay as we are', said Rose. 'We are not self-supporting on the funds coming in at the moment. In the absence of a better alternative to make money we have decided to form a new club, either to work with the Grecians' Association or to work independently of them.'

Vice-chairman George Gillin explained: 'Money is needed for players and to cover the popular end of St James' Park, as well as to provide social amenities.'

Concessions for old age pensioners and a guaranteed entry to all-ticket matches were two of the things on the agenda of the first meeting held by the newly formed Supporters' Club.

The plan was that membership of the new Supporters' Club would guarantee a ticket for all future all-ticket matches.

The Supporters' Club would also be represented at one City board meeting per month, and they had also planned more refreshment stands to be at St James' Park for home games, something that had been lacking in previous seasons.

It was announced that promotion to the Third Division had cost Exeter City around £11,000, the amount that the balance sheet showed as the club's loss for 1963–64.

To get out of the Third Division the club had to spend £13,000 on signing players, but this was said to be cancelled out with an increase of 100 per cent on the revenue side.

Whilst travelling and hotel expenses dropped by about £300 on the season before to £4,595, wages, salaries and bonuses rose by almost £3,000 to £30,972.

The final profit and loss account for the year showed that Exeter City Football Club's total deficiency was £45,052, compared with £42,893 the previous year.

The floodlights went out at St James' Park in October 1964 when Exeter City were informed by the Football League that the lights were simply not good enough, following reports by match officials and visiting teams.

The lights, it has to be said, had been criticised many times before that, as far back as the late 1950s when City keeper George Hunter said on occasions he couldn't see the flight of the ball when the opposition took a corner kick!

However, this time City had to conform to the League's wishes and a new set of lights was duly ordered. Exeter appealed to the League to be allowed to use the existing lights until the new set arrived, as there were two midweek fixtures scheduled before that would happen.

The League agreed, provided City would specially clean and overhaul the existing set for their next fixture against Brentford. A report of the state of the lights would then be submitted to the League by the match referee.

The game was played on 14th October 1964. But ironically there was a power failure as Brentford ran out on to the St James' Park pitch!

A cable fault had plunged half the ground into darkness. A frantic call was made to the South Western Electricity Board, who arrived at the ground and had the lights working again 25 minutes after the scheduled kick-off time.

Onto the field once more came the players and the match officials. And then? The lights went out again!

The referee decided to wait another 20 minutes to see if the problem could be finally resolved, or else he would have no other option than to postpone the game. Happily they did work and the match finally got underway in front of an attendance of a very patient and good humoured 7,500.

Another problem that arose when the crowd were stood or sat in total darkness waiting for the kick off, was that the tannoy system was also out of action.

Someone, in their wisdom, decided to walk around the perimeter of the pitch with a message chalked on a board with an update of the situation. But of course no one could read it unless they were in the front row of the terraces or stands!

The match referee was obviously not very impressed, nor were the Football League and a few

EXETER CITY
FOOTBALL CLUB

WEDNESDAY, 2nd DECEMBER, 1964
Friendly
EXETER CITY
VERSUS
ARSENAL
Kick-off 7.15 p.m.

Official Programme 6

days after the Brentford fixture, which had ended 0-0, Exeter City received a letter that stated that the club were not to use the lights again until a new set had arrived and been installed.

It was to be a few weeks before there was a friendly match to mark the official switch on of the new lights, when First Division Arsenal visited the Park on 2nd December 1964.

The game drew an attendance of 11,507, which included former Grecian and Gunners legend, Cliff Bastin, as the visitors paraded seven internationals in their team.

Arsenal won 4-1, with Frank McLintock scoring a hat-trick and George Armstrong adding their other goal. Adrian Thorne replied for the Grecians.

The new lighting system was described as being 'brighter than those at Wembley Stadium' – which seemed a bit of an over-the-top description. But at least they worked!

The teams that night were:

Exeter City: Shearing, Smyth, McDonald, Grace, Mitchell, Rutley, Welsh, Curtis, Carter, Ley, Thorne.

Arsenal: Burns, Howe, McCullough, McLintock, Neil (Ure), Court, Skirton, Sammels, Baker, Eastham, Armstrong.

Retired Metropolitan Police officer, Victor Meek, who lived at number 20, Old Tiverton Road, attempted to get an injunction to stop Exeter City Football Club from building their proposed £7,000 supporters' clubhouse on a site adjoining his land. Although work had started in November 1964, the foundations having been dug and some concrete laid, the project had come to halt.

Meek was to contact his solicitor to get the work stopped altogether because there was a covenant between himself, as the owner of number 20, and the Football Club, as owners of number 18, that they should not erect a building of that kind.

The covenant made in 1883 forbid any kind of building on that property except a dwelling house at the front or offices of a dwelling house at the rear. Meek said he was a keen supporter of Exeter City, as was his son, but that was not the point.

He wanted to hold the Football Club to that covenant, as it was not too long ago that planning permission had been refused to the club to have a bowling alley erected on the same land.

The main grounds for refusal was of possible noise, that it was primarily a residential area and of the danger of cars coming out on a blind corner.

Meek realised that the City Council had agreed planning permission for the building of the clubhouse, but failed to see that the objections had changed.

He contacted the Council, who were aware that the covenant existed, but they had told him that this did not affect the planning permission and was merely a matter between the parties involved.

Exeter City F.C. chairman, Reg Rose, was notified by letter by Meek that he suggested work on the clubhouse site should stop immediately pending clarification of the situation. It was to be a case of a written agreement for cessation of work or an injunction.

Meek added that the legal situation was such that if he allowed the building to be erected it would be too late to obtain an injunction to prevent it. He therefore had to act to stop the building or he would be burdened with a lawsuit to have it pulled down again.

Rose added that he knew nothing of restrictive convenants on the land. It had been cleared once before and the report had stated that it was in order to develop the site. However, he agreed he would look into the matter.

The second Supporters' Club building – 'The Centre Spot' – was behind the Big Bank and was demolished prior to the building of the new covered terracing. The first Supporters' Club premises were situated at the top of the Big Bank.

A few days later the board of directors decided that they would not contest the 1883 covenant. Instead they would move the building to a site in an unrestricted area on the same plot.

Rose said that he would not allow anyone to make a profit out of Exeter City Football Club, and therefore the club would not contest Meek and his claims about the covenant.

The board stated that the clubhouse would now be built on the practice pitch at the rear of the Big Bank terrace at St James' Park, which they understood, after checking via their solicitors, was free from any restrictions.

It was unfortunate that the clubhouse had to be moved as it would cost the club several hundreds of pounds to do so, having already spent money on the foundations etc.

A further problem would be that the club would now have to reapply for planning permission which would undoubtedly cause more delay and expense.

The Minister of Housing and Local Government was then asked to make a decision on the planning application by the Exeter City Council.

A Council spokesman said that this had been due to the large number of objections to the clubhouse plans by local residents in the area.

Amazingly City had to wait until January 1966 for a final decision to be made, as planning permission was indeed refused. They were told there had been 43 objections to the plan.

Flavius Maximus and his Roman colleagues liked both Exeter and Carlisle, although it is doubtful whether they were attracted to the respective places by the prospect of watching quality football.

Carlisle was a strategic point near to Hadrian's Wall, while Exeter was a West Country stronghold. This was long before the building of both Brunton Park and St James' Park. Presumably chariot racing was of more interest at the time.

There may be a few hundred miles between the two places, but Jimmy Blain liked both, although Exeter

Eric Welsh.

more than Carlisle. And what's more Eric Welsh had good times in both Exeter and Carlisle, winning full international honours whilst playing for the latter's football team.

Even today, the deal that involves a straight exchange of two players between the clubs seems an unusual one. It was also reported that the deal had been worth £20,000 to City, although one would assume that was based on the value of the players, not so much a cash transaction.

Yet, the moves for both players, and both clubs, proved to be beneficial, as Blain and Welsh enjoyed some of the best football of their careers.

Welsh had been brought across the Irish Sea by the Grecians in September 1959, where he had been playing for Distillery.

He quickly made an impression in the City reserve team and soon made his first-team debut against Crystal Palace in April 1960, a game that City drew 2-2. The winger went on to feature in 105 league matches for Exeter, netting 19 goals.

It was in October 1965 that the long-distance player exchange took place, with Welsh heading off to Carlisle and Blain arriving at St James' Park.

Welsh went on to play for Torquay United and Hartlepool United after leaving Brunton Park in June 1969, but not before he had won four full international caps for Northern Ireland, as well as appearing for their under-23 side.

Blain came to Exeter, having commenced his career with Everton, where he had worked his way through the junior sides to become a full professional in May 1959.

He had to wait until a move to neighbours Southport before he got his first taste of league action, where he scored 40 goals in 127 matches.

A short stay at Rotherham United was then followed by signing for Carlisle in April 1964, playing mainly as a winger, something he was to do when he first came to City.

Blain though, proved to be one of the most versatile players ever to have worn the Exeter shirt, appearing in most positions in the team and eventually settling down as a left-back.

Blain proved to be the best signing made by the then-City boss Ellis Stuttard, but the player was unable to prevent the Grecians sliding back into the Fourth Division by the end of his first season with the club.

The first chance City fans had of seeing Blain was against Bristol Rovers at the Park on 27th November 1965, although he had actually made his Exeter debut the week before in a 2-1 win at Brentford.

It wasn't until Frank Broome took over as manager of the Grecians for the second time in May 1967 that Blain was first tried as a defender, with a good deal of success.

The versatility of Blain was welcome in a wafer-thin squad of players, finances being almost non-existent at the Park.

Blain still got the occasional chance to play in attack, notably the night the City team took apart a Swansea Town side, winning 6-0, with Blain netting twice in what was a memorable performance.

After appearing in 320 league matches for the Grecians, netting 14 goals, Blain's career at St James' Park finally came to an end as he was given a free transfer at the conclusion of the 1973–74 season.

'There's only one Tofik Bakhramov!' He was of course the Russian linesman who became the centre of attention in 1966.

It was the World Cup Final at Wembley. West Germany had taken England into a period of extra-time, with the scores level at 2-2 after 90 minutes.

Then Geoff Hurst let fly with a thunderbolt of a shot that cannoned off the underside of the crossbar. Did it go over the line?

The England fans waited with baited breath. Tofik, though, was in no doubt that ball had done so and signalled a goal.

England had gone 3-2 up. The rest is history, as another Hurst goal, to complete his hat-trick, gave England a famous 4-2 win and the country's first and only World Cup win.

Whilst the vast majority of the nation celebrated by dancing in the streets, back in Exeter, Grecians' fans were still trying to get over the fact that the team had been relegated at the end of the previous season.

After waiting 60 years to achieve promotion in the first place – reaching Division Three in 1963–64 – the club's stay at this higher level lasted just two seasons before they were back in the basement league.

It had been a constant struggle during the two seasons, the first of which saw City end the campaign in 17th place.

But relegation could not be avoided in 1965–66, as they had slumped to 22nd place, and therefore fell through the trap door to the Fourth Division along with Southend United, Brentford and York City.

Not only had the Grecians endured a poor season of league football, but the cup competitions didn't bring any joy either.

City were on the end of a giant killing in the F.A. Cup at St James' Park as Southern League Bedford Town won 2-1 in the first round.

And the team fared little better in the Football League Cup first round, going down 2-1 to Colchester United, having made the long trip to Essex.

City managed just 12 league wins all season, three of which came in consecutive games against Brentford, Bristol Rovers and Gillingham, and all in the space of three weeks.

It proved to be a false dawn though, for the Grecians then went on a horrible run of games that lasted 14 matches, before they 'tasted' success once more – against Brentford.

In what was the biggest win of Exeter's season, they crushed relegation rivals Brentford 5-0, with goals from Alan Banks (2), George McLean (2) and Jack Kennedy.

Despite playing in what was a poor team, Banks went on to become the season's top scorer with 17 goals from 38 league matches.

Not surprisingly the manager, Ellis Stuttard, paid the penalty, as he was formally released from his contract in June 1966.

For the last three months of the season it was widely known that Stuttard was manager in name only, as trainer Jock Basford – his eventual successor – was entrusted with trying to guide Exeter out of trouble.

Basford was a keen advocate of giving young players a chance and he used his contacts, mainly at previous club Charlton Athletic, to bring in the likes of Ray Harford, Ray Keeley and Ray Elliott. Another newcomer was inside-forward John Evans.

With the team relegated, City fans could only hope that the success of England on the worldwide stage would help increase interest in the game generally, including Exeter.

Sadly this was not the case however. For despite being relegated the average crowd at St James' Park in 1965–66 was 5,590. By the end of the next season's Fourth Division campaign, the gate had dropped to 3,990.

The enthusiasm that England and their supporters had shown didn't rub off on Exeter City as the Grecians finished 14th.

On Guy Fawkes Day 1966, a story broke in the local press that Exeter City had approached a former Plymouth Argyle chairman with a view to him either joining the board of directors at St James' Park, or taking over the entire club.

City chairman Reg Rose confirmed that the Grecians had approached former Argyle chairman Ron Blindell, which would involve the investment of substantial money in the club.

Rose said that his colleagues on the board were aware that he wished to retire from the chair and directorship of Exeter City as soon as possible due to health reasons.

With full agreement of the board, Blindell was approached and the deadline for a decision was agreed when any or all of the proposition would be submitted to a full board meeting.

But three days later millionaire Blindell said he would not be joining Exeter City after negotiations had broken down.

'The deal is off', he said. 'They have had second thoughts and there is no deal, At 5.30 p.m. last evening everything had been agreed and laid down after five hours of talks, but they had a change of mind and so there is no deal. It would have been a challenge for me.'

With the deal having fallen through and Rose anxious to relinquish his position, it was agreed that he, along with director Fred Dart, would become joint chairmen of the club, thus lessening the workload of the City chairman.

On leaving the ground it was reported that Blindell said that his suggestion would have meant the club 'would have been liquid' and the proposed agreement would have made him chairman.

He added that he did not know what went wrong, and he would have enjoyed coming back into football, and the arrangements were such that he knew it would have been a success.

He was positive that with the co-operation of the board and with potential he felt there in the players, the club could have been put on its feet. He was prepared to invest a considerable sum in the club.

A statement to set the record straight was then issued on 14th November 1966 by the three directors of Exeter City Football Club concerning the negotiations that had taken place with Blindell.

The offer involved Blindell having a controlling interest by the directors selling to him some of their shares. Eventually the board agreed to accept the offer.

The statement read: 'On Monday Mr Blindell turned up with a completely new offer. He would take over St James' Park for £20,000. The present directors have got the ground covered for £20,000, so that it does not go to one man and had to agree to leave their £20,000 free of charge for five years.

'Mr Blindell agreed we could consider this for the next two or three days in case we changed our minds, and then he would come back and sign up all the arrangements.

'But when we had tentatively agreed to his proposals, he suddenly had a change of mind and immediately decided he wanted it all signed and sealed that evening before he left the ground.

'In view of this we reconsidered and some of present directors decided to make money available to the club, and on the advice of the club's solicitors and accountant, who were present at the meeting, it was rejected unanimously by the chairman and four directors.

'It was agreed that only a short formal statement be issued, but as different reports have since appeared and the three directors named as rejecting this offer, they thought they would put the facts before the footballing public.'

However a few days later, Blindell decided to put his side of the saga and stated that there was never any question of him having a controlling interest in the club:

'I was prepared to take over the chairmanship of the club putting £20,000 either on a mortgage or the purchase of the ground', he explained.

'The club had to pay neither interest nor rent if they were making a loss and the directors loans remained as they were, interest free for a minimum of five years.'

Blindell had also suggested that the all directors' shares should be pooled, so that everyone, including himself had an equal number:

'During all the discussions there was a desire that out of the money I put into the club, Messrs Cowley, Kerslake and Rodgers, wanted repayment of their loan', he added.

Blindell would not agree to this except to say that a repayment would be made within a specific

The Exeter City playing squad of 1966–67 who wore the unfamiliar all-white kit
Back row: Colin Buckingham, Roger Smith, Ray Keeley,
Ben Embery, John Evans, Bobby Nash, Peter Godfrey, Ray Elliott.
Middle row: Ken Thompson, Alan Goad, Ken Jones, Mike Balson, John Smout,
Richard McNeil, Ernie Wilkinson, Ray Harford.
Front row: Keith Harvey, Jack Kennedy, Bruce Stuckey, Jimmy Blain, Jock Basford (Manager),
Cecil Smyth, George Ley, George McLean, Bert Edwards.

number of years, because the cub needed the money he was prepared to invest.

Blindell said that his offer was £20,000 to purchase the ground, with a rent of £2,000 yearly, only payable if the club made a profit and that the lease to the club was to be perpetuated, which was a resolution of an annual meeting three years ago.

Alternatively his suggestion was a mortgage of £20,000 on which the rate of interest was 10 per cent, but again only payable if the club made a profit. Blindell added that the offer was rejected by three votes to two.

'I had been invited supposedly by a unanimous decision of the Exeter City board to become chairman and because in all probability, the three directors could not draw some money out of the club, they had a change of mind', he said.

In April 1967, in what was by now a familiar cost-cutting move, it was announced that there would be extensive cutbacks on the playing side of the club, as Exeter City were to withdraw their teams from the Western League and the Exeter and District League in order to save on costs.

This would leave just the first team, with a much smaller squad of professionals, to play in the Fourth Division of the Football League during the 1967–68 season.

The cuts were first announced the previous January, but a month later it was decided to keep a Western League side, but withdraw one of the Colts' sides from the Exeter and District League, as well as making a reduction in the full-time playing staff.

But by April 1967 the directors had changed their minds once again and the move towards the original cutbacks were confirmed by chairman Les Kerslake.

'This is not a negative step, but positive action to concentrate all the efforts of the club into a successful league side, which is the lifeblood of Exeter City', he said.

'The policy has already been adopted successfully by some Football League clubs, notably Portsmouth, and many more clubs are now following suit.

'This is a direct result of the lifting of the players' maximum wage restriction and the introduction of Selective Employment Tax.'

It was hoped that there would still be football on Saturdays for supporters to watch when the City were playing away from St James' Park though.

'Negotiations have already been started and there is a possibility that St Luke's College will play their Western League matches at St James' Park next season for the benefit of the 200 or so people who normally watch the reserve team in action,' explained Kerslake.

'Naturally there will be some snags to overcome, but the board are confident that with the financial economies that will be made, more money will be available for strengthening in the future which will be for the benefit of all supporters of the club.'

The move was likely to save City several thousands of pounds and was a way to curb the heavy expense sheet, but at the same time it was something of a gamble.

The directors had taken into account the few supporters who visited St James' Park for Western League fixtures and they also considered every item of expense, before arriving at the decision to dispense with the teams.

The fall in gate receipts is one of the biggest problems that the club faced. In 1966–67 for instance, they had dropped to an all-time low.

Between three and four thousand for a Fourth Division match was not regarded as enough by a long way and something had to be done to arrest the financial slide.

It was no good leaving matters indefinitely and the directors decided on a course of action that was not going to please everyone, but would certainly help keep football alive at the Park.

Supporters were hoping that the board of directors' confidence of more money being available to strengthen the team as a result of the cuts, would be justified.

Kerslake added: 'The policy decision that the board made was for next season and was not necessarily an everlasting solution. It would save the club several thousands of pounds a year.'

Unfortunately it was reported that City manager Jock Basford was not happy with the fact that there would be a smaller playing staff and only one team.

Within days Basford resigned and it was later announced that Frank Broome would be returning from Australia, where he had been coaching, to take over as manager for his second spell at the club.

One of the most popular men ever to have managed Exeter City Football Club was undoubtedly John Newman. The long-serving boss came very close to building a promotion-winning team and unfortunately left the club midway through the every season his hard work came to fruition.

A native of Hereford, Newman's football career started with his local side, and also winning county representative honours. The wing-half's big break came when he signed amateur forms with Birmingham City in July 1959 and as a professional two years later.

He enjoyed his first success, winning a Second Division Championship medal and then appearing in the 1956 F.A. Cup Final, but by November 1957, he had made the short move to join Leicester City.

From Filbert Street, Newman linked up with Plymouth Argyle in January 1960, where he appeared in nearly 300 league matches for the Pilgrims.

He was signed by Exeter City in November 1967, in a double deal that also saw the return of Alan Banks to St James' Park for a second spell with the Grecians.

After Frank Broome was relieved of his managerial duties by the Exeter City board of directors in February 1969, Newman was appointed in a caretaker role, but by April that year, he was officially City's player-manager.

It was to be the start of a long managerial association with the Grecians, although it might have been oh so different if matters had not been resolved in October 1971.

Rumours had been circulating that Newman was to hand in his letter of resignation to the directors, frustrated with the way things were going at St James' Park.

And on Monday 18th October 1971, the rumours were confirmed, as it was announced that Newman's letter would be discussed at a meeting of the directors on the following evening.

Newman had guided the Grecians to their best season for several years in 1970–71, but after the 3-1 home defeat against Southport a few days earlier, he left the ground immediately after the final whistle without making any comment or seeing his players.

The following day, 19th October, and before the meeting of the board, chairman Fred Dart and director Jack Cowley visited Newman at his home.

Just hours before the meeting of the board, the City directors wrote a letter to Newman urging him to reconsider and stay. The players also wrote to the directors stressing their vote of confidence in the manager.

Messrs Dart and Cowley chatted with Newman to try to get him to change his mind over resigning and as a result the City boss said he would give it some thought.

Later that day Newman met with the directors for a heart-to-heart talk and several things were straightened out. As a result, he withdrew his letter of resignation.

The City directors and players were delighted with his change of mind, for none of them wanted him to leave in the first place.

City full-back Campbell Crawford summed up the feelings of the players by saying: 'This is great news. All of the lads have considerable confidence in John Newman who treated players as players, and was fair to everyone.'

Newman went on to stay until November 1976, when the opportunity to take over as manager of Grimsby Town was simply too appealing to turn down.

The team that he built, with a few additions, then won promotion to the Third Division five months later, but this time under the guidance of another former Argyle defender, whom Newman had brought to the club, namely Bobby Saxton.

Newman went on to join Derby County in July 1979 as their assistant manager, and then manager between January and November 1982.

Returning to his home town, he was appointed manager of Hereford United in November 1983, a post he held until September 1987.

From there he became assistant manager of Notts County in July 1988, then similarly with York City, before moving on to become coach and chief scout of Mansfield Town in 1991.

It was cash bonanza time for Exeter City when they were paired with European Cup holders Manchester United at St James' Park in the third round of the F.A. Cup in January 1968.

Bobby Charlton, Denis Law, George Best, Nobby Stiles and Alex Stepney were the household names expected to be in the United side, and not surprisingly the tie was made all ticket, such was the interest in the game.

Stiles was the only member of the United side who played for them when visiting St James' Park for a Football League Cup tie back in 1960.

'We were lucky not to lose', recalled Stiles. 'Because Exeter were leading, and hit the bar, before we escaped with a 1-1 draw. It was a bit of an ordeal. The pitch was alright, but it seemed small and the crowd was so close they seemed to taking part in the game.'

Admission charges for the F.A. Cup tie were increased, so that stand tickets cost 12s 6d instead of the more normal 8s, and ground admission was increased from 5s to 6s, with juveniles paying 3s.

Chairman Les Kerslake said that based on the club's normal charges, Exeter's share of the gate receipts would be roughly £1,200. The board felt that the regular 4,000 supporters would not begrudge the club the opportunity of increasing the admission charges from the 'wandering thousands'.

Some 12,000 vouchers were made available for issue at the Fourth Division fixture at the Park against Southend United, which would guarantee a ticket to those who picked one up at the turnstiles.

Needless to say the attendance for the visit of Southend was boosted to 12,714! Some of those who went to the game, simply paid their admission, picked up a voucher and then went home!

In the days leading up to the game, with all the tickets for St James' Park having been snapped up, householders in St James' Road were turning down offers of more than £100 each to rent their upstairs windows for a guaranteed view of the match.

More than 4,000 Manchester United fans swarmed into Exeter on the morning of the match, many of whom did not have tickets.

Ticket touts were in evidence selling ground tickets for between £1 and £2 each and stand tickets for £3.

Prior to the game City manager Frank Broome had been asked by the BBC to give names of his 16 probables, to which he replied he only had 14 players anyway!

Broome was also concerned what might happen if Bobby Charlton unleashed one of his famous rocket shots.

'If he belts the ball upfield, he is liable to crack a few windows in St James' Road', added Broome. 'If he belts it downhill, then a few greenhouses could be in danger in the allotments.'

The two teams, before a capacity crowd of 18,500 lined up as follows:

Exeter City: Peter Shearing, Cecil Smyth, Jimmy Blain, Keith Harvey (David Pleat), Brian Sharples, John Newman, John Corr, Alan Banks, Alan Pinkney, John Mitten, Mike Balson.

Manchester United: Alex Stepney, Tony Dunne, Francis Burns, John Fitzpatrick, Steve James, Nobby Stiles, George Best, Brian Kidd, Bobby Charlton, Denis Law, Carlo Sertori.

City proceeded to give the European champions a real fight and a fright. City were actually in front after 15 minutes, and after an hour it looked as if they would earn a lucrative replay, but then two quick goals by United ended the Grecians' moment of glory.

Banks' goal for City was a textbook affair with a glancing header from Balson's free-kick. St James' Park erupted, as it did 18 minutes later when Corr ran the ball into the net, but the 'goal' was disallowed for an infringement that was not obvious.

Exeter's defence contained United's attacks with a display well above Fourth Division standards, then disaster struck in the 43rd minute. The defence was caught flat-footed and Fitzpatrick equalised from Dunne's pass.

City, however, were still in with a chance, but two United goals in the 60th and 62nd minutes were very much an anti-climax. Dunne's centre was deflected past Shearing by Newman and then Kidd hit the ball home after a shot from Law had been blocked on the line.

United had taken a long time to get to grips with the game, but once they went in front it was never going to be easy for Exeter. It proved to be a memorable occasion, even though the result was perhaps a little disappointing, but probably expected.

Exeter City 1968–69
Back row: Alan Pinkney, Campbell Crawford, Cecil Smyth, Jimmy Blain.
Middle row: John Corr, Dermot Curtis, Mike Balson, Peter Shearing, Brian Sharples,
John Kirkham, Keith Harvey, Bert Edwards (Trainer).
Front row: Keith Whatling, John Mitten, Frank Broome (Manager), John Newman, David Pleat.

Having disposed of First Division Sheffield Wednesday at St James' Park in the second round of the Football League Cup, Exeter City were paired with Tottenham Hotspur at White Hart Lane – the tie being played on 25th September 1968.

The massive interest in the game from City fans prompted the running of a special train to Paddington, which started from Newton Abbot and picked up at Teignmouth, Dawlish and Exeter St David's.

A week before the tie the City officials and players attended a civic reception at the Exeter Guildhall, arranged to acknowledge the victories in the first and second rounds over Plymouth Argyle and Sheffield Wednesday respectively.

The Mayor, Alderman J.B. Martin, congratulated the team on their victories and hoped that they would pull off another one at Spurs, or even bring them back to St James' Park for a replay.

The build up to the game dominated the local sports pages and the *Express & Echo* reported: 'Tottenham Hotspur are undoubtedly the most powerful combination that Exeter City has ever been called upon to meet. For they are likely to meet a side in which every player has gained international honours of one degree or another.

'They have a tremendous array of soccer talent, but in getting these players together the Spurs have spent around £700,000. Exeter earn that sort of money through gate receipts over a thirty-year period!

'It is the first time that the Spurs have played a Football League Cup tie at White Hart Lane and it will also be the first time that Exeter City have played on the ground.'

On the day of the game the platform at Exeter St David's station became a mass meeting place for hundreds of cheering City fans.

On arrival at Paddington the City followers made their way down into the Underground chanting the name of the club and the players.

They made sure that Londoners knew they were being invaded by a large party of Devonians, their chants echoing in the Underground tunnels.

At White Hart Lane it was estimated that well over 2,000 Exeter City fans were present, for in addition to the special train, several coaches and many cars had made the journey to the capital, with City selling 1,600 stand tickets alone.

The City team lined up as follows: Peter Shearing, Cecil Smyth, Jimmy Blain, John Kirkham, Keith Harvey, John Newman, John Corr (Dermot Curtis), Alan Banks, Peter Bullock, John Mitten, David Pleat.

The attendance was 25,798 and fans were treated to what amounted to a thrilling cup tie, and saw the Grecians twice take the lead, before eventually losing to the star-studded Spurs side, 6-3.

It took the genius of Jimmy Greaves to knock the City out of the cup as he scored a hat-trick, but it was Exeter who stole the show in the first half.

They took the lead in the 15th minute when a Newman free-kick rebounded off the Spurs defensive wall and Mitten ran in to drive a tremendous shot past Pat Jennings.

The lead lasted just five minutes when Alan Mullery put Greaves through to equalise, but City came swarming back and unbelievably went in front again, as Jennings could only parry a hard drive from Pleat and Banks dived headlong to force the ball into the net.

Again Spurs hit back, this time within two minutes when Terry Venables scored with a 20-yard shot into the City net via the post.

In the 43rd minute Spurs went into the lead for the first time as Greaves nudged the ball home after Shearing had initially saved a header from Alan Gilzean.

In the second half City began to be forced back and Jimmy Pearce made it 4-2 in the 67th minute from eight yards. The same player scored again eight minutes later, with another 25-yard effort.

City kept plugging away and got a third goal when

FOOTBALL LEAGUE CUP, 3rd ROUND

TOTTENHAM HOTSPUR

v.

EXETER CITY

Official Programme

Price SIXPENCE

SEASON 1968-69   Wednesday, 25th Sept., 1968
Vol. 61   No. 11   KICK-OFF 7.30 p.m.

The match programme from City's trip to Tottenham Hotspur in September 1968.

Pleat's cross reached Banks who headed past Jennings.

It was not until the last minute that Spurs got their sixth goal and Greaves completed his hat-trick.

City were far from being disgraced and made such an impression that they were applauded off the field by the Spurs fans at the final whistle. The team also drew praise form Spurs boss Bill Nicholson.

The Grecians had therefore played five matches in the Football League Cup that season and had been watched by 75,000 spectators. This prompted Chairman Les Kerslake to say that the club were much more stable financially than they had been 12 to 18 months previous.

Alan Banks was a footballing hero – and he certainly was on this particular day if you were an Exeter City fan, but definitely not if you were a follower of Colchester United.

It was 1968, the second round of the F.A. Cup, and the occasion when the Grecians travelled to Essex for what proved to be a monumental victory.

The cup run had started in relatively low-key fashion as far as Exeter were concerned as they had been paired with Newport County in round one.

The Grecians really struggled against the Welshmen and having been held to a goalless draw at St James' Park, many felt that the team had lost their chance to progress to the next stage.

With a string of injury problems to contend with, manager Frank Broome had to call upon the services of St Luke's College student Alan Pinkney for the replay, replacing the absent Banks.

City though, confounded their critics by winning the rematch 3-1. They had considerable help in doing so as Newport managed to gift Exeter two own goals, with defender Mike Balson being the other Grecians' scorer.

The reward, if one could call it that, was a lengthy cross-country trip to Colchester United. Despite the awkward journey there were plenty of City fans at Layer Road for the tie on 7th December 1968.

They were in good voice as they stood on the tiny Layer Road terrace, which at the time was still of wooden construction, where the Exeter supporters gathered.

Peter Shearing, Cecil Smyth, Jimmy Blain, John Kirkham, Keith Harvey, John Newman, John Corr, Alan Banks, Mike Balson, John Mitten and former Tottenham Hotspur and Luton Town boss David Pleat made up the City team that day.

Banks, scorer of so many goals during his career at the Park, was declared fit enough to return to the side.

And he was to net arguably one of his most important ever, a strike that proved to be the only one of the afternoon.

The vast majority of the 6,180 crowd were stunned as City took a tenth-minute lead and then had to hang on for dear life to their slender advantage for the rest of the tie.

The goal had been set up by a surging run from Blain, who raced half the length of the field before

Alan Banks.

slipping the ball to Banks, who dashed through the home defence to score with a precision shot.

Very little was seen of the City attack after that as the team had to defend corners and repel the Colchester strike force.

City were almost beaten by the gods when just six minutes from time the floodlights went out. With fears of abandonment in the minds of City followers, the referee, after consulting with his linesmen and the Colchester manager, decided to finish the match in the gathering gloom, without the aid of lights.

It proved to be a crucial decision, as City clung on to their 1-0 lead before being rewarded for their Herculean efforts by being paired with the mighty Manchester United in the third round.

Needless to say the publicity that the tie brought to the Grecians, let alone the cash bonus, was enormous in the days leading up to the tie.

City were not overawed and eventually went down 3-1 to United, but not before a certain Mr Banks had found the back of the European Cup holders' net.

The expectant crowd waited outside the *Express & Echo* offices. The gathering met once a week, on a Saturday night shortly after 6 p.m. They perhaps never saw one another apart from that one fleeting get-together.

These were the days of the Saturday football final, printed by the *Express & Echo,* and featuring the match report from Exeter City's game that afternoon.

The paper was especially eagerly awaited whenever City had been playing away, as a blow-by-blow match report was phoned through the paper's Sidwell Street offices in Exeter throughout the game, whilst being faithfully recorded by a copy typist.

Unfortunately the days of football editions of newspapers have rapidly disappeared, overtaken by the likes of the radio and most of all by the internet, where instant information is available instead of having to wait for the printed version.

In the 1960s match reports were phoned through by the then Exeter City reporter, Tony Phillips. Not only did the paper provide an in-depth match report, but there was always at least one page of City gossip on one of the inner pages as well.

There may not have been a dearth of senior clubs in the area, but there were numerous reports and stories printed from the local leagues, such as the Exeter and District League.

So along with Exeter City, you could read about Devon Valley Mill, Ottery St Mary or Barnstaple Town. The Grecians' 'A' team match report from their game in the local league that afternoon was also there to be read, although usually only from the first half.

It was pretty well impossible to send in details of the second period of the match in time before the paper was printed, although in the 'stop press' there was always a list of latest scores and sometimes scorers to give as up to date information as possible.

There are many tales of local correspondents having to cycle to the nearest phone box at half-time to ensure that their report was used, desperately hoping that no one else was using the box on a long call. No such things as mobile phones or laptop computers in those days.

The trouble was by the time they got back to the ground, the second half had usually started. This perhaps wasn't too much of a problem, except that when the reporter filed the final score to the Sidwell Street offices, it was wrong as he had missed a goal being scored during the time he was still cycling back to the ground!

Thankfully, Tony Phillips didn't have that problem, having the luxury of a press box at Exeter City's away matches and with it, the use of a direct phone line.

Tony travelled by train to many of City's Fourth Division matches, usually with Grecians' supporters doing likewise.

The team had the advantage of travelling the day before to the far north and staying overnight in a hotel, so as soon as Tony arrived, he would make contact with the City manager and glean the latest news, so that he could forward this to the *Express & Echo* prior to the game itself.

If City had played especially well and obtained an unexpected result on the road, there was an buzz amongst the huddle of fans waiting outside the office in Sidwell Street, or the paper's office in Exmouth for that matter.

When the paper appeared, and then sold, a silence descended once again, as the City fans made their way home to read about the latest City triumph or defeat.

Somerton Park, Newport, was a relatively short journey to make for Exeter City supporters when the Grecians played there. Others may have been there to watch the Exeter Falcons speedway team, as that sport was also staged at the ground.

Who could forget the infamous coconut mats, which were placed by the corner flags for Newport County's football matches, the turf having been cut away and rounded off to form the corners of the speedway track!

One visit that will always stick in the memory was during the 'monsoon season'. Yes, a monsoon! There is no other way to describe what struck Newport just as they were playing Exeter City.

The pitch at Somerton Park was notorious for being soft and muddy, waterlogged or both, or so it seemed. On this particular afternoon the playing surface resembled a lake.

City travelled to Newport for a Fourth Division fixture on 1st February 1969, with the Grecians team lining up:

Peter Shearing, Cecil Smyth, Mike Balson, John Kirkham, Brian Sharples, John Newman, David Pleat, Dermot Curtis, John Rowlands, John Mitten, Keith Whatling.

Rain, hail and gale force wind throughout the first half made life extremely unpleasant for the players and the 1,427 fans huddled under shelter.

Newport, playing with the wind at their backs, had hit Exeter with two early goals in the first ten minutes, both netted by Tony Buck.

However, the fun and games started at half-time. The heavens really opened and the pitch flooded in minutes.

Newport, South Wales? ... This was more like the monsoon season in Calcutta, without the temperatures.

Referee Mr E. Wallace, of Swindon, decided to wait to see if the conditions improved before commencing the second half, and so there was an interval that stretched from the then usual ten minutes to one of 30.

The referee made a couple of pitch inspections and many felt that there was no way the game could be restarted. Even though the rain did stop, the playing surface resembled a paddy field and was a sea of mud and water.

Yet amazingly the players were ordered out of their warm dressing rooms to continue and play the second half.

This prompted the *Express & Echo* to report: 'A ridiculous decision. It should have been abandoned at half-time without doubt.'

Although the rain had ceased and the wind had dropped, the players were ankle deep in mud and the pitch simply got worse as the half progressed.

Surprisingly, in view of the conditions, Exeter did reduce the arrears as John Kirkham netted in the 57th minute. And a great comeback could have been completed had Dermot Curtis not fired his shot wide when well placed.

The *Express & Echo* added: 'The pitch would have kept 22 youngsters happy who wanted to make mud pies for there was no shortage of material! It certainly did not make the 22 footballers happy, nor one imagines the Newport County groundstaff.'

The small gathering of supporters were not overly happy either, although it could have been worse as they may have only been treated to 45 minutes of football had the referee decided that the game should be abandoned, which he really should have done.

Despite this soggy experience, many City fans will have been saddened when Newport County dropped out of the Football League many years later, for there were so many other memories of the Grecians playing at Somerton Park.

As for the ground itself, the site was later used for building houses. One hopes that the drainage has been improved!

DID YOU KNOW?

Despite the 2-1 win by Newport County over Exeter City, the 1968–69 season was not a particularly memorable one as far as the Fourth Division was concerned. The Grecians ended in 17th place, whilst Newport had to apply for re-election to the Football League along with York City, Grimsby Town and Bradford Park Avenue.

Here was a player who really enjoyed playing football. His happy go lucky attitude was just the same on and off the field. He was also a more than useful goalgetter, as Exeter City supporters knew only too well.

Frederick Binney was born in Plymouth on 12th August 1946 and was brought up in the Barbican area of the city. A natural goalscorer he first came to the notice of Torquay United and after a short spell as an amateur earned a professional contract in October 1966.

He had been spotted playing for South Western League side Launceston and Devon Wednesday League side John Conway, although he had played prior to that for Plymouth Dockyard team, C.M. Department.

He soon started to bang in the goals for United's reserve team, totalling over 60 in three seasons, and before long he was given a first-team opportunity.

Perhaps surprisingly, such outings were few and far between, and so when Exeter City manager John Newman signed Binney on loan, the player got his first real run of consecutive games in the Football League.

Binney made his debut for the Grecians who were, at the time, struggling in the Fourth Division, on 24th February 1969 against Bradford Park Avenue at St James' Park. He made an immediate impact by scoring in the 4-2 victory, along with goals from Campbell Crawford, John Kirkham and John Mitten.

He returned to Plainmoor at the end of his loan spell having scored 11 goals in just 17 league appearances. It was to be another 12 months before Binney was to join the City on a more permanent basis, after several attempts were made to persuade Torquay United to part with the player. Indeed his past scoring record at Exeter no doubt inflated the transfer fee that United wanted for their player!

Binney eventually returned to the Park in a £5,000 deal in March 1970. And although he only had time to score once before the end of the season it was not long before his obvious goalscoring potential was realised once more.

In the 1970–71 and 1971–72 seasons he scored eight and 17 goals respectively. But it was in season 1972–73 that he really hit the goal trail. Binney couldn't stop scoring, so much so that he found the back of the net in league matches on 28 occasions, the most goals an Exeter City player had scored since Rod Williams way back in 1936–37! Binney was also that season, equal top scorer in the entire Football League.

The very next season was just as productive as he scored another 25 league goals. He was of course destined to become the club's Player of the Year, hugely popular with the St James' Park supporters, as are most goalscorers.

It was no surprise that other clubs started to cast envious eyes on him, and in May 1974 he moved to Brighton and Hove Albion for a fee of £25,000, plus two players moving in the opposite direction to Exeter, namely John Templeman and Lammie Robertson.

Binney made his Brighton debut against Crystal Palace in a 1-0 home win at the Goldstone Ground, and later was a member of the side that won promotion to the Second Division in 1976–77, although he did miss much of the season through injury.

In the summer of 1977 he was playing in the United States for St Louis All Stars. A transfer back to Devon followed in October 1977 when Binney joined his home town club of Plymouth Argyle. His goalscoring boots worked overtime again with another 39 league goals in 73 appearances.

Binney ended his league career with a short spell at Hereford United, moving to the Edgar Street club in January 1980. By the time he had left at the end of the next season he decided to take up a coaching position to the Malaysia national team.

Binney was to return to St James' Park in 1985–86 as first team coach, working alongside manager Colin Appleton. When Appleton was dismissed in December 1987, Binney left football to become the Recreation Officer at Plymouth University, where he later became president and coach of their football team.

It was an afternoon of mixed emotions at St James' Park as Exeter City players and supporters celebrated the seven goals they scored, whilst their opponents, Barrow, had to face the long trip back to Cumbria and the prospect of having to apply for re-election to the Football League.

Unhappily for Barrow, a few weeks later they were voted out of the League to be replaced by Hereford United, and so their fixture at Exeter proved to be their last, and very unhappy, game in the Fourth Division.

The visit of Barrow was also the last home match of the season for the Grecians, being played on 29th April 1972. A somewhat indifferent season at that, which saw City end in 15th place.

With very little to play for, apart from pride, the game only attracted 3,050 fans through the turnstiles, but those who were there, if they were Grecians' fans, will have enjoyed the ensuing 90 minutes as City recorded their highest league win for many seasons.

The Exeter team lined up: Bob Wilson, Campbell Crawford, Jimmy Blain, Graham Parker, Jimmy Giles, Mike Balson, Tony Morrin, Alan Banks, John Wingate, Fred Binney (John Neale), Dave Gibson.

Barrow probably arrived in Devon hoping that they could get a result, despite their poor season, having held the Grecians to a goalless draw at their Holker Street ground the previous month.

But the *Express & Echo* reported: 'The seven goal salute that Exeter City gave their supporters to mark their final Fourth Division fixture of the season at St James' Park was the biggest win for more than 18 years, and it also marked Alan Banks' 100th League goal for the club.'

Although there were eight goals, the first half of the game was best forgotten as City struggled against what was a weak looking Barrow side, which reflected their position in the league table.

Amazingly though, Barrow took the lead early on through Garbutt, much against the run of play, but the whole match was to change, especially in the second half.

On the half-hour mark, City finally woke up and they equalised, though it was courtesy of an own goal by Barrow full-back Knox.

What a transformation in the second half though, as Exeter claimed an exclusive hold on the midfield and ripped Barrow to pieces.

It was one-way traffic and really a matter of how many goals Exeter would score, with their supporters encouraging them at every opportunity.

City were in full cry, and they could easily have hit double figures had they taken all their chances. As it was, six second-half goals came in the space of 31 minutes to totally demoralise Barrow.

City's second-half scorers were Binney (2), Banks, Parker, Morrin and substitute Neale. Binney took his tally for the season to 17 as he topped the Grecians' scoring chart.

The best of the goals was the third one, when Gibson played a superb ball down the right to the overlapping Crawford, who centred perfectly for Banks to head home his 100th league goal for the club, and his seventh of the season.

At the end of the game youngsters invaded the pitch to salute the City players, and in particular Banks.

The *Express & Echo* summed the afternoon up by reporting: 'There have been times this season when Exeter City have failed to crush sides, but they made it happen against Barrow.'

DID YOU KNOW?

One of the City goalscorers against Barrow in the 7-1 win was Tony Morrin. He had been signed from Barrow at the start of the season! Morrin had also played for Bury, Burnley and Stockport, and after leaving St James' Park he had another spell with Stockport, before moving on to Rochdale.

Someone once said that a week was a long time in football. This aptly described a episode in Exeter City's history during October 1973.

The week started badly off the field for the Grecians as it was announced that the club had made a trading loss of £10,352 on the previous year.

However, the news was tempered by the comments of City chairman Fred Dart, which appeared in the annual report to shareholders.

'In a year of declining support, Exeter City were one of the few clubs to actually increase their overall attendances during the season', he said.

There was also praise for manager John Newman who had done well to foster team spirit and the happy atmosphere in the dressing room.

It must have been even happier in the dressing room just 24 hours after the report was released, for City had hammered Rotherham United 4-1 at Millmoor.

Having negotiated the first round of the Football League Cup by disposing of a Welsh challenge from Swansea City – the Grecians requiring extra-time at the Park to do so – Exeter were somewhat disappointingly drawn away in round two to Rotherham.

Millmoor on a Wednesday night in October, with all due respects to Rotherham United, is not a pretty place to be, the ground being hemmed in by a scrapyard in those days.

However, City got on with it and produced a magnificent display to win through to the third round stage of the League Cup and earn a trip to First Division West Bromwich Albion.

City's triumphant team took to the field at Rotherham as follows: Bob Wilson, Campbell Crawford, Mike Balson, Graham Parker, Jimmy Giles, Keith Clapham, Tony Scott, Fred Binney, Dick Plumb, Brian Joy, John Wingate.

Unfortunately, being a midweek fixture, there were not too many City fans to witness what the *Express & Echo* report described as: 'A wonderful night of triumph.'

City made the perfect start when Binney took advantage of a horrible mix up in the Rotherham defence to put his side in front after 14 minutes.

There was no further goal action until 20 minutes from time when the Grecians stepped up a gear and Parker fired home a second goal from Scott's cross.

Four minutes later City knew they had made it through to the next round as Wingate's shot was deflected into the Rotherham net.

Although the hosts immediately pulled a goal back through Gilbert, City put the icing on the cake with a fourth goal as Joy ensured that his team mates were equally in joyful mood following a cross from Plumb.

Such was the strange quirk of the fixture list that City were back at Millmoor just three days later, but this time for a Fourth Division fixture.

And, with the team having performed so well in midweek, there was a much bigger following of City supporters at the game hoping that the Grecians could continue where they had left off.

They didn't. And those who had travelled to the game were left wondering how such a change in fortunes could occur in a matter of days between the same two teams playing one another.

Having won 4-1 in the League Cup, it was disastrous for the City as they went down 0-4 to the Millers, and worse still they not only had a player sent off, but it was the wrong player!

Jimmy Giles was the player to take an early walk after 51 minutes following a linesman attracting the attention of the referee.

The trouble was that it had been Keith Clapham who had retaliated following a foul on Giles by Rotherham player, Wigg. But he got away with it. A real case of mistaken identity.

At that time Rotherham were leading 1-0, but the City had looked more than capable of getting something out of the game.

However, with a man short, the whole complexion of the match changed, and Rotherham added three further goals from Phillips (2) and Johnson.

City supporters left Millmoor shaking their heads in disbelief at what they had seen. How could a team win 4-1, only to lose 0-4 to the same opponents less than week later? Strange game this football.

Season 1973–74 resulted in Exeter City travelling to the West Midlands twice in a few weeks to fulfil Football League Cup ties, with very differing results.

It also led to transfer speculation for ace goalscorer, Fred Binney, as he had been playing exceptionally well, especially in the tie at the Hawthorns, where the Grecians surprised everyone by defeating West Bromwich Albion 3-1.

Despite Albion being two divisions higher than City, you would not have believed it on what was a wet night in the Black Country on 31st October 1973.

In winning, City reached the last 16 of the League Cup for the very first time, and the result was described as being one of the best for a very long time.

Cheered on by a train load of supporters, City chased, harried and produced some great football to surprise the Albion as the team lined up:

Bob Wilson, Campbell Crawford, Brian Joy, Tony Morrin, Jimmy Giles, Keith Clapham, Ken Wallace, Fred Binney, Dick Plumb, Dave Gibson, John Wingate.

City took a deserved 20th minute lead when a cross from Gibson was headed on by Wingate and Plumb moved in to score with a header.

However, five minutes later Albion equalised when Lou Costello and John Wile linked up to give Willie Johnston the chance to score from close range.

The excitement continued at either end, as first Joy headed off the City goalline and then debutant Wallace hit the Albion crossbar.

All square at the start of the second half, City once again looked dangerous going forward and it was no surprise that Binney netted a brilliant goal in the 67th minute, beating two defenders, before drilling a low shot into the net.

With 17 minutes remaining it was all over for Albion when Binney chased a long through ball from Morrin and produced a superb dipping shot into the net.

It was a night to remember for all City supporters, and their reward in the next round was? ... Another trip to the West Midlands, to face Albion's neighbours Wolverhampton Wanderers at Molineux.

A lot happened in the three weeks between the success at Albion and the trip to Wolves, not least of which was the country being gripped by a power workers' and miners' strike, which meant that there was a restriction on the use of electricity.

This affected many football matches, with games being switched to earlier kick offs and in the case of City's tie at Wolves, this was moved to a Wednesday afternoon, which prevented a lot of fans from travelling, due to work commitments.

City had also received an offer for Binney, believed to have been between £35,000 and £40,000 from Swindon Town, but that was firmly rejected.

Exeter had to contend with further problems prior to the game with Wolves, due to an ever-increasing injury list that meant they forced to make several changes to the team for the fourth round tie played on 21st November 1973.

The City team was: Allan Clarke, Campbell Crawford, Jimmy Blain, Brian Joy, Jimmy Giles, Keith Clapham, Ken Wallace, John Neale, Dick Plumb, Dave Gibson, John Wingate.

With an afternoon kick off, only 7,623 were in attendance, which included a handful of fans from Exeter, and with fortune not favouring the Grecians – they fielded their only 12 fit players (including one substitute) – City crashed to a 5-1 defeat.

Without the threat of the injured Binney, very little was seen of the City attack, however, they were only trailing by one goal at half-time netted by Kenny Hibbitt.

Although Wolves made it 2-0 early in the second half with Derek Dougan scoring, the Grecians fought back and managed to reduce the deficit when Joy's fee-kick was headed in by Plumb.

After that though, the difference in class between the sides told, and Wolves went on to win the tie comfortably with further goals from John Richards (2) and Hibbitt, all being scored in the space of nine minutes.

It was a brave performance by the Grecians against the odds, and sadly they never got the opportunity to reproduce the display that had brought them victory at West Bromwich Albion.

Exeter City refused to travel to fulfil a Fourth Division fixture at Scunthorpe United on Tuesday 2nd April 1974, even though they knew they would probably face the wrath of the Football League. However, they felt they had a watertight case to justify the decision.

The Grecians were backed by the club doctor who warned that there could have been health risks to some of the players had they played at Scunthorpe. The City therefore decided to act upon his professional advice, despite being told by the League that they must fulfil the fixture.

'In my view the club is perfectly correct in refusing to put these players at risk', said the doctor. 'I have issued nine certificates for injury and illness. I have written special certificates to be forwarded to the Football League confirming that these players are not fit to play.

'Last Saturday Exeter were forced to field a side against Peterborough United in which at least two players should not have played because of illness. They suffered a physical reaction afterwards.'

City chairman Gerald Vallance added: 'There is a meeting of the directors this evening when the whole matter will be discussed. One of the reasons I took this decision was because after Saturday's match one of the players had to be taken home to bed in the state of near collapse.

'I did not feel we could ask players in that condition to travel 350 miles to play a match. I would not even expect them to work for me in that condition.'

City secretary Pat Wakeham forwarded the doctor's certificates to the Football League with a full report to follow. The League refused to comment on Exeter City's action, but it would be discussed by a League Management meeting at the end of the month.

The nine certificates were issued for Fred Binney, Keith Bowker, Keith Clapham, Jimmy Giles, Tony Morrin and Graham Parker, who were all ill and Brian Joy, Tony Scott and Ken Wallace, who were injured.

With Mike Balson unavailable because of a two-match suspension, this left City with just nine players, including two goalkeepers.

City had twice contacted the Football League in an effort to get the game called off, but they refused.

Scunthorpe United showed no sympathy whatsoever with the Grecians' plight, as a club official was reported to have said: 'I just hope we will get the points out of this, and of course, the possible matter of compensation, but it is entirely up to the Football League.'

Scunthorpe manager Ron Bradley added: 'I am simply not prepared to accept Exeter City's excuse. I feel the Football League should award the game to Scunthorpe United.'

Despite medical advice the Football League decided they knew better and were more qualified to decide whether a player was fit or not, and at their meeting on 24th April 1976, they announced that they would fine Exeter City Football Club the sum of £6,094. A truly amazing decision that brought comment from far and wide about how unjust it was.

City were fined the sum of £5,000 for failing to fulfil the fixture to be paid by 1st June 1976 and ordered to pay Scunthorpe United £1,026 for the loss of their average gate receipts.

They were also ordered to pay Scunthorpe £68 relating to costs incurred for their match arrangements. Exeter were ordered to forfeit the match with Scunthorpe being awarded the points.

City manager John Newman said it was a shattering decision and he was dazed as to what the club could do about it. Vallance said the decision was disgraceful and terrible.

'It is a terrific financial blow to the club, The League Management Committee seems to have searched for every penny they could screw out of us', he added.

Although Exeter City subsequently appealed against the decision and had may well-known figures in the game speaking publicly on their behalf, it was to no avail and City had try to find money they could ill afford, which was helped by a public appeal fund against the injustice of the fine.

'It has been a worrying period', said Vallance. 'The injustice of the whole thing is quite appalling, But we have gone as far as we can. Many of the lawyers in football advised us to take the Football League to the High Court, but taking things into consideration, we decided against it.

'When we appeared before the League Management Committee it was no form of appeal. In fact we were told almost as soon as we entered the room that we had no chance of the fine being reduced. It really was a waste of time meeting the Committee.'

The amazing aspect of all this was that the Management Committee had obviously decided they were medical experts rather than considering the evidence submitted by the club doctor! Needless to say the whole episode left a nasty taste in the mouth and has never been forgotten.

Exeter City squad 1973–74
Several of these players were declared not fit to travel by the club doctor for the Grecians' match at Scunthorpe United in Apriil 1974, but the Football League took no notice of medical advice and ordered City to fulfil the fixture.
Back row: John Neale, Keith Clapham, Brian Joy, Graham Parker.
Middle row: John Newman (Manager), Dick Plumb, Bob Wilson, Mike Balson, Allan Clarke,
Dave Gibson, John Wingate, Jack Edwards (Trainer).
Front row: Jimmy Giles, Tony Morrin, Fred Binney, Fred Dart (Chairman), Jimmy Blain, Tony Scott, Campbell Crawford.

Goalscorers always take the plaudits in any team, quite rightly as goals win matches. However, they would be the first to admit that behind every good goalscorer are players who are creators.

Into that category and one of the most gifted ball players to have worn the Exeter City shirt would come Lamond (better known as Lammie) Robertson.

A player whose skill deserved to be seen at a higher level, although it was only the case for the briefest of times when he played for Leicester City.

But he was also a player who had more than a few run ins with referees, his competitiveness and temper getting the better of him, which led to bookings or worse still a sending off.

Having said that, Lammie only missed a handful of matches during one of the Grecians' most successful seasons – 1976–77 – when the team achieved promotion from the Fourth Division for only the second time in the club's history.

In that successful City squad were the likes of Alan Beer, John Templeman, Nicky Jennings, Graham Weeks, Peter Hatch, Richard Key, Bobby Hodge, Tony Kellow, John Hore and player-manager Bobby Saxton.

Lammie was a native of Paisley and not a long goal kick from the River Clyde, but the Scotsman actually started his playing career with Burnley, the club he joined as an apprentice.

He never made a first-team appearance at Turf Moor and had to wait for his Football League debut until moving to neighbouring Bury in June 1968.

His stay with the Gigg Lane club was a short one though and eight months later he had signed for Halifax Town where he established a regular place in their side, making a total of 149 league and cup outings, scoring 20 goals.

Lammie's next move was to the south coast as he was signed by Brighton and Hove Albion in December 1972. It was from there that he moved to Exeter City in May 1974.

The transfer to the Grecians saw striker Fred Binney move to Brighton for a fee of £25,000 with Lammie and John Templeman moving to St James' Park as a player exchange, as part of the overall deal.

His City debut came in 1-0 defeat at Barnsley on the opening day of the 1974–75 season, when the City team lined up: Bob Wilson, John Rutter, Peter

Lammie Robertson.

Hatch, Tony Morrin, Jimmy Giles, Hedley Steele, John Neale, Lammie Robertson, John Templeman, Nicky Jennings.

Robertson was immensely popular with City supporters and he went on to feature in no less than 133 league and cup matches in red and white, netting 25 goals, during his stay at the club.

His form throughout the promotion season of 1976-77 and for the following campaign attracted the attention of First Division Leicester City, who paid a £15,000 fee to take him to Filbert Street in September 1977.

He then went on to play for Peterborough United and Bradford City, before ending his career in the Football League in 1980, when he linked up with non-league Northwich Victoria.

After retiring from the game he was believed to have taken over the running of a restaurant in Hebden Bridge in the Pennines. However, the *Sunday Times* newspaper, which featured the City team in a 'Where Are They Now?' article, thought he was running a night-club in Leeds.

It has to be said that probably suited his flamboyant style, which City supporters became accustomed to when he was playing for the Grecians.

Not for the first time in the club's long history, Exeter City were facing a cash crisis in November 1974. They seemed to have constantly been battling to try to balance the books over very many years and this time it was reckoned that the Grecians were losing £300 per week, and it simply could not continue, or the club would go under.

Club chairman Gerald Vallance said: 'I feel confident that we will see out the season. Whether we see out the following season is a different matter.'

The grim warning came at a time when professional football was facing a national crisis as crowds dipped alarmingly across the country, not just at St James' Park.

The Grecians needed an attendance at home games of between 4,500 to 5,000 to generate enough income to cover the running costs of the club – they eventually averaged 3,435 for the 1974–75 season.

The club were about £3,000 down on gate receipts compared with the same number of games the previous season. The club's average wage bill was £850 per week, whilst other costs put the weekly outlay up to £1,300 per week. In return the gate receipts generated £1,000 per match.

Vallance explained: 'We are losing about £300 per week at the moment. I feel we will be reducing the loss when we start receiving our share of the pools for the Football League Cup, F.A. Cup, television and football pools.

'But generally speaking we do not receive the first payment until December or January. That is a major income we are not receiving at the moment.

'The figure of £300 is true at this stage, but I belive it is a false figure if your finances are spread over a 12-month period. However, we do have a cash problem, because not enough is coming in to meet the expenses.

'The critical period for Exeter City is between now and the new year. The crisis has really come in the last six weeks basically, through the drop in gate receipts.'

Exeter City had reported a net loss of £6,120 on the last year, almost identical to the amount that refusing to play Scunthorpe United in April 1974 cost the club in fines and compensation.

Without that fine City would have only lost £26 on the season. The net loss in the previous year was £10,352 and the debit balance at 31st May 1974 was £69,985.

Vallance added: 'We can look back on the 1973–74 season as being reasonably successful since we finished in tenth position in the league and a run in the Football League Cup.'

Despite the comments about receiving money from the Football League, F.A. Cup etc., it seems that the club were still in a precarious position by the following August, for manager John Newman gave an indication as to just how bad the finances were.

'The club has had an extremely sticky time to get through the summer period', he said. 'We have jumped through a little crisis and it will depend on the season ahead whether we are able to keep the present situation going.

'I'm not pleading poverty on the club's behalf, but at the moment we are in a position where we have to look closely at every penny spent. The secretary and I had a meeting with the playing staff. We discussed everything with then. If we can pull through this period, we will be a bigger and stronger club.

'We only have a fringe policy on youth football at the club because we are unable to implement anything further owing to our present financial position.

'We have not therefore run it at the kind of level we would have liked. The youth policy is, however, very worthwhile and people have worked hard on this aspect of the club.'

Plough Lane was a ground of character. A typical Southern League ground of that time. Yet it was to host Football League matches for a few seasons following the meteoric rise of Wimbledon Football Club.

Of course, the story of Wimbledon F.C. and Milton Keynes Dons has been well documented, but the Dons fans of August 1975 could not have predicted what was to happen in years to come.

It was a strange but hugely enjoyable friendly fixture for Exeter City to have as they travelled to south-west London as part of their build-up to the new 1975–76 season.

However, there were a good number of City fans present, for the curiosity value if nothing else, for that first-ever meeting between the sides.

In the Wimbledon team was a certain Dickie Guy, whose heroic goalkeeping display in the F.A. Cup had made him a national figure on the sports pages. Guy went on to become the president of AFC Wimbledon.

There was also another well-known name in the Dons team that faced Exeter City that afternoon – Dave 'Harry' Bassett who was to make his name as a manager with several clubs.

Exeter had begun their pre-season preparations with a fairly low-key 2-0 win over Colchester United at St James' Park.

Two goals inside a minute just after half-time secured victory, as Mike Jordan found the back of the net, and then John Wingate added number two.

The second match of City's build-up to the new season involved them making the journey along the south coast on a Friday evening to Southern League Poole Town.

City goalkeeper Bob Wilson was unfortunately punished for his second-minute error to give Poole the lead. However, the Grecians equalised in the 65th minute through Alan Beer.

Twenty-four hours later City were on the road again to Wimbledon, but sadly there is no record of the actual team that the Grecians used on the day.

However, the four-page match programme listed the squad as: Bob Wilson, John Templeman, Alan Hooker, Brian Joy, John Wingate, Keith Clapham, Bobby Hodge, Keith Bowker, Lammie Robertson, Alan Beer, Nicky Jennings, Tony Morrin, Hedley Steele, Mike Jordan.

The programme, incidentally, is now quite a rare item amongst collectors and one can expect to pay considerably more for it today than you would have done at the actual game.

Exeter were surprised by their opponents as Wimbledon ran out 2-0 winners in a keenly fought game, considering it was a pre-season friendly.

City did of course return to Plough Lane at a later date to play the Dons in a Football League fixture, but much has happened to both clubs since those days.

Most notable of course is the fact that both are now run by a supporters' trust, although obviously AFC Wimbledon are a completely new club from the old Wimbledon, which was moved to Milton Keynes amidst much acrimony.

DID YOU KNOW?

So what happened to those City players who were listed in the programme for the game at Wimbledon after they left Exeter City and moved elsewhere?

Bob Wilson (never played for another Football League club); John Templeman (Swindon Town); Alan Hooker (Dorchester Town); Brian Joy (York City); John Wingate (no further club); Keith Clapham (emigrated to Australia); Bobby Hodge (Colchester United); Keith Bowker (Cambridge United); Lammie Robertson (Leicester City); Alan Beer (retired through injury); Nicky Jennings (no further club); Tony Morrin (Stockport County); Hedley Steele (Dorchester Town); Mike Jordan (Bideford).

Exeter City were expected to name a new club chairman following a special board meeting between the remaining four directors in April 1976. The meeting was called following the walk out of Gerald Vallance, who had been chairman for the previous two years and a director of the club for six years. Vice-chairman Clifford Hill said that a statement would be issued after the meeting.

Vallance confirmed that he quit after a disagreement at a board meeting, which concerned the appointment of other directors to the board.

'I asked to strengthen the board which seemed reasonable with the present financial difficulties and wanted to spread the load', said Vallance.

The two people Vallance wanted in the boardroom to increase the number of directors from five to seven were Exeter Speedway promoter John Richards and former Exeter City goalkeeper and Cockwood publican Bert Hoyle.

'I wanted these people to join the board, but the rest of the directors would not confirm it. They turned it down. I could not stay then', added Vallance.

Within days it was announced that Clifford Hill would be appointed the new chairman of Exeter City Football Club, and he immediately spoke of the board of directors' one basic concern.

'That Exeter City should continue as a viable and successful football club', he said. 'We have a good staff and we appreciate this. I have every faith in Exeter City as a viable soccer club.'

Following the emergency meeting and the appointment of Hill as chairman, the new man at the helm issued the following statement:

'At the unanimous request of my colleagues, I have agreed to become chairman, with Wally Rice as vice-chairman, with a view to resolving the continuity of Exeter City as a progressive football club. The financial implications have obviously been referred to our legal and finance advisors, and a full statement will be made at a later date. Until I am advised on those meetings I have conducted, I cannot make a full statement on the steps that the club is taking.'

All was seemingly not well in the boardroom, however, and following another personal statement made by Clifford Hill published in the *Express & Echo,* the newspaper posed several questions, which the new City chairman said he would answer.

1) In your opinion was Exeter City Football Club heading for bankruptcy?

2) Why did two directors threaten to resign if the two men proposed by Mr Vallance joined the board?

3) Did the two men proposed by Mr Vallance impose any conditions before they were prepared to join the board?

4) Why did Mr Vallance threaten to resign at a meeting four days earlier?

5) What were the differences between Mr Vallance and the rest of the board over the financial management of the club?

6) Why in your opinion has the club's solvency of two years ago turned into an annual debt running into tens of thousands of pounds?

7) Why has the board allowed Mr Vallance to establish a position on which he can call in the large sums of money he has lent to the club?

8) What do the board intend to do to restore the club's solvency?

The saga rumbled on and on 16th June 1976 the board issued another statement that read:

'Mr Vallance, having renounced the controversial conditions which led to his resignation from the chair in April, has expressed his desire to rejoin the board. The Exeter City board of directors will therefore be meeting to discuss the situation when he returns from his holidays.'

On 1st July 1976, this unhappy situation appeared to have been resolved as following a board meeting, Vallance said: 'Forget the squabbles of the past and let us concentrate on getting a promotion side together for next season.'

This proved to be a prophetic statement for City were indeed promoted the very next season!

Back as chairman of Exeter City, Vallance added that he still wanted to strengthen the number of directors, but this would not now lead to the dispute that led to his resignation the previous April. The two men that Vallance had in mind were no longer interested.

The board of directors issued yet another statement that read:

'Certain outstanding problems have been resolved. The directors of Exeter City have unanimously decided to request that Gerald Vallance rejoin the board and resume his chairmanship of the club, which he was pleased to accept.'

To become a legend as a player you have to be very special indeed. In recent years there have been two such players who have appeared for Exeter City, who have been bestowed that honour by the club's fans.

Firstly there was Alan Banks, whose goals in the mid and late 1960s were such a feature of the Grecians' matches.

Secondly and more recently, although it is over 20 years since he last wore a City shirt, it has to be Tony Kellow.

He was such a character off the field, and still is, that it was inevitable that the supporters would immediately take to the Falmouth-born striker.

A late arrival on the Football League scene, Kellow was 24 years old when he was snapped up by City manager John Newman from Western League side Falmouth Town in the summer of 1976.

What a signing he proved to be! In his very first season with the club he helped the Grecians to win promotion, as he hit 22 league and cup goals in 49 appearances.

He announced his arrival on the league scene for City with a two-goal salvo in the opening fixture of the season as Exeter drew 2-2 at Hartlepool United on 21st August 1976.

Kellow continued on the goal trail and by the time Blackpool paid Exeter City, what was then a club record fee received for a player, £105,000 in November 1978, the amiable striker had totalled 40 league goals in 107 matches.

However, the move to Blackpool proved to be an unhappy one for Kellow as he never really settled on the Lancashire coast, despite netting 23 goals in 57 games.

He jumped at the chance to rejoin Exeter when manager Brian Godfrey parted with a club record fee of £65,000 in March 1980.

It was transfer deadline day, and one that also saw Godfrey sign a young Welsh striker by the name of Ray Pratt from Merthyr Tydfil for a further £10,000.

It didn't take Kellow long to return to the Grecian goalscoring trail, for in his second match back (the first back at the Park) he netted from the penalty spot as City defeated Barnsley 2-1.

The 1980–81 season proved to be an excellent one for Kellow, for although the team only achieved a mid-table placing in the Third Division, he topped the goal charts with 25 in 46 matches.

But possibly more memorable was the hat-trick he netted against Leicester City in the 3-1 F.A. Cup fourth round replay victory at St James' Park in January 1981.

Kellow played a major part in City's run to the quarter-final stages of the competition, where they succumbed to Tottenham Hotspur at White Hart Lane.

The following season – 1981–82 – Kellow was again City's top scorer with 21 goals this time, but with the team struggling badly in 1982–83, and by his standards, ten goals from 33 league matches was a poor return for the striker.

After a handful of matches under manager Gerry Francis, the almost unthinkable happened – Kellow was sold to … Plymouth Argyle!

Once again, life away from St James' Park was not a success and after just two goals in ten matches, he was signed by Swansea City in October 1984.

However, Kellow made just the one substitute outing for the Swans and a month later he moved back along the South Wales coast to link up with Newport County where he hit eight goals in 20 appearances.

Kellow just couldn't keep away from Exeter City though, and he was back at the club for a third spell when signing in July 1985.

Once more he went on to top score for the Grecians, although again it was in a struggling team, and he only managed nine league goals.

Fifteen goals in 33 league matches proved to be a better return for the then 34 year old in 1986–87, and finally his last season as a player at the Park came in 1987–88, when he scored four goals in 16 league matches.

The great man had been a fantastic servant to Exeter City and he played his last league match for the club when being introduced as a substitute as City lost 1-0 at home to Tranmere Rovers on 30th January 1988.

It wasn't the last City fans saw of Kellow though for he had spells as commercial manager and running the social club.

He moved back to his native Cornwall to live, but not before he became a pub landlord in Exeter. Kellow has been guest of Exeter City on more than one occasion, notably to officially open the new club shop in the rear of the main grandstand in 2006.

Still extremely popular, the Cornishman is welcome back at the Park at any time and is a true Exeter City legend.

Bobby Saxton had been signed by Exeter City manager John Newman from Plymouth Argyle in September 1975, where they had also previously been team mates.

It was therefore ironic that when Newman left the Grecians to take over at Grimsby Town, it was Saxton who was appointed by Exeter in his place in January 1977.

Newman had worked long and hard, with moderate success, to try to build a promotion-winning team, and was undoubtedly one of the most popular managers ever to be in charge at St James' Park.

But it was Saxton who took over and within four months triumphantly led the Grecians to promotion, with a quite amazing run of results when the team only lost one out of their final 14 league matches.

In doing so, he had bolstered the playing squad with the signings of Geoff Gay and Lee Roberts, both on loan from Bolton Wanderers and Shrewsbury Town respectively.

Saxton also introduced St Luke's College goalkeeper John Baugh into the side, following a broken ankle sustained by regular keeper Richard Key in a rare 2-0 defeat at Crewe.

Saxton, a centre-half, came to the Park with immense playing experience. The Yorkshireman had started his career with Denaby United, before signing for Derby County in February 1962.

He signed for Plymouth Argyle in February 1968 for a fee of £12,000 where he went on to make 256 league outings for the Pilgrims.

The Grecians were seeking a central defender and Newman returned to his former club to sign Saxton for a fee of £4,000, and he eventually totalled 107 league and cup appearances, scoring three goals. He also featured in the 1976–77 promotion team when he made 28 league appearances.

With City settling into life in the Third Division, Saxton was lured back to Plymouth as their manager in January 1979. Unfortunately from the Grecians' point of view, Saxton also took assistant Bert Edwards, physio Tony Long and chief scout Jim Furnell with him from City to Home Park, which didn't go down too well with the supporters at St James' Park.

By then City had become an established middle of the table side, and eventually finished the

Bobby Saxton – manager of Exeter City's promotion-winning side of 1976–77 – pictured on his return to St James' Park in 2008 for a reunion of the victorious squad. (www.cheggerspics.co.uk)

season in a very creditable ninth place, albeit with Brian Godfrey in the Park hot seat by that time. However, many felt that had Saxton stayed at Exeter, such was the momentum that he may well have brought success to the club once more.

After that he became manager at Blackburn Rovers (May 1981–December 1986). Following a spell as an advisor to Preston North End, Saxton became manager at York City in June 1987, but had left the club by September 1988.

After a short time on the coaching staff at Blackpool, Saxton then became assistant manager of Newcastle United in 1989, and even had a spell as caretaker manager of the Magpies in March and April 1991.

More recently he has been involved at Sunderland (assistant manager to Peter Reid between 1995 and 2002) and then did some scouting for Bolton Wanderers.

In 2005–06 Saxton came out of retirement to assist Niall Quinn during his time as acting manager at Sunderland. When Quinn stepped back from the management role and brought in Roy Keane in August 2006, Saxton agreed to stay on briefly as part of his coaching staff, before becoming Director of Scouting at the club two weeks later. He was later sacked as Keane brought in his own backroom staff, but then became a scout for Newcastle United.

The promotion-winning squad of 1976–77
Back row: Harry Holman, Tony Morrin, Mike Jordan, Nicky Jennings, Tony Kellow.
Middle row: John Hore, John Templeman, Mike Green, Phil Howe, Richard Key, Graham Weeks, Keith Clapham, Alan Hooker.
Front row: Lammie Robertson, Alan Beer, Bobby Saxton (Player-Manager), Bobby Hodge, Peter Hatch.

There were unprecedented scenes outside the Guildhall in Exeter's High Street as around 2,000 people congregated to hail their heroes – the Exeter City squad of 1976–77 – who had just won promotion for only the second time in the club's history.

Supporters and well-wishers gathered to greet the players before a reception being held by the Mayor of Exeter, John Landers. Many ran behind the open-top bus that carried the players, their wives and club officials through the city centre.

The noise was deafening as the cheering and chanting continued as the players arrived. They went onto the Guildhall balcony to wave to their supporters.

The *Express & Echo* reported: 'The chants rang out – "We want Saxton." Many of the fans waited outside the Guildhall whilst the hour-long reception continued. When the players reappeared the fans roared – "We will be playing Plymouth Argyle in the Third."'

Although player-manager Bobby Saxton quite rightly took the plaudits, many remembered the huge input that former manager John Newman had on the squad. Newman had departed earlier in the year to take over at Grimsby Town.

Earlier that afternoon – Saturday 14th May 1977 – City had played their final Fourth Division fixture of the season at St James' Park before an attendance of 10,751.

It was almost as if the match was in the way of the celebrations, but nonetheless the Grecians ended the season in style as they won 3-0 with goals from Bobby Hodge, Alan Beer and Nicky Jennings.

Prior to kick off the visiting Aldershot team formed a tunnel of honour and sportingly clapped the Exeter City team onto the pitch.

A reunion of the Exeter City promotion-winning squad was arranged by the Supporters' Club in 2008, and a number of players returned to the acclaim of the St James' Park crowd as they were introduced during the half-time interval of the Grecians' Blue Square Premier League fixture against Northwich Victoria.
Pictured left to right are: Harry Holman, Mike Jordan, Graham Weeks, John Baugh, Bobby Hodge, Alan Beer, Lammie Robertson, Bobby Saxton, Peter Hatch, Richard Key, John Hore, Tony Kellow. (www.cheggerspics.co.uk)

On each occasion City scored the pitch was invaded by ecstatic fans, but it was all good humoured and they quickly took their places back on the terraces.

As the whistle sounded for the end of the game, the players and match officials sprinted for the dressing rooms, pursued by hundreds of supporters who went onto the hallowed turf.

Minutes later the players reappeared in the directors' box to acknowledge the tributes from their supporters, before returning to the dressing room to celebrate their success with champagne.

The *Echo* summed up the occasion and party atmosphere perfectly by reporting: 'Asking the fans not to invade the pitch would have been like trying to put a cork back in a champagne bottle.'

As the jubilant City fans enjoyed the occasion, it was left to player-manager Bobby Saxton to sum up the promotion season:

'I think the lads have done very well', he said. 'To be truthful I am not surprised that we have done it. When I took over I could see that we would have a chance of doing something this season and I always thought we were good enough to go up.

'Even so, I cannot believe it, for it is a fairy tale that has meant a lot of hard work and dedication by everyone. Reactions from the fans and the people of Exeter have been marvellous.'

The team had shown great consistency in the final 12 games, suffering just one defeat, winning ten and drawing the other. The win at Workington on 26th March started the run, and it almost came to an end at Barnsley where they found themselves 3-0 down at half-time, only to stage one of the greatest comebacks in the club's history to win 4-3.

City chairman Gerald Vallance said: 'It has been a wonderful achievement and I hope we can repeat it again next season. I am absolutely delighted we have won promotion.

'I feel it is a wonderful achievement considering the small staff that we have had to work with. I have never been with a promotion team before and I must admit to being left feeling a little shell shocked.

'I would like to place on record our thanks to John Newman for what he did for the club. All this of course in no way detracts from the marvellous impetus and drive that Bobby Saxton has given the team in the comparatively short time he has been in charge.'

Exeter City were three minutes away from F.A. Cup glory. That was all that remained on the watch when Wolverhampton Wanderers substitute Daly hit a terrific volley from the edge of the penalty area that screamed into the net to save his First Division side from a giant-killing act.

City had looked more worthy of that crown in this F.A. Cup round three tie played at St James' Park on 7th January 1978, but they were cruelly robbed of their deserved glory.

Wolves had taken the lead in the 24th minute when Carr saw City keeper Richard Key off his line and he cleverly flighted his free-kick into the net. Six minutes later though, City were back on terms as Lee Roberts beat two defenders before unleashing an 18-yard shot past the Wolves keeper.

City completely ran the show in the second half and it was no surprise that they went into the lead after 67 minutes following a scramble in the Wolves penalty area. As the ball bobbled around, Harry Holman fired home.

The fact that Wolves snatched an undeserved equaliser spared the Midlanders blushes, when they knew only too well that they were a beaten side for most of the game.

The City team lined up: Richard Key, John Templeman, Peter Hatch, Keith Bowker, Jimmy Giles, Bobby Saxton, Colin Randell, Tony Kellow, Harry Holman, Lee Roberts, John Hore.

The crowd of 14,377, including several hundred from Wolves, were then stunned at the final whistle, as they witnessed scenes that had never been seen, nor have they since, of wanton destruction.

A large section of the First Division club's 'fans' raced onto the pitch and proceeded to break the crossbar of the goal at the Big Bank end of the ground. They tried to smash the goalposts to the ground. The mindless destruction continued outside the ground as well, when hooligans ripped off pieces of fencing and brickwork to use as weapons, smashing windows of nearby houses.

In Well Street and Victoria Street, terrified residents ducked for cover as windows were broken by flying bricks and bottles. Within minutes Exeter City found themselves besieged by a group of very angry residents demanding that their windows be replaced at the club's expense. Immediately officials found two builders among the club's vice-presidents and began the work of boarding up the windows.

Trouble had begun long before the match started as railings and barriers were pushed over. Twice during the tie, play was halted by pitch invasions by Wolves fans, despite the blue line of 35 police officers trying to hold them back. Some 23 arrests were made and City commercial manager Ray Ellis estimated that the damage to the crush barriers alone would cost £1,000 to put right.

The head of Exeter police, Chief Superintendent John Proctor said: 'It was frightening to be among the Wolves fans. It was pure lunacy. There were about 1,750 people behind the St James' Road goal, but about 500 of those were out for trouble.'

It was Mr Proctor in consultation with Exeter City Football Club officials who decided to impose a crowd limit of 16,000 at the ground for the match, but he saw no reason to reduce that for future games.

'Despite the fact that barriers were broken, there was still plenty of room inside the St James' Road enclosure', he added. 'Exeter City can in no way be blamed for what happened.'

Exeter City directors held a board meeting to discuss the incidents and chairman Gerald Vallance said that they expressed sympathy to nearby residents whose windows were broken by the Midland mob, but said that the club could not accept liability for the damage.

He added that the broken railings in the ground would be repaired with stronger ones and the work would be done in a such a way that a cage could be constructed above them if necessary.

In the match programme for the replay, a tie that City lost 2-1, Tony Kellow netting for the Grecians, the Wolves manager Sammy Chung wrote as follows: 'There was one aspect of the atmosphere at Exeter which thoroughly depressed me. I refer to the senseless and stupid behaviour of a certain so-called group of Wolves supporters.

'I can only apologise to all Exeter City directors, players and supporters, and assure them that the vast percentage of our supporters are well behaved and sensible followers of our great sport.'

One of Exeter City's greatest ever comebacks was against a shell-shocked Doncaster Rovers in the Football League Cup, second round, second leg, played at St James' Park on 5th September 1979.

Having defeated Hereford United 5-2 on aggregate in the first round, which included a fine 3-1 win at Edgar Street, City were a little disappointed to be paired with Doncaster as their reward.

Exeter had played really well at Hereford, including one memorable goal netted by Keith Bowker, who went on to complete a hat-trick, when the perseverance of Dave Pullar saw him pull the ball back across the goal area from the tightest of angles.

The Grecians travelled to Doncaster's Belle Vue for the first leg in the second round, and must have felt that the tie was almost beyond them when they suffered a 3-1 defeat.

The City goal had been scored by winger Pullar, who had also been on target against Hereford at the Park in the second leg of the first round.

It was disappointing for much of the first half for the 3,201 spectators at St James' Park as Exeter attempted to claw back the two-goal deficit.

However, there was a glimmer of hope when, after 35 minutes, Peter Hatch crashed home a shot from 20 yards.

Unfortunately for City, Doncaster refused to roll over and Gavin Warboys, later to play for the Grecians on loan, netted at the start of the second half to make it 4-2 on aggregate.

The game then took a sensational twist as City scored again in the 70th minute when the lively Peter Rogers was pulled down in the area and up stepped Steve Neville to coolly dispatch the penalty kick.

Six minutes later City were awarded another spot-kick. Neville was fouled and he picked himself up to take the kick once again, only to see it saved. Had City blown their chance?

Exeter, by then, were in full cry with Doncaster grimly hanging on as attack after attack bore down on the visitors' goal, the team being roared on by the crowd.

Jimmy Giles saw his header hit the Doncaster crossbar and, with time fast running out, Exeter finally levelled the scores – 4-4 on aggregate –

John Hore – pictured in 2008 – was a member of the City team that staged a terrific comeback against Doncaster Rovers in the Football League Cup. (www.cheggerspics.co.uk)

when John Sims finished off a move by getting on the end of a cross from Hatch.

It had been a magnificent fight back by the City, but there was more to come as they scored in each half of extra-time.

Substitute Bowker made it 4-1 on the night as he headed in Pullar's cross, and the same player scored again when he hit a blistering drive past the keeper to complete a memorable night for the Grecians and a miserable one for Doncaster.

The City team that night lined up: Vince O'Keefe, Phil Roberts (Keith Bowker), John Hore, Jimmy Giles, Martyn Rogers, John Delve, Dave Pullar, Steve Neville, John Sims, Peter Rogers, Peter Hatch.

The *Express & Echo* match report report read: 'Exeter City are through to the third round of the Football League Cup in one of the most amazing and exciting cup games seen at St James' Park in years.'

Exeter did even better in the third round, as they travelled to St Andrews and caused a huge shock by defeating Birmingham City 2-1, both the goals being scored by Neville.

The Grecians then got the plum draw they wanted in round four as they were paired with Liverpool at Anfield.

They put up a tremendous performance before a large gathering of travelling fans, and it wasn't until the latter stages of the tie that the men from Anfield finally broke the resilience of the Grecians, going on to win 2-0.

For the second season running, Exeter City had progressed to the fourth round of the Football League Cup, and they were then faced with a Herculean task of visiting and playing First Division giants, Liverpool, on 30th October 1979.

To reach that stage, the Grecians had beaten Hereford United (5-2 on aggregate) in the first round; Doncaster Rovers (6-4 on aggregate in round two); and then achieving a brilliant 2-1 win at Birmingham City in the third round.

Hundreds of City fans made the journey to Merseyside to see the Grecians take on the League Champions, many of whom had specially taken the day off work for the big match.

It was reported that some Exeter school children had also taken the day off to attend the match, but they were warned that if they did so without permission from school teachers they would be in a good deal of trouble!

A half-filled Anfield – the attendance being 21,019 – saw the teams line up as follows:

Liverpool: Ray Clemence, Phil Neal, Alan Kennedy, Phil Thompson, Ray Kennedy, Alan Hansen, Kenny Dalglish (David Fairclough), Jimmy Case, David Johnson, Terry McDermott, Graham Souness.

Exeter City: Vince O'Keefe, Tony Mitchell, Peter Hatch, John Hore, Jimmy Giles, Dick Forbes (Peter Rogers), Steve Neville, Ian Pearson, Keith Bowker, John Delve, David Pullar.

It was not the foregone conclusion that many people had predicted as City matched their illustrious opponents and held out until the hour mark, more than matching anything that Liverpool could produce.

Although eventually beaten 2-0, the Exeter supporters had every reason to be proud of their team, and there was no doubt that the City had

earned the standing ovation that they received from the appreciative Liverpool crowd at the end of the cup tie.

The difference between the teams on the night was the introduction of Liverpool super-sub David Fairclough. He was a second-half replacement for Kenny Dalglish and he proceeded to change the course of the game with two goals in the 62nd and 88th minutes.

The fact that Liverpool had to wait until two minutes from time to clinch the game was purely down to City pushing forwards in search of an equaliser and thus leaving holes at the back.

Not surprisingly City goalkeeper Vince O'Keefe had plenty to do and his performance drew praise from his counterpart in the Liverpool goal, England's Ray Clemence.

Tony Mitchell was outstanding and the way he man marked Dalglish out of the game was a real feature of the first half.

City did get the ball in the Liverpool net once, when a shot from Ian Pearson beat Clemence, but the effort was ruled out for offside.

Liverpool manager Bob Paisley was full of praise for Exeter City and said: 'All credit to Exeter. I thought they did extremely well. I always expected it to be hard. I thought the Exeter goalkeeper Vince O'Keefe was magnificent. He was as good as any goalkeeper who has been here this season.'

Needless to say City boss Brian Godfrey was equally praiseworthy and proud of his players:

'We were playing against the Football League champions and there are plenty of clubs who go to Anfield and do not do as well as we did', he said. 'I just hope we can carry the spirit we showed into our league games. We won't be playing Liverpool every week.'

DID YOU KNOW?

After defeating Exeter City 2-0 at Anfield in the fourth round of the Football League Cup, Liverpool went on to beat Norwich City 3-1 to set up a semi-final meeting with Nottingham Forest. They lost 1-0 in the first leg at Forest, and then drew 1-1 back at Anfield to go out of the competition.

It was reported in December 1979 that a group of seven people were formulating plans to make a takeover bid for Third Division Exeter City.

It seemed all very secretive, as none of the consortium were named, however, it was believed that two were farmers and the rest successful businessmen.

Their spokesman, a wealthy Exeter company director who had tried before to invest in shares in the club, revealed that they did not necessarily want to unseat the current City chairman, Gerald Vallance.

It was reckoned that Vallance had between £50,000 and £60,000 invested in the club at one time, although that amount had been reduced in recent years.

'Our concern is not with the chairman. He would be an asset to any board', said the consortium spokesman.

'But we feel there is not nearly enough being done to sell the club along the right lines. There is potential in the city to have a successful Second Division club. Yet Exeter could find themselves back in the Fourth Division if they are not careful.

'The St James' Park ground looks a right mess and crowds are down to between 3,000 and 4,000 when they should be nearer 10,000.

'There have been a constant stream of players who have refused to sign for Exeter City this season. There has to be a reason apart from the players' wives refusing to move to the West Country. Manager Brian Godfrey has lined up some exciting signings but the club has not played its role and sold Exeter to the players.'

The consortium told the *Express & Echo* that they had the cash to buy out most, if not all of the existing five-man City board.

'It would probably take around £200,000 to give us control, but that does not bother us', added the spokesman.

'We are all local people born and bred and having made our money in the area have Exeter City close to our hearts. We want Exeter to have the best of everything, but there is no chance of that if some of the present board of directors are allowed to stay on.

'The club needs facelift as simple as that. People have got to be attracted back to St James' Park and every member of the consortium would want only to plough money back into the club.'

Exeter City had recently announced a record profit on their last financial year of over £100,000 and one crucial fact was that the club owned their own ground, which Vallance estimated to be worth anything between £600,000 and £1 million.

Vallance was reported to be 'amused' by the consortium's plan and said: 'I don't think they appreciate the money involved. In law you cannot withhold the transfer of shares, but I can't honestly see the situation reaching that stage. In fact at a board meeting tomorrow, we are likely to announce a new director joining us.

'It will be interesting to learn the outcome of the consortium's next move, because in certain areas they are right in what they are saying.'

A major brewery had previously tried to buy St James' Park as part of an arrangement whereby they were prepared to sponsor the social club at a cost of £35,000, but they were quickly turned down.

Nothing more was heard about the proposed takeover in the following weeks and the status quo remained.

DID YOU KNOW?

Exeter City manager Brian Godfrey had previously been in charge of Bath City between July 1976 and January 1979. He stayed at St James' Park until the end of the 1982–83 season and subsequently managed Weymouth, Bath City (again) and Gloucester City. He then worked in various capacities for Shortwood United, Cinderford Town, Newport AFC and returned to Gloucester City. Godfrey retired in 2003 to live in Cyprus.

'It's Liverpool and Cup fever' reported the *Express & Echo* as the Grecians were paired with the Merseyside giants in the second round of the Football League Cup, played over two legs, in October 1981.

It was to be a return meeting of the two clubs, as Exeter City had travelled to Liverpool in the fourth round of the same competition in October 1979, where they lost 2-0.

As soon as the draw was announced the telephones never stopped ringing at St James' Park with supporters wanting to know about ticket and travel arrangements.

It was decided to give everyone attending the Football League fixture at the Park against Millwall a voucher as they came through the turnstiles that would guarantee them a ticket for the second leg against Liverpool.

This boosted the attendance for the visit of the Lions to 7,169, and they were treated to a nine-goal thriller as City won 5-4, Mike Lester netting a hat-trick for the Grecians.

With excitement building, City had to negotiate the first leg at Anfield played on 7th October 1981, a tough game against the reigning European Champions.

Nonetheless, hundreds of City fans made the journey north, by special train, car and coach, and it was estimated that around 700 would be cheering on manager Brian Godfrey's men. The teams lined up:

Liverpool: Bruce Grobbelaar, Phil Neal, Alan Kennedy, Phil Thompson, Mark Lawrenson, Ronnie Whelan, Kenny Dalglish, Sammy Lee, Ian Rush, Terry McDermott, Graham Souness.

Exeter City: Len Bond, Martyn Rogers, John Sparrow, Steve Davey, Joe Cooke, Lee Roberts, Frank Prince (Dave Pullar), Peter Rogers, Tony Kellow, John Delve, Mike Lester.

It proved to be too much of a task for the City and they found themselves trailing 3-0 at the interval after goals were scored by Rush, McDermott and Dalglish.

Liverpool added two more in the second half

through Rush and Whelan, however, the Grecians did have two efforts cleared off the line by Lawrenson, who blocked goalbound attempts from Peter Rogers and Lee Roberts.

It was a disappointing night for City watched by an equally disappointing crowd of just 11,478, and ensured that, despite still having the second leg to play back at St James' Park, the tie was effectively all over for the Grecians.

The return meeting took place on 28th October 1981, and this time there were 11,470 present to see how the City would cope after such a beating in the first leg.

Unfortunately it was worse! For this time the Grecians lost 6-0, and therefore appeared in the record books as being on the receiving end of the highest aggregate winning margin in the Football League Cup at that time. The teams lined up:

Exeter City: Len Bond, Martyn Rogers, John Sparrow, Steve Davey (Peter Hatch), Nicky Marker, Phil Roberts, Dave Pullar, Peter Rogers, Tony Kellow, John Delve, Mike Lester.

Liverpool: Bruce Grobbelaar, Phil Neal, Mark Lawrenson, Phil Thompson, Ray Kennedy, Alan Hansen, Kenny Dalglish, Ronnie Whelan, Ian Rush, Terry McDermott, Kevin Sheedy.

For Nicky Marker, it was a real step up for the apprentice professional who, prior to the game, modestly said: 'It will certainly be a bit different to playing for the "A" team at Willand Rovers.'

There was no lack of effort or spirit from the City team, but they were simply outclassed and outplayed by a Liverpool team whose possession football made it look so easy.

Rush put them in front in the 16th minute and there were further first-half goals from Dalglish and McDermott.

Sheedy made it 4-0 early in the second half and the rout was complete when Marker, who had earlier cleared a Dalglish shot off the line, turned the ball into his own net after the same Liverpool player had fired against the post. Three minutes from time, Rush made it 6-0.

The newspaper headline was 'Exeter City Cup Sensation' – and it really was a sensation as the Grecians had held First Division Newcastle United to a 1-1 draw at the other St James' Park in the fifth round of the F.A. Cup in February 1981.

The Grecians' magnificent run in the cup had just kept going, having already disposed of Leatherhead, Millwall, Maidstone United and Leicester City (after a replay).

The game at Newcastle though presented the greatest test that season, and the odds were very much against a City result, but once again the team defied those odds in front of an attendance of 37,420, which included thousands of Grecians' followers who had made the long trip to the northeast.

The teams lined up as follows:

Newcastle United: Kevin Carr, Steve Carney, Peter Johnson, Nigel Walker, Stuart Boam, Bruce Halliday, Bobby Shinton (Alan Shoulder), John Trewick, Ray Clarke, Ken Wharton, Chris Waddle.

Exeter City: Len Bond, Martyn Rogers, John Sparrow, Dick Forbes (Ray Pratt), Lee Roberts, Phil Roberts, Ian Pearson, Peter Rogers, Tony Kellow, John Delve, Peter Hatch.

The *Express & Echo* reported: 'Hail the heroes of Exeter City! They shook those redoubtable F.A. Cup fighters of Geordie land – Newcastle United.

'With six minutes to go and the majority of the crowd urging on the home side who were leading by a single goal (scored by Shoulder in the 57th minute), Exeter struck an almighty blow and the 2,000 or so City supporters went wild as Lee Roberts hooked the ball over the keeper's head for the equaliser.

'How those City supporters celebrated. It was fairy tale stuff as Exeter sensed that the seemingly impossible task of earning a replay was about to become reality. It was a sensational finish by City.'

But even more euphoric scenes were to follow, as the Grecians faced Newcastle United back at the Park for the replay four days later in front of a packed ground and an attendance of 17,668.

Tickets for the replay had been like gold dust and were soon snapped up as soon as they were put on sale, grandstand tickets costing £3 and ground admission being £2.

The gates were closed 45 minutes before kick off, the capacity of the ground having been

reached. Outside the main entrance ticket touts were selling grandstand tickets for £9 each.

Police estimated that there were around 3,000 Newcastle supporters in the ground. They had 170 police officers on duty and were planning to escort the supporters back to their coaches and out onto the motorway after the game.

There were no changes made to the City team from the first meeting, whilst Newcastle made just the one, bringing in Shoulder to start the game instead of Shinton.

The *Express & Echo* report takes up the story of the game, and for those who were lucky to be present, it proved to be another unforgettable night:

'This was no act of traditional giant killing, but a ruthlessly professional performance by a head and shoulders better side that enabled Exeter City to turf First Division Newcastle United unceremoniously out of the F.A. Cup and reach the quarter-final for the first time in fifty years.

'City's tremendous triumph was created by a first half of champagne football mixed with ice cool finishing. They lashed in three goals in that opening 45 minutes that rocked the Geordies to their very foundations.

'And then their total determination and will to win was enough to contain Newcastle in a second half spell in which they threw everything they had in trying to get back into the game.'

Exeter went ahead in the 14th minute when a Hatch inswinging corner took the keeper by surprise and it squeezed into the net. Five minutes later it was 2-0. A Hatch long throw fell to Pearson who scored with a spectacular overhead kick.

Nothing was stopping Exeter, who were roared on by the crowd, and with four minutes of the half remaining Peter Rogers took advantage of a hesitant defence to net a third goal.

If Newcastle were in shock, so were the City fans! Despite the visitors throwing everything at City in the second half, the Grecians still managed to add one further goal to complete a fantastic 4-0 win, as Martyn Rogers netted from a Kellow cross.

Manager Brian Godfrey commented: 'It was a fabulous result. We were by far the better team and showed just how well we can play. The crowd were tremendous. They were like an extra man for us.'

Midfielder John Delve added: 'I think we probably made it easy for ourselves by working so hard in the first half. The game was all over by half-time, The biggest problem we had was trying to calm everyone down. It will certainly give Tottenham Hotspur something to think about in the next round.'

EXETER CITY'S MAGNIFICENT F.A. CUP RUN OF 1980–81

22nd November 1980: round one:
Exeter City 5 Leatherhead 0
City team: Len Bond, Martyn Rogers, Lee Roberts, Phil Roberts, John Delve, Peter Hatch, Dick Forbes, Ian Pearson, Tony Kellow, Peter Rogers, Dave Pullar.
City scorers: Kellow (2), Pearson, L. Roberts, Hinshelwood (own goal).

13th December 1980: round two:
Millwall 0 Exeter City 1
City team: Len Bond, Martyn Rogers, Lee Roberts, John Delve, Phil Roberts, Peter Hatch, Dick Forbes, Ian Pearson, Tony Kellow, Peter Rogers, Dave Pullar.
City scorer: P. Rogers.

3rd January 1981: round three:
Maidstone United 2 Exeter City 4
City team: Len Bond, Martyn Rogers, Lee Roberts, John Delve, Phil Roberts, Peter Hatch, Dick Forbes, Ian Pearson, Tony Kellow, Peter Rogers, Dave Pullar.
City scorers: Pullar (2), Kellow, P. Rogers

24th January 1981: round four:
Leicester City 1 Exeter City 1
City team: Len Bond, Martyn Rogers, Lee Roberts, Phil Roberts, Frank Prince, Peter Hatch, Dick Forbes, John Delve, Tony Kellow, Peter Rogers, Dave Pullar.
City scorer: Pullar.

28th January 1981: round four replay:
Exeter City 3 Leicester City 1
City team: Ian Main, Martyn Rogers, Lee Roberts, John Delve, Phil Roberts, Peter Hatch, Dick Forbes, Ian Pearson, Tony Kellow, Peter Rogers, Dave Pullar.
City scorers: Kellow (3).

14th February 1981: round five:
Newcastle United 1 Exeter City 1
City team: Len Bond, Martyn Rogers, Lee Roberts, John Delve, Phil Roberts, John Sparrow, Dick Forbes, Ian Pearson, Tony Kellow, Peter Rogers, Peter Hatch.
City scorer: L. Roberts.

18th February 1981: round five replay:
Exeter City 4 Newcastle United 0
City team: Len Bond, Martyn Rogers, Lee Roberts, John Delve, Phil Roberts, John Sparrow, Dick Forbes, Peter Rogers, Tony Kellow, Ian Pearson, Peter Hatch.
City scorers: Hatch, Pearson, P. Rogers, M. Rogers.

7th March 1981: quater-final:
Tottenham Hotspur 2 Exeter City 0
City team: Len Bond, Martyn Rogers, Lee Roberts, Dick Forbes, Phil Roberts, John Sparrow, Ian Pearson, Peter Rogers, Tony Kellow, John Delve, Peter Hatch.

Exeter City chairman Clifford Hill and his fellow directors had been one of the busiest boards in the country, reported the *Express & Echo* in August 1983.

They had saved the club from extinction by digging deep into their own pockets and using every ounce of their considerable business expertise. But their work was not finished by a long way according to Hill who felt it was now the turn of the players and fans to do their bit.

Hill warned that City's future depended on a concerted effort by directors, players and supporters, and without that joint effort there would not be the success that everybody was praying for.

'There has been a lot of talking and doing behind the scenes. It is now time for action on the field and for the fans to get behind us', he said.

'After a traumatic end to the previous season, and the hectic bustle of the last few months, perhaps I can take a breather to review our current position at the beginning of what could be seen as our most important year.

'In October of last year Exeter City was foundering with a loss of £250,000 and at times was within a hair's breadth of closing down.

'We also had to contend with the Chester Report and major – and at times drastic – changes in the format of football affecting the fortunes of all clubs and in particular those in the lower divisions.

'There is for example the new dependence of clubs on their home gates. Our survival is now a matter of history, but our predicament then created a great awareness of where our future lay.

'We either went forward with ambitions for the Second Division or languished in what ultimately has to become regionalised football.

'With this in mind the board gathered support and set their caps at future promotion. We mustered all resources and, believing that success has to be engineered from the top, obtained the services of Gerry Francis as manager.

'Our massive debt will not go away until we reduce it from profits. The directors have already provided an unacceptable level of unsecured loans and our creditors have been mainly satisfied.

'It is now up to the public to support us through the turnstiles and if they don't then they will have squandered perhaps the last chance for Exeter City to be recognised as part of the national soccer scene.'

On his appointment as player-manager Gerry Francis explained to the gathered press how ambitious he was for the Grecians:

'I want to get them in the Second Division in one year – and I want to be playing in the First again in two years.

'I am realistic and I realise that I have inherited a team that was a point above relegation to the Fourth Division last season. I have got no illusions about the difficulty of the job I have got to do.

'But I am an ambitious person. I was as a First Division player and I will be just as ambitious as a manager.'

Exeter City were also hoping to attract a sponsor to display their name on the team's shirts in a one-year contract worth £10,000.

One possible link involved newly appointed director and former World Boxing Champion, Alan Minter, who had hinted that transport giants Daf Trucks might be persuaded to take an interest in the Grecians as he himself had a contract with them for promotional work.

The bookmakers, Coral, never quite shared the same hopes that had been displayed by the club, for at the start of the season they were offering odds of 40-1 for City to win the Third Division championship.

Sadly the club's optimism never materialised. Francis had left the club by the end of the season, Exeter City were relegated to the Fourth Division, and attendances had averaged 3,380.

The Exeter City squad prior to what proved to be a truly disastrous 1983–84 season
Back row: Martyn Rogers, Ray Pratt, Nick Marker, Graeme Kirkup, Frank Howarth, Tony Kellow.
Middle row: Martin Ling, Darren Clifford, Symon Burgher, Len Bond, Leon Smith, Michael Lane,
Adrian Robson, Malcom Musgrove (Trainer).
Front row: Dick Forbes, Tony Dennis, David Harle, Gerry Francis (Player-Manager),
Keith Viney, Peter Rogers, Steve Neville.

It's probably true to say that the 1983–84 season is the worst seen at Exeter City in their history, yet at the start of it, optimism for the future and success being brought to the club was at its highest for a very long time.

Fans were excited by the prospect of former England international Gerry Francis taking over as player-manager of the Grecians, yet in a few short months, the move had proved to be a complete disaster both for Francis and the club.

The Chiswick-born player was a talented midfielder who was captain of Queens Park Rangers during the 1970s. He won 12 caps for England between 1974 and 1976, which including captaining his country on eight occasions.

By the time he arrived at St James' Park, Francis, then 32, had made 419 league appearances with Queens Park Rangers (in two spells), Crystal Palace and Coventry City.

Although he still had a year left on his contract

Coventry, they released him to become player-manager at Exeter, and it had been reported that he had been approached before his predecessor Brian Godfrey had left!

Arriving in a fanfare of publicity, and attending pre-season road shows at places such as Tiverton and Exmouth, hopes were high for success. However, although the City directors had done well to secure such a high-profile appointment, they then failed to back him up with money to spend in the transfer market.

The result was a team of free transfers, loan signings and non-contract players, and it soon became obvious that City were never going to compete in the Third Division with such an assortment of players.

Signings made by Francis included Stan McEwan (Blackpool), Tony Dennis (Plymouth Argyle), Joe Auguste (Hounslow Town), Jim Hicks (Exeter University), Peter Taylor (Maidstone United), Mark

140

O'Connor (Queens Park Rangers), Hugh Atkinson (Wolverhampton Wanderers), Simon Webster (Tottenham Hotspur) and Roy McDonough (Southend United).

City supporters had to wait until 3rd December before they saw the team win at St James' Park, a 2-1 success over Hull City.

Early exits were also made in the Football League Cup and the F.A. Cup, both in the first round against Cardiff City and Maidstone United respectively.

After a terrible run of just one win in 22 games, Francis was sacked in May 1984. He had made 28 appearances for the Grecians, scoring three goals, but the team eventually finished rock bottom of Division Three and were therefore relegated.

During his time as manager at Exeter, Francis continued to live in Bagshot, Surrey, which brought some comment as to how he could do the job living so far away.

By the time of the last outing made by Francis at the Park against Scunthorpe United, crowds had dipped to just 2,003 and the alarm bells were very much ringing.

Francis went on to play for Cardiff City, Swansea City, Portsmouth and Bristol Rovers, all on short-term deals, before eventually being appointed manager of the latter team.

Despite his experience at being manager at Exeter, Francis was a success at Rovers. In 1990 he guided the Pirates to the Third Division title, but a year later he returned to Queens Park Rangers as their manager.

In November 1994 Francis left Loftus Road for Tottenham Hotspur, and although he enjoyed reasonable success, he left in November 1997 with Spurs battling against relegation from the Premiership.

In September 1998, Gerry Francis was named as Queens Park Rangers manager for the second time, but by then the club were struggling for Division One survival. He resigned as manager in February 2001.

The bad days at Exeter City must have seemed a long time ago as Francis' association with Queens Park Rangers was rekindled for a brief spell as Director of Football at Loftus Road.

He then began his second stint as manager of Bristol Rovers in June 2001. However, less than six months later, Francis left the club.

EXETER CITY SEASON 1983–84

League appearances (substitute outings in brackets):
Len Bond 45; Keith Viney 42; Steve Neville 40(3); Martin O'Connor 38; Graeme Kirkup 36; Ray Pratt 30(6); Nicky Marker 28(3); Hugh Atkinson 28; Gerry Francis 28; Stan McEwan 28; Simon Webster 26; Peter Rogers 25; Martin Ling 23(6); Roy McDonough 15(1); John Sims 12(2); Steve Harrower 10(3); Peter Taylor 8; Joe Auguste 7(3); Tony Kellow 7(1); Frank Howarth 6(5); David Harle 6; Russell Musker 6; Ian Evans 4; Tony Dennis 3(1); Jim Hicks 3; Richard Crabtree 1; Michael Lane 1.

League goalscorers:
Ray Pratt 16; Stan McEwan 9; Steve Neville 9; Peter Rogers 5; Gerry Francis 3; John Sims 3; Hugh Atkinson 1; Steve Harrower 1; Martin O'Connor 1; Keith Viney 1.

Exeter City froze admission and season ticket prices for the 1989–90 season as a big thank you to the supporters for their loyalty over the previous 12 months. The figures make fascinating reading, especially the admission prices, in comparison to those of today.

In May 1989, City's financial director, Murray Couch, said that despite the fact the club were in debt to the tune of around £500,000 and that there were strong economic grounds for putting up charges at St James' Park, the board of directors had decided otherwise.

'We had been very appreciative of the increased hard core support this season', he said. 'We felt, as a board, that we didn't want to put the prices up. From a financial point of view there ought to be a rise, but there won't be as a sign of gratitude for the loyalty of our supporters.'

Therefore match day admission remained at £5 for the grandstand and £3 for the rest of the ground, with reductions for senior citizens and children.

Grandstand season tickets remained on sale at £100 and those for the terraces at £60, and there were special cut-price offers on tickets bought before 3rd June 1989. Supporters could save up to £30 by booking their grandstand seat by that date.

There were also concessionary rates for family season tickets with some attractive bargains to be had with reductions of up to £128 for a pass covering two adults and two children.

'What we are looking for is for more people to become season ticket holders and we are appealing for them to take advantage of the early purchase savings. That will help us through the difficult summer period', said Couch.

City had a total of 338 season ticket holders during the 1988–89 campaign, but it was hoped that figure would increase as attendances overall had done so for matches at St James' Park during the past 12 months.

The total league attendance at City's home games during 1988–89 was around 60,000, thus giving an average per game of 2,680.

Top gate that season was 4,243 for the Devon derby against Torquay United in October 1988, but Park attendances topped 3,000 on four other occasions – against Hereford United, York City, Burnley and Stockport County respectively.

Couch added: 'We have had a mildly successful season by our recent standards and when we start getting gates of 3,000 plus, we're getting to a more viable position.

'Without the support this season we would not have been able or willing to go into the transfer market so heavily.

'We won't be making a profit this season, but we feel we have invested in the future of this club by backing manager Terry Cooper's judgement.'

City's spending on players had been modest in comparison to some of their Fourth Division rivals. Tranmere Rovers, for example, splashed out £60,000 on goalkeeper Eric Nixon alone, and Scarborough were all set to part with £120,000 for Hereford United striker, Phil Stant, the division's leading goalscorer.

But £10,000 for Steve Neville, £10,000 for Richard Dryden, £7,000 for Brian McDermott and an impending £5,000 payment for Richard Young represented a major change in policy for the City, whose directors had been more interested in selling rather than buying in previous years.

Their refusal to accept anything less than Cooper's £300,000 valuation for skipper Shaun Taylor when one or two clubs had made tentative enquiries for the big defender, underlined the board of directors' new and more adventurous outlook under chairman Ivor Doble.

'We all believe we have got every opportunity next season of being promoted with the ground work that has been done this year', added Couch.

This prediction was to be spot on as City ran away with the Fourth Division championship 12 months later.

You could say that Terry Cooper was the most successful manager at Exeter City, for he is the only person so far to have brought a league championship title to the club, the Fourth Division title in 1990. This he did in some style.

A typical, forthright Yorkshireman, who was not afraid to voice his opinion on players, matches etc., Cooper's side went unbeaten at St James' Park during the triumphant 1989–90 season.

A former England international full-back, Cooper was born in Knottingley in July 1944, and started his playing career with Leeds United as an apprentice, originally as a left-winger.

Cooper went on to win a string of honours under Leeds manager Don Revie, including playing in the 1968 League Cup winning side and the successful team that lifted the Inter Cities Fairs Cup.

In 1969, Leeds won the league championship with Cooper making his contribution. They also won the Fairs Cup again in 1971.

Had he not been sidelined for 20 months recovering from a badly broken leg, Cooper would surely have added greatly to the total of 250 league outings and seven goals.

He had won 20 caps for England, including featuring in the 1970 World Cup Finals.

He joined Middlesbrough in March 1975 for a fee of £50,000, and played a further 105 league games for them. Aged 34, Cooper moved to Bristol City in July 1978 for £20,000. After a short spell as player-coach, he then became player-manager of cross-city rivals Bristol Rovers in April 1980.

It was not the best of times to be manager of the club, for not only did they have their off-the-field troubles when the grandstand burnt down at Eastville, but they were also relegated.

After leaving them in October 1981, Cooper went on to Doncaster Rovers and then returned to Bristol City as their player-manager in May 1982, not retiring from playing until 1984.

He proved to be very successful at Bristol City, taking them to promotion to Division Three in 1986 and winning the Freight Rover Trophy in 1987. He had also become a director of the club, and was therefore player-manager-director!

Cooper was appointed manager of Exeter City in May 1988. In his first season at St James' Park the team ended in tenth place in the Fourth Division, but what a difference 12 months later!

With Darran Rowbotham in magnificent

Darran Rowbotham – City's leading goalscorer during the 1990 Championship season.

goalscoring form (had he not been injured, he would surely have added to his 20 goals in just 32 appearances), the Grecians stormed to the Fourth Division championship.

Cooper was not adverse making changes to the team when needed and as a result, brought in several players who only made a few appearances between them, such as Tony Coyle, Gary Elkins, Karl Goddard, Paul Eshelby and Clive Stafford.

Other players who featured in the successful City team that season were: Dave Walter, Jim McNichol, Chris Vinnicombe, Lee Rogers, Shaun Taylor, Clive Whitehead, Danny Bailey, Brian McDermott, Steve Neville, Richard Dryden, Scott Hiley, Richard Young, Ian Benjamin, Ben Rowe, Steve Harrower, Paul Batty, Tony Frankland, Kevin Miller, Angus McPherson, Tom Kelly and Kevin Summerfield.

Cooper was highly thought of by club and fans alike, understandably so, however, not for the first time, just as the Grecians looked to be making progress, Cooper left and was appointed manager of Birmingham City. He found it difficult at St Andrews and was subsequently dismissed in the autumn of 1993.

Cooper was to return to take over as manager again at Exeter City, but they were sorry times at the club, as the Grecians went into administration, but despite managing to survive the club ended in bottom place in the Football League in 1994–95,

only to survive the drop into the Conference due to Conference champions, Macclesfield Town, not having a sufficient ground grading to win promotion.

Ill health forced Cooper to stand down as City manager, and he was replaced by goalkeeper Peter Fox. He has not returned to management since then, but has for some years worked as an overseas scout for Southampton.

The Exeter City squad for season 1990–91
Having won the Fourth Division Championship the previous season, the Championship trophy can be seen in the front of the team. Manager Terry Cooper is in the back row first left.

The Football Association came down hard on Exeter City Football Club and its directors when they delivered their verdict following an investigation in December 1990.

The F.A. dished out bans and fines after finding the club, three directors and one former board member guilty of misconduct. One director (chairman Ivor Doble) was banned for 12 months and fined £5,000; another two (Murray Couch and Archie Gooch) were banned for three months each and fined £3,000 and £2,000 respectively, whilst another (Mike Holladay) was fined £1,000. In addition Exeter City Football club were fined £7,500.

A three-man F.A. disciplinary commission reached the verdicts after a 14-hour meeting. The hearing was launched into serious allegations of a £27,000 overpayment in grant aid by the Football Grounds Improvement Trust (FGIT).

An F.A. team visited the ground in April 1990 just as City were poised to clinch the Fourth Division championship, and chairman Ivor Doble said that he had drawn FGIT's attention to the fact that they had received more cash than they were entitled to and paid back £27,000 out of his own pocket.

Following the announcement by the Football Association, Doble spoke of his amazement at the severity of the punishment.

He said: 'I am absolutely astonished. There is no way we deserve this. As chairman I expected to bear the brunt of it. I give out jobs to people on the board, but as chairman I take overall responsibility.

'The buck stops with me. But in no way did I expect this. All we have ever done has been for the sake of the club, and I don't want to harm Exeter City in any way.'

Exeter City's financial director Murray Couch added: 'We have the best team, the best manager and in my opinion the best chairman in the club's history. I am distraught at the commissions findings.'

Grecians' manager Terry Cooper was shocked at the 12-month ban from football handed to chairman Ivor Doble:

'I am shocked, I have no idea what happens next. The ban situation needs clarifying', he said. 'We don't exactly know what it means. Until we do know, I cannot make any decision or further comment.

'I have had the privilege to manage under two gentlemen. One was Des Williams at Bristol City,

Ivor Doble cuts the ribbon to officially open the new Big Bank terracing development at St James' Park. Doble, along with his fellow directors' kept the club financially afloat for several years. An out and out City fan, he always did what he thought best for the club.

the other is Ivor Doble. Some managers are not lucky enough to get one such chairman.

'The worrying thing is if the likes of Mr Doble pull their money out of the club, Exeter City will be around £250,000 in debt, and let's face it, there is nobody likely to put up that kind of money.

'My fear is that I will have to sell our top players just to keep the bank happy. The club and ultimately the supporters are the losers of all of this.'

The following day the sentences imposed upon the club and the directors became clearer and in fact were even harsher than first thought.

Ivor Doble was banned for a year, fined £5,000 plus £2,000 costs; director Murray Couch was suspended from all football for six months and fined £2,500 plus another £2,000 costs; Mike Holladay was ordered to pay £1,000 with £2,000 costs; and the club itself was fined £7,500 with £2,000 costs. A total of £24,000 would have to be paid to the F.A.

The *Express & Echo* were to later reveal the financial input to the club of the various club directors, who they reckoned had a £250,000 interest.

Mr Doble they said, had loaned the club a total of

£125,397 and that included a payment of £46,397 to cover a pressing tax bill. On top of that he also had £20,000 of shares in the club.

Director Peter Carter loaned £25,100 and was also owed £20,000 for work on the new vice-presidents' club at St James' Park.

Mike Holladay's investment was £17,500 and he helped towards the signing of Steve Neville, paying the first £5,000 instalment of the transfer fee to Bristol City two years earlier.

Murray Couch's loan was £15,500, but that figure nearly doubled when the club was in more desperate financial straits.

Club president Clifford Hill had an existing loan of £12,500 although his investment was higher when he was chairman. Hill's wife also owned the Cat and Fiddle training ground and charged Exeter City a rent to use it.

Archie Gooch and Gino Vece were repaid £12,500 when they left the board of directors earlier in 1990 and former chairman Byron Snell was paid back £19,000.

City's outstanding debts totalled nearly £270,000. They owed Exeter City Council £16,800; the brewers Bass Wales £32,600; and National Westminster Bank £150,000, with around £70,000 due to other creditors.

The opening of the new Big Bank covered terracing took place in February 2000. Pictured are directors Stuart Dawe, the late Paul Dobson, Ivor Doble, Murray Couch, former team manager Peter Fox and Peter Carter.
The redevelopment of St James' Park continued apace and following the demolition of the much-missed Cowshed terrace, this was replaced by a brand new seated stand in 2001, with executive boxes etc.
In honour of the club's former chairman, it was named the Ivor Doble Stand.
Successful Exeter-based businessman, Mr Doble, is an Exeter City F.C. honorary president, and regularly attends matches at St James' Park.

Had anyone prophesied on that magnificent day in 1966 when England won the World Cup, that one of the players would later become manager of Exeter City, you would not have believed them. However, much later on, it was indeed true.

Who would have thought that the 'little human dynamo' Alan Ball would be in charge at Exeter? With a glittering playing career, and perhaps a less successful managerial career, nonetheless, it was City director Stuart Dawe who set things in motion by contacting Ball and eventually the former England midfielder accepted the role as manager.

Ball had been named man of the match in that World Cup Final, the youngest member of the England squad, but now he faced a big challenge to try to turn the fortunes of the Grecians around, with a limited budget at his disposal.

Ball, who was born in Farnworth, was on the books at Wolverhampton Wanderers as a schoolboy, but they decided not to offer him a contract, nor did his local club, Bolton Wanderers, who told him he was too small.

Blackpool signed Ball as an apprentice in September 1961, turning professional the following May, and the young player never looked back.

After starring in the World Cup Final it was inevitable that he would be on the move to a bigger club, and that proved to be Everton who paid £110,000 for him in August 1966.

Playing in the 1968 F.A. Cup Final and then as part of the Everton team that won the Football League Championship in 1969–70, Ball continued to appear for England as well.

Arsenal was his next stop, the Gunners parting with a then record fee of £220,000 in December 1971. Apart from injury, he was a virtual ever-present as more success came his way as a player.

However in December 1976, after 52 goals in 217 appearances, he was transferred to Southampton for £60,000 where he helped the Saints to a League Cup Final, also appearing in well over 100 league matches for them.

Ball then went on to play in the North American Soccer League with Philadelphia Fury as player-coach in May 1978, and then onto Vancouver Whitecaps in May 1978.

Returning to England he was appointed player-manager of Blackpool, but he didn't prove to be a success and the parting of ways came in February 1981.

Alan Ball.

A month later though he was back at Southampton for a second spell with the club and he added a further 63 league matches to his career tally.

He left Southampton in October 1982 to play for Hong Kong side Eastern Athletic, before joining Bristol Rovers in January 1983, where he remained until his retirement the following season. When Ball finally retired from playing, he had played 975 competitive games in 21 years.

Ball resumed his managerial career in May 1984 with Portsmouth and was a huge success. They just missed out on promotion to the First Division in his first two seasons as manager, and he finally guided them to the top flight in 1987. However, they were relegated after just one season back among the elite, and Ball was sacked in January 1989 for failing to mount a serious promotion challenge.

The following month he joined Colchester United as assistant manager and in October 1989 took up a similar post at Stoke City. Within two weeks though Ball had been promoted as a manager. His time there proved to be very disappointing as Stoke suffered relegation to the Third Division and he was sacked in February 1991.

Disillusioned with the managerial side of the game, Ball was in no hurry to return, so it was a big surprise that when he did, it was with Exeter City.

He was appointed manager in July 1991 and was

confronted with a squad of players who were clearly not good enough as shown by the early results (losing 6-3 at West Bromwich Albion and then 6-1 at Shrewsbury Town).

Ball immediately set about reshaping the squad, bringing in a number of players and eventually he managed to guide the team from what appeared to be a disastrous season, to one that at least meant survival in the Third Division.

He soon became noted for his trademark flat cap that he wore whilst in the dug out directing the City team and for his 'squeaky' voice with a strong Lancastrian accent.

Whilst at Exeter, Ball also had the honour of working alongside England boss Graham Taylor as his team coach between February and August 1992.

After taking the Grecians to the third round of the F.A. Cup and a home tie against Aston Villa in January 1994, within days Ball had left St James' Park to become manager of his former club, Southampton.

Ball had left a legacy of not being afraid of trying out young players who had come through the City youth system under the guidance of Mike Radford, and one in particular, Martin Phillips, was later to be sold to Ball for a record fee of £500,000.

By that time Ball had moved on to become manager of Manchester City, a position he held until just three games into the 1995–96 season.

In February 1998, Ball returned to Portsmouth as manager but his contract was terminated on 9th December 1999 after the club endured a near-fatal financial crisis and came close to relegation from Division One.

Ball continued to be seen on national television as a football pundit, and he made a few return visits to Exeter City for matches and functions.

The world of football was truly shocked when Ball died very suddenly in April 2007, aged just 61. He had been a popular figure during his time at Exeter, with his coaching ability second to none and his passion for developing young players.

ALAN BALL'S FIRST SEASON AT EXETER CITY 1991–92 (LEAGUE RESULTS)

Date	Opponent	H/A	Score	Date	Opponent	H/A	Score
Aug 17	West Bromwich Albion	A	3-6	Jan 18	Preston North End	A	3-1
Aug 24	Brentford	H	1-2	Jan 25	Fulham	H	1-1
Aug 31	Shrewsbury Town	A	1-6	Feb 8	Wigan Athletic	H	0-1
Sep 4	Torquay United	H	1-0	Feb 11	Chester City	A	2-5
Sep 7	Huddersfield Town	A	0-0	Feb 15	Swansea City	H	2-1
Sep 14	Hartlepool United	H	1-1	Feb 22	Bolton Wanderers	A	2-1
Sep 17	Stockport County	H	2-1	Feb 29	Bournemouth	H	0-2
Sep 21	Peterborough United	A	1-1	Mar 3	Preston North End	H	4-1
Sep 28	Reading	H	2-1	Mar 7	Fulham	A	0-0
Oct 5	Hull City	A	2-1	Mar 10	Bradford City	A	1-1
Oct 12	Darlington	H	4-1	Mar 14	Leyton Orient	H	2-0
Oct 19	Bury	H	5-2	Mar 21	Stoke City	A	2-5
Oct 26	Wigan Athletic	A	1-4	Mar 24	Bournemouth	A	0-1
Nov 2	Leyton Orient	A	0-1	Mar 28	Birmingham City	H	2-1
Nov 6	Bradford City	H	1-0	Mar 31	Hartlepool United	A	1-3
Nov 9	Stoke City	H	0-0	Apr 4	Huddersfield Town	H	0-1
Nov 23	Birmingham City	A	0-1	Apr 10	Stockport County	A	1-4
Nov 30	Chester City	H	0-0	Apr 14	Bury	A	1-3
Dec 14	Swansea City	A	0-1	Apr 18	Peterborough United	H	2-2
Dec 22	Brentford	A	0-3	Apr 20	Reading	A	0-1
Dec 26	Shrewsbury Town	H	1-0	Apr 25	Hull City	H	0-3
Dec 28	West Bromwich Albion	H	1-1	May 2	Darlington	A	2-5
Jan 1	Torquay United	A	0-1				
Jan 11	Bolton Wanderers	H	2-2				

City finished in 20th place in the Third Division.

The Football League ordered Exeter City to end their half-time entertainment, which involved chasing a turkey across the pitch and shooting it.

Their directive, received by the club in October 1992, followed a complaint made to the League by a Plymouth Argyle supporter who was upset and concerned that City's turkey, dressed in an Argyle shirt and then shot, was not in the best of taste.

It was felt that this stunt could incite trouble when the two clubs were due to meet at St James' Park on Boxing Day morning.

The stunt got its first viewing when Exeter City commercial manager Steve Birley, who thought of the idea, unleashed the seven-foot turkey in an Argyle shirt onto the pitch during the half-time interval of the Grecians' Coca Cola Cup tie against Oldham Athletic, a game that City lost 1-0 before an attendance of 4,375.

'The turkey is being used to promote the club and create interest by making guest appearances', said Birley, who was no stranger to that sort of activity, having once dressed up in a gorilla suit whilst working at Reading F.C., in their commercial department.

After first appearing in an Oldham Athletic shirt, the turkey underwent a half-time transformation wearing a Plymouth Argyle shirt and was introduced to City fans as a top goalkeeper, Helter Skilton.

Birley would normally shoot the turkey with a blunderbuss, but at the Coca Cola tie the turkey was there to let in three penalties against a charity team from British Gas.

'It is not meant to incite hatred', Birley stressed. 'But it is meant to incite a bit of passion. I wanted the 4,000 fans there to make as much noise as the 9,000 at Home Park.'

However, the funny side of the antics did not amuse the powers that be, and the Football League decreed that it was not in the best of taste.

'The problem is that somebody has complained to the Football League as the result of an article that appeared in a local Sunday newspaper', said Birley.

'That being the case the League have contacted me, quite rightly asking for further details. As a result the club have been asked to tone down the half-time stunt. In fact we can no longer dress the turkey in a team's colours ... and indeed ... shoot it!'

Exeter City 1991–92
Back row: George Kent (Community Officer), Steve Birley (Commercial Manager), Eamonn Dolan, Dave Cooper, Ronnie Jepson, Kevin Miller, Scott Daniels, Jon Brown, Craig Taylor, Jim McIntyre, Mike Radford (Youth Development Officer), Alan Ball (Manager).
Middle row: John Hodge, Alan Tonge, Toby Redwood, Mike Chapman, Scott Hiley, Peter Whiston, Danny Bailey, Andy Cook.
Front row: Richard Pears, Martin Phillips, Kevin Darch, Mark Hutchings, Jimmy Ball, Anthony Thirlby, Mark Brown, Matthew Harris, Phil Lafferty, Gary Rice, Steve Allen.

'In actual fact the paper concerned forgot to mention that prior to the turkey wearing a Plymouth Argyle shirt, it also wore an Oldham Athletic shirt to promote the Coca Cola Cup tie. There were no complaints about that.

'It is sad that the stunt has been curtailed in what was only meant to be a piece of fun. We have had a good laugh but not at the expense of anybody else. We have simply used the turkey as a focal point to get people talking.'

However it wasn't clear at the time that the turkey would be banished altogether, as Birley then added:

'Perhaps we should have stuffed the turkey?

Shooting it was perhaps over the top, so we are going to have to tone it down a bit.

'The turkey will most definitely still make an appearance, but it won't be shot. There are other means. Of course the turkey will be happy as he will not be shot for the Christmas table.'

Ironically the seven-foot tall turkey did appear in the most unlikeliest of places – at Home Park, Plymouth – when the City travelled there on Easter Saturday 1993, for there stood right at the back of the Barn Park terrace, could be seen a turkey head amongst the City travelling fans! Exeter won the game 3-0.

EXETER CITY SEASON 1992–93 – THE SEASON OF THE TURKEY!

League appearances (substitute outings in brackets):
Kevin Miller 44; John Hodge 41(1); Jon Brown 40; Ronnie Jepson 35(3); Scott Hiley 33; Andy Cook 32; Danny Bailey 27; Peter Whiston 27; Scott Daniels 26; Andy Harris 23(5); Tom Kelly 20(2); Steve Moran 19(4); Kevin Bond 17(1); David Cooper 16(4); Alan Tonge 13(2); Jim McIntyre 12(3); Jason Minett 11(1); Chris White 11; Eamonn Dolan 10(9); Stuart Storer 10; Steve Williams 8(4); Eamonn Collins 8(3); Joe Gallen 6; Richard Evans 5; Toby Redwood 3(3); Gary Chapman 3(1); Craig Taylor 2(3); Mark Loram 2(1); Vince O'Keefe 2; Martin Phillips 0(6).

League goalscorers:
John Hodge 9; Ronnie Jepson 8; Steve Moran 8; Eamonn Dolan 4; Stuart Storer 4; Scott Hiley 3; Jim McIntyre 3; Peter Whiston 3; Scott Daniels 2; Richard Evans 2; Jon Brown 1; Gary Chapman 1; Andy Cook 1; Tom Kelly 1; Alan Tonge 1; own goals 2.

John Hodge.

Kevin Miller.

What could have been a triumphant first-ever appearance at Wembley Stadium ended in compete disaster and disappointment.

The Grecians has fought their way through to the Southern Area Final of the Autoglass Trophy, where they were paired with Port Vale, the prize of a trip to the twin towers being decided over two legs.

City travelled to Vale Park for the first game, staged on Tuesday 16th March 1993, with around 500 fans giving the City team their backing.

The Grecians lined up: Kevin Miller, Jon Brown, Andy Cook (Alan Tonge), Danny Bailey, Scott Daniels, Peter Whiston, Toby Redwood, Jim McIntyre, Ronnie Jepson, Steve Moran (Eamonn Dolan), John Hodge.

However, they were stunned as early as the 14th minute when Vale took the lead through a Kerr penalty after Andy Cook had brought down an attacker in the area.

City though fought their way back to be on level terms nine minutes from the break when a rare 30-yard strike from Danny Bailey beat the keeper.

It was looking good for the Grecians to at least be able to start the second leg back at St James' Park all square, but Vale were to break their hearts when 15 minutes from time they won the game 2-1 as Taylor netted.

City boss Alan Ball though was disappointed overall with the Exeter performance saying: 'There is no point in trying to kid ourselves, we were poor. But we worked hard and I am delighted to go into the second leg just 2-1 down.'

City had to wait until Wednesday 21st April for the second leg back at St James' Park, when 7,060 attended the match that could, with a bit of good fortune, have seen Exeter City go on to make their first-ever appearance at Wembley.

In the days leading up to the game, not surprisingly with such a big prize on the end of it, there was much speculation and coverage in the local press, and the club produced a brochure to mark the fact that they had reached the Area Final.

It was honours even when the whistle signalled the half-time break, although City had enjoyed the lion's share of possession, without being able to unlock the Vale defence.

That was to change though after 63 minutes when John Hodge, who posed numerous problems for the visitors, delivered a superb far-post cross.

Eamonn Dolan found space to power a header

Jim McIntyre, Ronnie Jepson and Eamonn Dolan, the three City goalscorers who sent the Grecians into the Autoglass Trophy Southern Area Final.

towards goal which keeper Musslewhite could only parry, and Jason Minett followed up quickest to push the ball into the net.

The Grecians were caught out, however, 11 minutes later, when Vale surged forward and Foyle's through ball allowed Bernie Slaven to fire past Kevin Miller from 18 yards.

City's dream of Wembley all but disappeared after that as they strove to score again without success.

Grecians' manager Alan Ball commented: 'It was a magnificent effort. My players scrapped and fought for everything and I am really disappointed for them that it was not to be.

'We were mugged. Although we didn't produce top quality entertaining football and didn't carve out a lot of chances, I cannot recall us being under any real pressure.'

City's team for the second leg lined up: Kevin Miller, Andy Harris, Jim McIntyre, Danny Bailey, Scott Daniels, Jon Brown, Kevin Bond, Jason Minett, Steve Moran (Martin Phillips), Eamonn Dolan, John Hodge.

Comedian Freddie Starr made an offer to take over Exeter City Football Club in September 1993. He offered club president Clifford Hill a 100 per cent profit on his major shareholding, plus the money back that he had invested in the club.

Starr said that he had faxed an offer to the club and that Hill would remain as honorary president should the deal be accepted. The *Express & Echo* reported that Starr, a friend of manager Alan Ball, had already visited the Cat and Fiddle training ground and spent some time alongside the players.

Starr added that if his offer was accepted, he would visit St James' Park with his accountant and solicitor to sort out all the details and take it from there.

'I believe that Exeter have some good youth players coming through, but I would probably buy one or two players to start with', he said. 'I would have to take the advice of Alan Ball, because after all, he is the manager and the directors should keep quiet.'

Starr went on: 'I think the club could be 100 per cent better than it is now, The supporters deserve better and they are the most important people.

'Refreshment and toilet facilities need improving and I would hope to build a stand on the Big Bank. I am doing this for the club and its supporters.

'It is a dream that I have always had to own a football club and I can assure the Exeter fans that I am a quick learner.'

Star revealed that he had already met with Hill at an Exeter hotel the previous week and claimed that the president had told him he wanted a six-figure sum for the club and an agreement that the ground would not be sold for building development.

A short statement was immediately issued by Allen Trump, Exeter City's chief executive:

'The board does not consider the approach by Mr Starr to be in the best interests of Exeter City Football Club.'

Twenty-four hours later Hill also rejected Starr's bid for the club and described the offer as 'laughable'.

Hill said that Starr's offer for his 51 per cent stake in the club had failed to impress the directors.

Meanwhile Starr had decided that he would attend the City fixture at St James' Park against Wrexham to show the Exeter supporters his desire to get involved.

The quickly moving scenario then took a twist

Entertainer Freddie Starr (pictured right) mounted a takeover bid for City. He is seen presenting the Man of the Match award to Stuart Storer.

when Starr approached former City chairman Ivor Doble to set up a meeting with him, and added that Doble seemed to have suffered a raw deal from the club and he would want to find out if he would consider returning to the board.

After the meeting took place at the Clarence Hotel, in Cathedral Yard, Exeter, Doble said: 'Mr Starr's commitment to Exeter City surprises me. I asked him why Exeter City and he said he felt he could put the club on the map. He has got some tremendous ideas to improve everything at the City and to get the fans back through the turnstiles.'

Starr then doubled his offer to Hill to buy his controlling stake in the club and hoped it would be a package that could not be turned down.

He tabled a bid of £200,000 to buy out Hill, and he reckoned that with the debts the club had, the bid was worth about £500,000.

After watching Exeter City defeat Wrexham 5-0 with Ronnie Jepson netting four of the goals, a chant went up around the ground of 'Freddie Starr's red and white army'.

However, once again the comedian's offer was rejected, and as a result one of the club directors, Stuart Dawe, resigned from the board.

Reading a prepared statement, Chief Executive Trump said: 'The board has unanimously supported the president's rejection of Mr Starr's final offer. Mr Dawe has resigned as a director.'

Another attempt was made to buy the club, this time by a four-man consortium, which included Starr, Doble and former directors Peter Carter and Dawe.

But by 12th October 1993, Starr pulled out of any involvement with the club as he had been told by Doble that one of the conditions of the sale of the shares by Hill was that he and former director, Dawe, should not be allowed on any future board.

As a result of that Starr contacted his solicitors and accountants and they advised him not to get involved with Exeter City Football Club.

Starr said: 'I just hope that Alan Ball is not forced out for introducing me to the club. Please pass on my thanks to Ball and his staff, but particularly the fans for supporting me. I hope that Exeter City continue to rise up the table.'

Exeter City 1994–95
Back row: Exeter City apprentices.
Second row: Scott Daniels, Toby Redwood, Stuart Storer, Peter Fox, Chris White, Jason Minett, Andy Harris.
Third row: Peter Whiston, Ronnie Robinson, Gary Worthington, Russell Coughlin, Jon Brown, Mark Brown, Craig Taylor, David Cooper.
Fourth row: Danny Bailey, Ronnie Jepson, Mark Chapman (Physio), Alan Ball (Manager), Mike Radford (Youth Development Officer), George Kent (Community Officer), Alan Tonge, Jason Percival.
Front row: Exeter City apprentices.

Exeter City chairman Ivor Doble ruled out any possibility of the club moving from its St James' Park home to an out-of-town site, but was also seeking to make major changes to the ground that had been home for the Grecians since 1904.

In January 1994 the City board of directors met with architects to discuss the most dramatic facelift to the ground in the club's history.

City were considering total redevelopment of the Big Bank end of the ground, turning the terracing into an all-seater grandstand, with a pub and leisure facility beneath the structure.

'These proposals are at a very advanced stage', said Doble. 'We have not drawn up the plans yet, but we are certainly looking into the feasibility of a complete rebuilding of that end of the ground.

'First and foremost we want to improve facilities for Exeter City fans. The Big Bank has been there in its present form for 80 years. We believe it is time for an improvement and we are talking with architects and structural engineers to see what ideas they can come up with.'

Doble admitted that he had been impressed by Torquay United's Ellacombe End development, built with the help of a £300,000 grant from the Football Trust.

'We are thinking on something similar', he added. 'We know that there are various grants that we might be able to claim to help fund a project of this type.'

The City directors were keen that any redevelopment would not reduce the capacity of the Big Bank, which at that time stood at 3,500.

With the latest set of club accounts revealing that they made a loss of almost £350,000 in the 12 months up to June 1992, City were anxious that any redevelopment should be a profit-making venture.

'We believe that a new supporters' club incorporated in the project could be very well supported and that would be good for the club', added Doble. 'The Centre Spot is falling to pieces. It is like a rotten pear. We feel our supporters should have better facilities than that.'

Early indications were that the bill for the extensive rebuild would run into seven figures, but it did not put Exeter City off the project.

Doble ruled out the possibility of the club moving to an out-of-town site.

'This is something we have looked at in the past but it definitely not on the agenda now', explained Doble. 'I know that Torquay United were thinking of a similar move some time ago and they are glad that they have stayed where they are.

'You would not have the same number of people visiting the club facilities on a normal working day either. The way forward is for the club to press on with plans for improvements for our present ground. Why throw away everything you have got? Why not just make the very best of it you can?'

Three months later – in April 1994 – after announcing the plans for the redevelopment of the Big Bank, Doble said that they may have to be shelved if the planners imposed a height restriction on the £1 million-plus project.

He believed that the plans could be thrown out over concerns that the four-storey cantilever stand was too high and to reduce the size of the stand would make the project unviable as they would lose the option of having executive boxes on the top floor and as a result revenue of £60,000 per year.

DID YOU KNOW?

It was a disastrous season for Exeter City as they finished rock bottom of the Football League in 1994–95. Fortunately for the Grecians, they avoided the drop into the Conference as champions Macclesfield Town were deemed not to have a ground meeting required league standards.

In May 1994 the *Express & Echo* reported that Exeter City could be about to quit St James' Park for a new out-of-town stadium. Directors had been locked in discussion with local developer Rockeagle over the possibility of moving to the Matford Marshes site on the southern outskirts of the city.

Despite the previous announcement that the club would not leave St James' Park, the City directors were thought to be re-examining the viability of leaving the Park as ambitious proposals to give the ground a facelift seemed certain to be vetoed by the city planners.

It was felt that a switch to a new out-of-town stadium would cure long-standing problems with parking and traffic congestion around St James' Park.

However, a move to Matford Marshes was anything but clear cut. Although Rockeagle were given permission to redevelop 18 acres of the 127-acre site, there were fierce objections from residents and conservationists that could have led to the plan being the subject of a public inquiry.

The redevelopment plans for the Big Bank were, as expected, rejected by the City Council and this prompted the club to seek an alternative site.

'We will now have to explore all other alternative avenues', said City chairman, Ivor Doble. 'We are very disappointed that the planners have blocked the redevelopment that we considered vital to safeguard the future of the club.'

The City Council then called for a meeting with the football club to try to find a solution for Exeter City's need to expand and improve its ground.

As well as Matford Marshes, it was revealed that land earmarked for a shopping development could be another possible site for a new football stadium.

The former Digby Hospital site at Rydon Lane and some surrounding land was regarded as an ideal site, as the land owned by the Council had already got planning for leisure facilities.

Exeter City's commercial manager, Steve Birley, came out strongly in favour of a move to a new site, away from St James' Park.

'It is widely accepted that the facilities at dear old St James' Park are archaic to put it mildly', he said. 'A move to a purpose-built stadium is a must if Exeter City Football Club is to maintain a place in the modern game of professional football.'

On 1st June 1994 it was reported that the club were confident that they could raise up to £10 million required to build the new out-of-town stadium.

Doble, and fellow director, Peter Carter, had attended a meeting in London with a three-man delegation from the Football Trust.

'They could not make any promises, but will definitely provide some of the money we need', said Doble. 'We have now got to go away and put a precise figure on what it will cost to build the stadium.'

The City board would try to seek outline planning permission for a 15,000 all-seater stadium at Matford Marshes, a site owned by Rockeagle, and negotiations over a land swap deal with the developer, which would give them the club's St James' Park headquarters, possibly for housing.

The next major announcement came in July 1994, when the proposed ground move to Matford Marshes was put on hold.

It was believed that the City Council preferred the Grecians to move to a site at Digby alongside the new railway station that was to be shortly constructed there on the branch line to Exmouth.

Unfortunately for City, the club's financial position took a dramatic turn for the worse, the Grecians then found themselves in administration, and the plans for a ground at Matford Marshes were rejected by the Council.

EXETER CITY FOOTBALL CLUB'S

PLAN FOR <u>SURVIVAL</u>-NEEDS <u>YOUR</u> SUPPORT!!
THE CITY OF EXETER WILL NOT BE THE SAME
WITHOUT ITS LEAGUE FOOTBALL CLUB

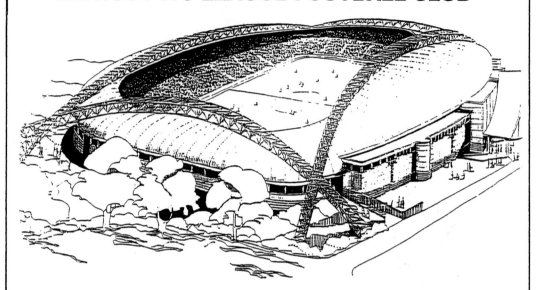

The only way that Exeter City FC can secure its future is by a development proposal to build a modern stadium at Matford. This can only be financed by development elsewhere, i.e. at no cost to the local ratepayer nor handouts from the City Council. The Administrator David Peacock of accountants Ernst & Young has said that: "Without this proposal <u>he would with regret have to close down the Football Club and League football in Exeter would be finished.</u>"

If you would like to see League football <u>SURVIVE</u> in Exeter whether you are an active supporter or not please write a <u>LETTER OF SUPPORT</u> as soon as possible to:

The Director of Planning
Exeter City Council
Civic Centre, Exeter EX1 1JN

WE NEED EXETER CITY COUNCIL TO SUPPORT US-PLEASE WRITE TODAY.

Thank you in anticipation of your support
Ivor Doble (Chairman)

Exeter City AFC Limited, St James Park, Exeter, EX4 6PX

EACH MEMBER OF A HOUSEHOLD MAY WRITE A LETTER

Not for the first time in its history, Exeter City Football Club's very future was threatened. In administration in 1994–95, the following passionately written article from the match programme considered the situation at the time:

'Once upon a time there was a professional football club in Exeter. It represented the city and surrounding area for 91 years (1904–1995). It was not what you could call successful, but it did have its moments and brought a lot of joy and happiness to people who celebrated with the club in its time of glory.

'It also brought a lot of publicity to the city of Exeter and no sooner the club did achieve a bit of glory, F.A. Cup runs, Fourth Division Championship, then all of a sudden it gained a lot of friends, supporters and sponsors. All bathed in the success achieved by Exeter City Football Club. everyone felt part of the club and wanted to be associated with it.

'There were also the lean or simply indifferent years, the struggles. No glory, just a hard slog. Then in November 1994, just over four years after one of the greatest moments in the club history – Exeter City Football Club were declared financially ill.

'The "illness" was soon announced as critical by the administrators who had been called in by the club to try and arrest the situation and plan ahead for the future. Plans for a new stadium at Matford, which would have secured the club's well being were rejected by the City Council. But the creditors of Exeter City F.C. allowed the club to try and find another solution, but it had to be found quickly. They couldn't wait forever.

'All of a sudden, those so-called supporters and sponsors disappeared (apart from the hard core with the club at heart). The club directors were left to take the criticism. The administrators were criticised for not telling the supporters what was going on. The City Council were blamed for not allowing the club to build a new stadium at Matford. Everyone was blaming each other as time ran out for the Grecians.

'Results on the field suffered. There was even a move to blame the situation on the team manager and his assistant. The administrators, directors, players and management were concerned what would happen, as were the dwindling band of supporters who still paid their money at the turnstiles. The true supporters of the club who one could rely on through thick and thin.

'Too many people though appeared to be blaming each other, instead of trying to pull together and find a solution. The whole situation was becoming nasty at times. Why couldn't everyone simply stick together for the good of the club? Was that too much to ask in the hour of need?

'The Football League wanted an answer by 18th May 1995 as to whether there would be an Exeter City F.C. in existence for the following season. The administrators at Ernst & Young, were working hard to ensure that there would be a future, but would their efforts be enough?

'Four schemes were proposed for new stadiums, two of which were eventually withdrawn, leaving the clear favourite, the Old Rydon Lane site.

'Then there were Beazer Homes who still liked the idea of a site at Matford. Both were allied to other development (a mixture of housing, leisure uses etc). Both schemes had their opponents, plenty of NIMBYs (not in my back yard).

'The City Council could not discuss them until the very last minute – possibly a day before the Football League deadline. The uncertainty dragged on, the administrator seemed a little more hopeful, but the supporters were still very worried.

'The last Football League fixture of the 1994–95 season was played at St James' Park against Fulham on 29th April. Even the pages of the match programme were black edged, Still the future of the club was not known.

'Two days before the game the scheme for the Old Rydon Lane site was withdrawn, causing even more gloom about the dire situation the club now found itself in.

'The 8,000 fans who had been present for an F.A. Cup match against Aston Villa 12 months earlier had disappeared. This despite the fact they were "life long supporters". For the game against Fulham, only half that number were likely to be present. Where were the rest?

'The match ended. Everyone went home with more than a little sadness in their hearts, not knowing whether they would be able to take their places on the St James' Park terraces ever again.

'The City directors, back room staff and players,

the supporters, administrators and the creditors, all waited for the final decision that would either guarantee the existence of a club that had faithfully served the community for 90-plus years, or one that would condemn it forever.

'The day of reckoning arrived. Interested parties waited with baited breath. The Football League was finally informed ... the decision was ... tears of happiness and relief ... or tears of sadness or despair?'

EXETER CITY FOOTBALL TRUST

THIS TRUST FUND HAS BEEN SET UP FOR THE PURPOSE OF SUSTAINING THE EXETER CITY FOOTBALL CLUB FOR THE SEASON 1995/6.

FUNDS RAISED WILL BE KEPT IN A NEW BANK ACCOUNT UNDER THE CONTROL OF THE TRUSTEES AND NOT MIXED WITH ANY FUNDS HELD BY THE ADMINISTRATORS OR DIRECTORS.

THE FUTURE OF LEAGUE FOOTBALL IN EXETER IS AT STAKE AND TIME IS RUNNING OUT!

WE CALL UPON THE CITIZENS OF EXETER TO ASSIST WHERE POSSIBLE BY SUPPORTING AT LEAST ONE OF THE FOLLOWING FUND-RAISING ACTIVITIES:.

WORKPLACE COLLECTIONS
CLUB AND PUB COLLECTIONS
SATURDAY SHOPPING COLLECTIONS
COLLECTION IN SHOPS
COLLECTIONS IN SCHOOLS & COLLEGES
SPONSORSHIP FOR VARIOUS ACTIVITIES

MONEY MAY BE PAID INTO: EXETER CITY FOOTBALL TRUST
c/o NATIONAL WESTMINSTER BANK
59, HIGH STREET, EXETER

WE NEED YOUR HELP NOW!

Exeter City may have been struggling both on and off the field, but all that was forgotten as they produced one of the shocks of the F.A. Cup third round when they held Premiership Everton to a goalless draw at St James' Park on 10th December 1999.

What made the result even more remarkable was the fact that the Grecians were forced to field a substitute keeper, as regular custodian Stuart Naylor, who had performed first-half heroics keeping Everton at bay, was injured and had to be replaced by rookie keeper Jason Matthews.

With St James' Park in the throes of rebuilding, it was a three-sided ground that greeted the Everton fans as the old, open to the elements, Big Bank terracing had been demolished to make way for a brand new covered terrace. This much reduced the capacity and 6,045 squeezed into the ground, with many thousands more watching on BBC TV's *Match of the Day* later that evening.

Exeter City: Stuart Naylor (Jason Matthews), Jon Richardson, Rob Dewhurst, Chris Curran, Jon Gittens, Graeme Power, Paul Buckle, Jason Rees, Geoff Breslan (Steve Flack), Lee Boylan (Barry McConnell), Gary Alexander.

Everton: Paul Gerrard, Abel Xavier, David Weir, Richard Dunne, David Unsworth, Nick Barmby (Michael Ball), Don Hutchison, John Collins, Mark Pembridge (Joe-Max Moore), Kevin Campbell, Francis Jeffers.

Everton really should have taken one of their numerous chances throughout the game, but the grit and determination of the City players prevented them doing so.

Even when Exeter lost Naylor at half-time, Everton were unable to find a way past the inexperienced replacement. Jason Matthews' saves, when called upon, earned him the sponsor's Man of the Match award, and quite deservedly so too, for it was him, and him alone, who kept Exeter's hopes alive and if everyone was honest, they wanted just that. Everton wanted it just as much towards the end – a replay back at Goodison Park.

Because of the reduced ground capacity, City had approached the Football Association, with Everton's agreement, to ask if the tie could be switched to Goodison, but this was turned down. So it was ironic that the teams would now battle it out on that very ground, albeit in a replay.

Andrew Longmore, in his match report for the *Independent*, described the afternoon: 'Two

Stuart Naylor.

goalkeepers, one summoned from redecorating his house to play for one final season, the other imported from the Screwfix Direct League on a free transfer, kept Exeter's Cup hopes alive for another lucrative fortnight. Who said the magic of the F.A. Cup died with Manchester United's defection? Exeter thoroughly deserved their standing ovation at the final whistle.'

Speaking about Matthews who replaced the concussed Naylor, City manager Peter Fox said: 'He was on decent money as an electrician. Now he's not! I wasn't surprised by Jason's performance and nor were the players. He's determined to make it and I'm sure he will.'

Cup hero Matthews, gave up his job as an electrician to try his luck in professional football. The career move was costing him nearly £300 a week. He said: 'I am a lot worse off coming to Exeter City, but being a professional footballer is the best job in the land. I was dead nervous at first.'

As for Naylor and the injury he sustained, it was after a one-two with Jeffers that Campbell surged through and as he jumped over Naylor, caught the goalkeeper's head. 'I saw Campbell trying to avoid me', Naylor said afterwards, 'and that's the last I remember.'

To be fair, the gulf in class was vast, and on another day Everton would have won easily, but they hadn't planned that they would be facing, not one, but two goalkeepers who were on the top of their form.

Little was seen of the Exeter City attack, and the man in goal at the other end of the park, had very little to do in comparison to the Grecian goalkeeping duo.

But at the end of the game City were delighted just to earn a replay and a lucrative pay day from their visit to Goodison Park.

No one gave the Grecians a chance at Goodison Park, the replay being played on 21st December 1969, yet once again City defied all the odds and almost took their Premiership opponents to a period of extra-time, before the deadlock was eventually broken five minutes from the end of normal time.

Everton had decided that the tie would not attract their usual attendance and as an incentive cut the entry prices, however, only 16,869 turned up, and that included hundreds of Exeter fans.

Once again, little was seen of Exeter as an attacking force, with huge amounts of possession from Everton, but it wasn't until the 85th minute that the tie was eventually settled when a deflected shot from Collins was pounced on by Nick Barmby who tucked away the vital winner.

The teams lined up as follows:

Everton: Paul Gerrard, David Unsworth, Richard Dunne, David Weir, Alex Cleland, Nick Barmby, Don Hutchison, John Collins, Mark Pembridge, Kevin Campbell, Francis Jeffers.

Exeter City: Stuart Naylor, Graeme Power, Jon Gittens, Rob Dewhurst, Jon Richardson, Jason Rees, Paul Buckle, Chris Curran, Geoff Breslan (Barry McConnell), Gary Alexander, Jamie Robinson (Steve Flack).

Everton manager Walter Smith said: 'I was beginning to prepare for extra-time. Any mistakes that Exeter made went unpunished and we made life hard for ourselves. But the most important thing is that we are through.'

City boss Peter Fox added: 'I am proud of my players. But if we are honest, it was the right result. I did not even dare to plan for extra-time, because I've been caught out by football too many times in the past.'

HOW THE GRECIANS REACHED THE THIRD ROUND

29th October 1999: round one
Exeter City 2 Eastwood Town 1
City team: Stuart Naylor, Jon Richardson, Jamie Robinson, Shaun Gale, Chris Curran, Jon Gittens, Peter Smith (Paul Buckle), Jason Rees, Steve Flack, Shayne Bradley, Kofi Nyamah (Geoff Breslan).
Scorers: City – Flack 40th, Gale 47th
Eastwood – Smith 56th
Attendance: 2,441

19th November 1999: round two
Exeter City 2 Aldershot Town 0
City team: Stuart Naylor, Jon Richardson, Graeme Power, Paul Buckle (Rob Dewhurst), Chris Curran, Jon Gittens, Jamie Robinson, Jason Rees, Gary Alexander (Robert Speakman), Steve Flack, Lee Boylan (Chris Holloway).
Scorers: City – Alexander 32nd, Flack 55th
Attendance: 4,151

The article below, written at the time by Neil Le Milliere for Supporters Direct, sums up the events of the torrid 2002–03 season:

'The colourful 12-month reign of John Russell and Mike Lewis at Exeter City did offer signs of hope and better things to come amid the recriminations, unpaid bills, boardroom rifts and threats to the very existence of the club.

'But there was to be no happy ending for City's embattled – and eventually embittered – co-owners who, in the end, were left isolated, unloved and ultimately with little option but to exit St James' Park.

'Russell and Lewis arrived at Exeter City for the start of the 2002–03 season warning: "We have no magic wand to wave."

'"We are practical, reasonable men", insisted Lewis upon the duo's arrival. "Our target within three years is to get the club back to a position where it is washing its face again – by that I mean not losing money."

'The involvement of celebrity spoonbender Uri Geller and son Daniel – who were listed as co-chairman and co-vice-chairman – undeniably raised the profile of the club. And the surreal sight of pop megastar Michael Jackson parading around St James' Park in a vintage car set the tone for a madcap 12 months.

'Russell and Lewis even made a failed first attempt to lure Paul Gascoigne out of semi-retirement, but the homecoming of championship hero and ex-Premiership goalkeeper Kevin Miller maintained the feel-good factor at the club.

'And when former England and Manchester United winger Lee Sharpe signed on the dotted line in time for the second game of the season – in return for a fee of £3,000 per game and against the wishes of manager John Cornforth – the sky seemed to be the limit.

'But the duo's incessant tinkering in team affairs – as highlighted by the disastrous recruitment of Argentinian flop Sebastien Scalise and the quick exit made by Sharpe – was starting to take its toll on Cornforth.

'On 11th September the club posted record £500,000 losses in the year up to June 2002. A few days later the duo revealed how they planned to cut City's £1.8m debts – by knocking down the old grandstand, replacing it with a shallower stand and earmarking surrounding land and the old Centre Spot clubhouse for housing development.

'The only drawback being that St James' Park was owned by Exeter City Council, who showed little enthusiasm for the project.

'But by cost-cutting and the slashing of administration staff at the club, the pair announced they had managed to trim City's weekly losses from £8,500 to £5,000.

'Supporters were divided over the sacking of Cornforth just 12 games into the season – they would soon become united in their condemnation of rookie successor Neil McNab on the recommendation of World Cup legend and former Grecians' boss Alan Ball.

'Ex-Darlington boss Gary Bennett was appointed as assistant boss even though he had never before met the new man in charge at St James' Park.

'And as pressure mounted on the ex-Spurs midfielder, it also increased for Lewis and Russell as stories of employment tribunals, unpaid bills, uneasy creditors and threats of winding-up orders began to surface.

'The city council then publicly demanded to know why charities had received no cash from Jackson's summer appearance – as did firms still waiting for payment for the equipment and services they supplied for the event.

'By early December, nine companies had lodged county court judgments against the club and the Sheriff of Devon had even taken "walking possession" of the floodlights at St James' Park.

'Following a public spat with the Exeter City Supporters' Trust over board representation, it emerged that the Gellers had failed to officially register themselves as directors of the club.

'On 24th February 2003, after just three wins from 20 league games and five straight defeats, McNab and Bennett were finally shown the door.

'A replacement was appointed just 24 hours later – and Gary Peters soon discovered the harsh realities of managing Exeter City Football Club.

'McNab had used up the club's entire allocation of loan deals in his fruitless search for success, a transfer embargo was imposed for failing to meet an instalment of Devine's fee, six directors resigned following an F.A. report into the state of City's finances and the Gellers left the board on the advice of concerned officials at the Football League.

'Peters threatened to quit over a planned fans' protest against Russell and Lewis before the pair were ordered to vacate their St James' Centre clubhouse over rent arrears owed to holding company OTR (Exeter) Ltd.

'And despite the prayers of Geller – and a remarkable return of 20 points from Peters' 13 games in charge – the Grecians lost their fight against relegation on the final afternoon of a fraught 2002–03 campaign.

'Geller promptly dropped another bombshell by announcing he had "disassociated" himself from Russell and Lewis following an incident at the club – and the next day called on the pair to quit St James' Park for the good of Exeter City.

'On 12th May, Lewis and Russell turned up at St James' Park to find the locks to their offices had been changed by landlords OTR, who then agreed to let them use a single room in the building.

'The pair's revelation that they were considering entering into a Creditors' Voluntary Agreement – a move designed to address the debts of a struggling company – raised the prospect of a points deduction before the start of next season.

'And there was no way back after Lewis, Russell and his wife Gillian were arrested and interviewed – but not [at the time] charged – by fraud squad officers investigating alleged financial irregularities at the club.

'Russell emerged from Heavitree Road Police Station in typically defiant mood, vowing to clear his name and promising to return to his desk the following day. Lewis, on the other hand, drove off to his partner's home in Swansea saying: "I won't be going back at all, ever – not the way I feel tonight."

'And his wish soon became the command of Ivor Doble, former chairman, club president and majority shareholder at St James' Park. Once Doble had publicly called on the duo to quit the Grecians, Russell was forced to admit: "It is quite obvious now that we can't stay under these circumstances."

'Companies House was officially notified of the pair's departure – paving the way for the Supporters' Trust to complete their takeover at St James' Park.

'Peters signalled his intention to leave within hours of this changing of the guard, leaving the club without a manager, with only an interim board and needing to raise £100,000 in seven days just to meet its monthly wage bill.'

DID YOU KNOW?

Manager Neil McNab, and his assistant, were appointed by Exeter City in October 2002. Exeter were 21st in the Third Division after picking up just three wins from their opening 13 games.

'Both Neil and Gary come with the highest recommendations', said Exeter chairman John Russell. 'When we mentioned their names to other managers in the game we got a massively positive feedback. What we like most about them is that they are both hungry and will live and eat Exeter City.'

Exeter City had to forget about how Swansea City were faring against Hull City, concentrate on the task in hand and win against Southend United at St James' Park.

This was a make or break game, and even if City won, then their fate could have been decided by the Swans. If the Welshmen won their game, then the Grecians' proud Football League history would come to an end.

Unfortunately that is exactly what happened. The Grecians duly defeated Southend United 1-0, but Swansea won at the Vetch as well, thus condemning Exeter to life in the Conference.

Saturday 3rd May 2003 would go down as one of, if not the darkest day in the club's history. The end of a turbulent season both on and off the field.

Prior to the game City boss Gary Peters said: 'There is only one right way to approach this game and that is as a football match. We've just got to go out and win the game and collect three points. We've got to do our job and not be concerned with what Swansea or Hull might do.'

Exeter City never seemed to be out of the headlines during the ill-fated season and many described the club as being more like a 'circus' show, rather than one that concentrated on playing football.

The Grecians had attracted showbiz personalities such as psychic celebrity Uri Geller and illusionist and escapologist David Blaine. They had made pop icon Michael Jackson honorary director, signed former England and Manchester United winger Lee Sharpe and even bid for Paul Gascoigne.

But now, on this final day of their Football League history, nerves were on edge for most of the 9,036 capacity crowd, with many more locked outside the ground.

The kick off was delayed for quarter of an hour because of crowd congestion and by the time the teams emerged the gates were closed with the hundreds still outside anxiously reduced to snatching a view from window ledges and any other vantage points they could find.

Peters, brought in as the club's third manager of the season, following on from John Cornforth and Neil McNab, had transformed the playing fortunes, but it was to prove to be too late.

'If you equate the results since I've taken over, we're playing like a play-off team. We've beaten Wrexham, who are already promoted, and Lincoln and York, who are in the play-offs shake-up', said Peters.

For City co-chairman John Russell, he was to hold an unwanted record of being the first and only man in charge of two different clubs (Scarborough being his former club) to be relegated to the Conference.

It was the off-the-field shenanigans that grabbed the headlines far too often in the months leading up to the final game.

Directors had resigned in April 2003 following a report by the Football Association's Financial Advisory Unit that concluded Exeter were insolvent and highlighted practices that the outgoing directors called 'deeply disturbing'.

Geller, named as the club's co-chairman even though he was never registered as a director, also departed and the club was left in the control of two men, Russell and Mike Lewis.

But even after the club had suffered relegation to the non-league ranks, the two men were still talking up the club's prospects promising that season ticket prices would be frozen.

Lewis acknowledged that the year they had been in charge had contained 'many changes and some trauma', but pledged better times.

Geller, who wept at the final whistle as the reality of relegation sunk home, said: 'This has been a terrible day for me and for all the fans. I never thought this could happen. I just hope we can manage to keep the club going. We just have to survive because there is no way we can let down the people of Exeter and the supporters of this club.'

Russell added: 'I feel like we have been shovelling crap uphill for the last 11 months trying to stay afloat but we won't give up and are determined to get through this. We must find a way of getting rid of the debt and then we can take the club forward.'

The team that represented Exeter City in their final match in the Football League lined up: Kevin Miller, Scott Hiley, Chris Todd, Santos Gaia (Ciaran Kilheeney), Phil Baker, Justin Walker, James Coppinger, Kwame Ampadu (Glenn Cronin), Sean Devine, Carl Pettefer.

How long would it be (if ever) before the Grecians found themselves back in the Football League?

A group of Exeter City supporters took control of Exeter City F.C. in May 2003, hopefully bringing to an end a traumatic period in the club's history.

The three fans – all members of the Exeter City Supporters' Trust – had the tough task of turning around the debt-ridden club's fortunes, which was reported at the time to be around £2.5m in debt.

Trust chairman Ian Huxham, chief executive Terry Pavey and Julian Tagg, took over from chairman John Russell and vice-chairman Mike Lewis – who formally left the club on Thursday 22nd May 2003.

The new board believed that the key to saving the club could be the possible backing of Exeter City Council. Mr Russell and Mr Lewis took the decision to quit the club after just 12 months in charge.

It followed City's relegation to the Conference – and the arrest of Russell and Lewis following complaints of financial irregularities.

They had been bailed to report back to Exeter police the following September. Both had strenuously denied the claims, with Russell reportedly describing the arrests as 'an absolute joke'.

As part of the handover of power, the club's biggest shareholder Ivor Doble was likely to be asked to hand his shareholding over to the Trust to give them a controlling interest.

The outgoing Exeter chairman said he was glad to be getting out: 'It's an absolute mega-mountain off my back – it's a relief', he told BBC Devon Online. 'We should never have got involved there in the first place. For much of the past 12 months, all we've done is battle against the media, past and present directors, and some of the supporters.'

'Hand on heart, we have made mistakes, I have to admit that – we're only human. But it's taken us several months to know the state of play here. We now know what is owed. That's one advantage the Trust has which we didn't have. We wish the members of the Trust all the best and we hope they turn things round. It's a challenge we started to lose in the end. They'll give it a very good go, and they're getting help from certain bodies which didn't give us any help.'

Local businessman Mr Huxham, admitted the new directors had taken on a huge job, but said that the future of Exeter City could have been 'catastrophic' had they not made the move.

He said: 'This was actually an easy decision, because we all love Exeter City Football Club. If it can be saved, we'll do all we can to save it.

'I think when the chips are down, a lot of people in this city will stand up and help save the club. I would love to think that the city council would help the Trust – we want this to be a community club.'

Huxham said he hoped the Trust would be involved in the long-term future of the club, but at the moment, they were taking things one step at a time.

He added that Russell and Lewis had not asked for any cash to buy out the club. At the time the Trust had around 350 members, and was raising thousands of pounds towards the cause.

Huxham was to subsequently leave his role as managing director of Exeter City F.C. and later unsuccessfully pursued a wrongful dismissal case against the club.

FINAL LEAGUE TABLE (BOTTOM SECTION ONLY) – FOOTBALL LEAGUE SEASON 2002–03

Nationwide League Division Three

	P	W	D	L	F	A	W	D	L	F	A	Pts
Darlington	46	8	10	5	36	27	4	8	11	22	32	54
Boston United	46	11	6	6	34	22	4	7	12	21	34	54
Macclesfield Town	46	8	6	9	29	28	6	6	11	28	35	54
Southend United	46	12	1	10	29	23	5	2	16	18	36	54
Leyton Orient	46	9	6	8	28	24	5	5	13	23	37	53
Rochdale	46	7	6	10	30	30	5	10	8	33	40	52
Bristol Rovers	46	7	7	9	25	27	5	8	10	25	30	51
Swansea City	46	9	6	8	28	25	3	7	13	20	40	49
Carlisle United	46	5	5	13	26	40	8	5	10	26	38	49
EXETER CITY	**46**	**7**	**7**	**9**	**24**	**31**	**4**	**8**	**11**	**26**	**33**	**48**
Shrewsbury Town	46	5	6	12	34	39	4	8	11	28	53	41

Life after the Football League began for Exeter City on 9th August 2003. The Grecians now found themselves in uncharted territory – the Nationwide Conference.

This season they wouldn't be playing the likes of Swansea City, Hartlepool United, York City or AFC Bournemouth, now City had trips to Woking, Leigh RMI, Margate and Morecambe.

But was this 'new' venture so very different to what they had become accustomed to since 1920? For their first-ever opponents were a familiar name – Halifax Town – who City had met on many previous occasions in the Football League.

This time though, the fixture was a non-league one, a fact that took some getting used to for the supporters of Exeter City, but at least the opening match was at St James' Park.

An attendance of 3,722 was at the Park, not a lot different to what City were attracting when in the League, and they were curious to see how the Grecians would fare, not just in this game, but throughout the season.

City lined up: James Bittner, Barry McConnell, Alex Jeannin, Glenn Cronin, Scott Hiley, Chris Todd, James Coppinger, Kwame Ampadu (Martin Thomas), Steve Flack, Reinier Moor (Sean Canham), Gareth Sheldon (Les Afful).

The Grecians came within minutes of winning their first Conference fixture and making the perfect start, but Halifax had other ideas.

The *Express & Echo* report of the game read: 'Five minutes left on the watch and a new chapter in Exeter City's future was being deliciously coated in a momentous victory.

'Steve Flack's header looked to have powered the Grecians to confident first stride on their journey back towards the Football League.

'The plot had already been hatched and the day mapped out by the boisterous band of City supporters who flocked to a sun-drenched St James' Park.

'A wave of optimism had spread around an encouraging opening day crowd of 3,722 – the Conference's second highest of the day – and as the countdown began to the final whistle it looked every bit as though everything had gone exactly according to plan.

'The late smash and grab raid courtesy of a Lewis Killeen goal was like an arrow through the

Scott Hiley. (www.cheggerspics.co.uk)

heart of a side that had battled so valiantly for the entire encounter.

'As the Halifax players leapt into the air to celebrate, the look on their faces suggested they had been dealt the perfect get out of jail card.'

City had taken the lead when Moor was hauled back by a defender. The subsequent free-kick was duly dispatched by Kwame Ampadu and as the ball curled its way menacingly towards goal, Flack towered above everyone to power a header into the roof of the net.

Despite a 15-minute spell at the start of the second half when City tore into Halifax, they were unable to increase their advantage and as a result were made to pay for it.

In the 85th minute, an outswinging corner from the right evaded the City defence and as Parke delicately flicked on, Killeen was stooping at the far post to nod home the equaliser. It was a hammer blow that City had not deserved.

So City could not get off to a perfect start in the Conference, but the quality of football on show wasn't a lot different to what had been seen at the Park the previous season in the Football League, so maybe life in the world of non-league football wasn't as bad after all.

How long it would be before City gained promotion though, was another question that remained unanswered, as they then faced trips to Telford United and Margate in the space of a week.

In October 2003 Exeter City successfully reached an agreement with the club's major creditors that ensured the immediate future of the club. The Grecians who were believed to have had debts of around £3.5m–£4.5m, met with creditors and thrashed out a Corporate Voluntary Arrangement (CVA).

Under the terms of the agreement, those owed money would receive 10p in the pound, to be paid off over the following five years. Among the creditors were former members of the board including ex-chairman Ivor Doble, the Inland Revenue and building firms who worked on redeveloping St James' Park.

Club chairman Ian Huxham said: 'This is a huge relief. This gives us a real chance now to take this club forward. But we shouldn't be under any illusion that this is anything other than the start of it – the hard work has still to come.'

It emerged that 88 per cent of the people and businesses owed money by the club agreed to accept the deal – well above the 75 per cent needed. If the deal hadn't been struck, the club would probably have gone into liquidation.

Even though the creditors had agreed to write off most of the debts, it still left City needing to find 10 per cent of the money owed – as well as the ongoing week-to-week running costs.

City's financial adviser Stephen Allinson was reported as saying that the club wasn't out of the woods: 'The important thing for everyone to realise is that this is the start, not the finish. But the club is committed to raise the 10p in the pound – and raise the money for ongoing expenses.'

The football club, run by the Exeter City Supporters' Trust, inherited terrible problems when it took over the previous month. David Treharne of the Trust sympathised with those who were owed money, but said it was down to bad housekeeping in the past.

He said one of the keys to City's long-term

THE TRUST

Exeter City Supporters' Trust

survival would be renegotiating deals made last year, and grooming the club's own youth players – as that would reduce City's big wage bill.

It was revealed that the major creditors were the builders Mowlem, owed around £800,000 for building two stands at the ground; £500,000 outstanding in tax and VAT; a £160,000 loan from the Football Foundation; plus £1.1m in loans from former directors.

The Supporters' Trust hoped that the CVA would enable them to deal with the debts built up over years, which they inherited, and begin the long climb back to respectability for the club.

Former Exeter City F.C. chairman, Ivor Doble had previously asked the Supporters' Trust, which was relatively newly formed, to take over the running of the club, which it agreed to do even though it had no significant shareholding.

In August 2003, the Trust approached Doble to ask about buying his shares in the club. A month later a deal was struck that gave the Trust Doble's 63 per cent holding in Exeter City F.C.

The Grecians became the sixth English club, following Lincoln City, Chesterfield, York City, Enfield and AFC Wimbledon, to become majority-owned by supporters via the democratic, mutual model propounded by the government-backed initiative Supporters Direct.

Supporters Direct's development officer Dave Boyle said: 'As so often, the supporters stepped in when nobody else would, and with their club in crisis. They have steadied the ship so far and will be doing all they can to ensure the club doesn't die. It proves yet again that the future of clubs lies with their supporters, not sugar daddies.'

It was probably the most important F.A. Cup draw ever in the history of Exeter City. With the club having gone through an extremely serious phase financially and still battling to pay creditors, when the Grecians were paired with Manchester United, someone above must have been listening and smiling upon them.

The sound of sheer joy and delight resonated throughout the city of Exeter, and much further beyond, as it was announced: 'Manchester United will play – number 64 – Exeter City.'

Within minutes all hell broke loose. What a game. What a prospect. What a way forward for the club who would now earn enough from the one big pay day at Old Trafford to almost wipe out their entire deficit at a single stroke.

City had beaten Braintree Town, Grimsby Town of League Two and Doncaster Rovers of League One to reach the third round, and the Sunday afternoon draw proved to be the saving of the club. A trip to Manchester United on 8th January 2005 beckoned.

The days leading up to the game were best described as manic, as supporters by their thousands arranged travel to and from the game and queued for tickets when they went on sale at St James' Park.

Exeter City manager Alex Inglethorpe said: 'We're really looking forward to the game at Old Trafford. It is the plum draw in the F.A. Cup to face Manchester United.

'No disrespect to everyone else in the Premiership, but the allure of playing United at Old Trafford is the tie that every non-league club dreams of.

'We are taking 9,000 fans with us up to Manchester. We are so proud that we can give this opportunity to our supporters. They are the ones who have been travelling all round the country to cheer us on at places like Tamworth and Burton. So to be able to offer them the chance to see us play at Old Trafford is a great way to say thank you to the fans.

'The F.A. Cup is a very welcome distraction, but our league position in the Conference is the most important thing. We really need to make sure that we do our best to gain promotion this season.

'The problems that Exeter have had are well documented. The F.A. Cup tie means that we could potentially start next season with an almost clean sheet of paper.

'It won't give me any more cash to spend on players or whatever. But it will mean that the club can continue forward without owing lots of money.

'I am not sure of the exact figures, but potentially the tie will bring in an awful lot of finance for us.'

Since the formation of the Premiership, no non-league team had beaten a side from the top flight in the F.A. Cup. Inglethorpe was philosophical about Exeter's chances against mighty Manchester United:

'Without sounding too corny, it is 11 men versus 11 on the pitch. I am sure United will have a lot more of the ball than us and create plenty of goalscoring opportunities. But there has to be a chance that we could win.

'Otherwise, we wouldn't play the game. If we didn't think we could get something out of it, then we wouldn't turn up! We would be wasting everyone's time! So we have to believe that there is a chance for us to do well at Old Trafford.

'We are not under any pressure to go and get a result. No one expects anything from us. So it is a match where we can go out and do the very best that we can. We need to be as organised as possible and just see what happens.'

The F.A. Cup has a history of producing upsets, none more so than what proved to be a truly incredible result as City held Manchester United to a goalless draw, and therefore earned not only a replay back at St James' Park, but potentially another money-spinning pay day.

Exeter City's 9,000 supporters in the crowd of 67,551 danced in near disbelief up in the stands as their Conference team humbled Manchester United on their own ground.

Manager Alex Ferguson put out a near second-string team and suffered the consequences. He sent on Paul Scholes, Cristiano Ronaldo and Alan Smith in a desperate attempt to stave off the replay, but Exeter held out to earn what seemed an unlikely replay.

The draw was no more than Exeter deserved. They played with a spirit and commitment you would expect, while United were in disarray for much of an afternoon that plunged them into an ever deeper state of embarrassment.

Deep into stoppage time it seemed United might still find a way through but Paul Scholes pushed the ball tantalisingly beyond the far post. The Exeter players raced towards their fans to join in the celebrations, as a bedraggled United sought refuge in the dressing room.

City boss Inglethorpe said:

'The whole experience has been an honour for everyone involved with the club. I always thought that if we got off to a good start and concentrated we would grow in confidence. That is what happened.

'I felt a great sense of pride, not just in the way we played, but in the way we conducted ourselves overall.

'I thought Sir Alex Ferguson showed a lot of regard for us. He had us watched twice and the players he put on the bench – like Ronaldo, Alan Smith and Paul Scholes – showed what he thought.

'He had a lot of internationals and experience in the side. I am immensely proud of my players and I think Sir Alex felt that too. He was very complimentary after the game and that means a lot.'

As for Sir Alex, after the disappointment and embarrassment of the result, he added:

'In my 18 years at the club that was the worst performance we have ever produced in the F.A. Cup. It is hard to get your head around it.

'If someone had told me before that the game would end 0-0, I would not have believed them. I know we played some young players, but that is not an excuse and we expect much more of them than that.'

Manchester United: Tim Howard, Phil Neville, Wes Brown, Gerard Pique, Jonathon Spector, Chris Eagles (Cristiano Ronaldo 63), Eric Djemba-Djemba, David Jones, Liam Miller (Paul Scholes 63), David Bellion (Alan Smith 76), Kieron Richardson.

Exeter City: Paul Jones, Scott Hiley, Gary Sawyer, Santos Gaia, Alex Jeannin, Marcus Martin, Danny Clay (Kwame Ampadu 66), Andy Taylor (Jake Edwards 89), Dean Moxey, Sean Devine, Steve Flack (Les Afful 74).

Exeter City club sponsors Flybe organised special flights to Manchester for the cup tie.

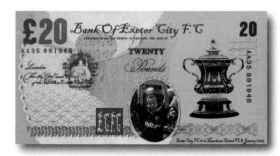

All manner of collectables were produced including this Bank of Exeter City F.C. £20 note!

After the Grecians' heroics in the first game at Old Trafford, they knew they would be facing a much stronger Manchester United team for the F.A. Cup third round replay.

In front of a full house of 9,033 and before the television cameras, City took the field knowing that they still had an almighty mountain to climb if they were to progress to the fourth round.

However they were safe in the knowledge that, from a financial point of view, the two games would be a lifeline and one that would virtually clear all the debts that had been hanging around the club's neck.

Prior to the replay, staged at St James' Park on Wednesday 19th January 2005, City boss Alex Inglethorpe calmly explained that 'it is all about us tonight, not them. We didn't do badly first time around, so we will prepare in much the same way for this match.'

Sure enough Manchester Untied manager Sir Alex Ferguson rang the changes and it was a team full of internationals that was to grace the St James' Park turf as the Old Trafford side attempted to put behind them the embarrassment of being held to a goalless draw by the Grecians in the first match.

City fought all the way throughout the 90 minutes, but in the end it was goals from Cristiano Ronaldo and Wayne Rooney that evaporated Exeter City's dreams. The Grecians though, to their immense credit, never made it easy for their illustrious opponents.

United enjoyed the greater share of possession in the first half, but they also spurned chances. They did, however, grab an early lead through Ronaldo who capitalised on some indecisiveness in the City defence, and for a while one wondered whether the flood gates would open and Exeter would be deluged as a consequence.

But City dug in and ran and ran. Little was seen of the Grecians as an attacking force, but for sheer work rate, they could not be faulted.

In the second half City enjoyed a much greater say in the proceedings and the longer the game went on, one hoped that a little piece of magic from someone would provide the equaliser.

And when Sean Devine stabbed the ball home from close range in the 75th minute, the explosion of celebration around the ground was brought to an abrupt halt as Devine had been ruled offside.

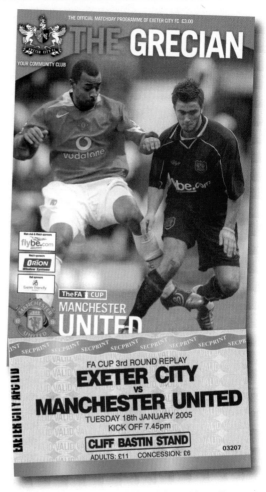

THE OFFICIAL MATCHDAY PROGRAMME OF EXETER CITY FC £3.00

THE GRECIAN

YOUR COMMUNITY CLUB

flybe.com

ORION

The FA CUP

MANCHESTER UNITED

EXETER CITY AFC LTD

FA CUP 3rd ROUND REPLAY

EXETER CITY
vs
MANCHESTER UNITED

TUESDAY 18th JANUARY 2005
KICK OFF 7.45pm

CLIFF BASTIN STAND

ADULTS: £11   CONCESSION: £6   03207

Eventually it took a last gasp finish from Rooney to kill off City's hopes. Substitute Louis Saha picked out the England striker and he went around keeper Paul Jones to roll the ball into an empty net.

City may have lost 2-0, but as the *Express & Echo* reported:

'The Grecians had mixed it with the millionaires over two matches and have won many friends along the way – quite a feat for a club, who 18 months ago, were faced with obscurity.'

Inglethorpe, naturally proud of his players added: 'Ultimately the best team won over the two cup games. They had the more chances and were the better team.

'But our players can sleep easy knowing that they have given all they had to give. The cup run was always going to be over at some point.

'I am very proud of the team. After conceding an early goal, it would have been easy to have feared the worst, but we showed we could be solid and we kept going.

'We took some risks towards the end because it's a one-off game – you may as well lose 2-0 as 1-0 in the end. We didn't have many chances so those we did have it was important to take.'

Ferguson, no doubt relieved that United made no mistake in the replay, said that Exeter City deserved a lot of credit:

'These two games have been absolutely fantastic, not just for Exeter, but for football as a whole', he said.

'I was listening to the radio this morning and all the talk was about Exeter City. It is just brilliant for them.

'It was a big drop when they went out of the Football League and fell into the Conference, but maybe these games can help lift them back up again.'

Exeter City: Paul Jones, Scott Hiley, Gary Sawyer, Danny Clay, Dean Moxey, Santos Gaia, Andy Taylor (Marcus Martin 86), Steve Flack (Jake Edwards 74), Kwame Ampadu (Les Afful 67), Alex Jeanin, Sean Devine.

Manchester United: Tim Howard, Gary Neville, Phil Neville, John O'Shea, Liam Miller (Darren Fletcher 66), Quinton Fortune, Paul Scholes, Eric Djemba-Djemba (Mikael Silvestre 80), Cristiano Ronaldo, Ryan Giggs (Louis Saha 70), Wayne Rooney.

WATCHING WAYNE: City's Andy Taylor and Kwame Ampadu fight to foil Manchester United striker Wayne Rooney

It's United... but City make them toil

MATCH REPORT PAGE 26 ● REACTION PAGE 28 ● THE FANS PAGE 30 ● ON THE BOX PAGE 32

The Express & Echo *special supplement the day after the City versus Manchester United replay.*

Paul Jones. (www.cheggerspics.co.uk)

Dean Moxey. (www.cheggerspics.co.uk)

DID YOU KNOW?

After defeating Exeter City in the third round of the F.A. Cup, Manchester United progressed all the way through to the final where they eventually lost 5-4 on penalties to Arsenal. After the two matches against the Grecians, they beat Middlesborough, Everton, Southampton and Newcastle United to reach the final.

Despite the disappointing outcome, 20th May 2007 will remain as one of the most important days in the history of Exeter City Football Club, only to be eclipsed 12 months later.

You had to pinch yourself to believe that you were actually watching the Grecians at England's foremost football stadium – and a brand new one at that – Wembley.

There were frenetic scenes in and around St James' Park in the days leading up to the actual Conference play-off final against Morecambe, as it seemed everyone wanted to be there, and that involved getting a ticket and arranging travel to London.

The City office staff and many volunteers burned the midnight oil to ensure that the whole operation ran as smoothly as possible, with a ticket agency actually taking over the worries of that aspect of things.

The trouble was, instead of the usual 3,500 regulars, all of a sudden City had a fan base of 30,000!

Some said they had been lifelong supporters (!), others just wanted to support their local club and cheer them onto a place back in the Football League, whilst there were even those who had never been to a football match before, but were caught up in the hype surrounding the game, and having the chance to visit the new-look Wembley Stadium was simply too good to miss.

City reached the final the hard way, as they are inclined to do! Playing Oxford United in the semi-final of the play-offs over two legs, the Grecians lost the first leg at St James' Park by the only goal of the game, in front of an attendance of 8,659.

With a lot to do in the second leg, City fans turned out in force for one of the most memorable games they were ever likely to see, as well over 1,000 Grecians made themselves heard.

At the end of 90 minutes Exeter were leading 2-1, so it was 2-2 on aggregate. City could have been down and out when Oxford netted first after just 27 minutes and therefore led 2-0 on aggregate, but they fought back like tigers to level matters with goals from Lee Phillips (39th minute) and Adam Stansfield (70th).

With neither team making the breakthrough in extra-time, the dreaded penalty shoot out took place with City winning 4-3 – Steve Tully firing home the winner – amidst unheralded scenes of joy.

Exeter were off to Wembley. Unbelievable, but true, and they would play Morecambe, a team they had a great record against, the Christie Park club having never previously beaten City.

At the end of the roller-coaster match at Oxford's Kassam Stadium, City manager Paul Tisdale said: 'It's fantastic – we're going to Wembley! But this is a step. The next step is winning and getting promotion.

'The players did us proud, they did the club proud, they did me proud and more importantly they did themselves proud. I'm very pleased for the club and the supporters.

'Ten days ago step one was to get into the play-offs, step two was to get to Wembley. Step three is to gain promotion. We've had a little celebration because it's hard not to, but we've quickly regained our composure. The celebrations lasted five minutes and we deserved them, but we know we've got a job to do.'

The great day arrived and Exeter emptied as trains, coaches and cars, full of City fans, headed to the 'big smoke' to help swell the attendance to 40,043, which proved to be the best ever for a Conference final at the time.

It was City's first-ever appearance at Wembley and many felt it was also the biggest day in the club's 103-year history, with the huge prize of a place back in the Football League at stake.

The first shock of the afternoon occurred before even a ball was kicked, as it was announced that goalkeeper Martin Rice, who had been in the team for the last few matches of the Conference season and for the play-off semi-final, was not playing and was replaced by Paul Jones, thus Exeter went into the game without a substitute goalkeeper when Rice did not take up his place on the bench.

City though, got off to the best possible start when taking the lead in the eighth minute as Jon Challinor's cross was headed home by Phillips.

Morecambe gradually got back into the game and were awarded a penalty in the 30th minute when Chris Todd was penalised for a foul on Danny Carlton.

However, late call up he may have been, Jones produced a brilliant save as he parried Gary Thompson's spot-kick and then blocked the follow-up effort from Wayne Curtis.

Unfortunately Phillips, who had started the game so well, then had to leave the field in the 37th

Exeter City at Wembley? Who would have thought it? Manager Paul Tisdale and his players acknowledge the vast army of City fans prior to kick off. (www.cheggerspics.co.uk)

minute with a hamstring injury and was replaced by Stansfield.

City never seemed to be quite the same after that and Morecambe duly equalised three minutes before the break when Thompson lofted the ball over Jones via the underside of the crossbar, after pouncing on a mistake by defender Billy Jones.

City manager Paul Tisdale made two changes early in the second half, replacing Wayne Carlisle and Lee Elam with Richard Logan and Jamie Mackie.

For long periods of the second half neither team threatened, but disaster struck the Grecians in the 82nd minute when a goal worthy of any final was scored by Carlton, with a terrific, unstoppable 25-yard shot to make it 2-1 to Morecambe.

City tried to get back into the match, but frustration got the better of Matthew Gill as he was red-carded in added time for an apparent head-butt on Craig Stanley.

The final whistle only proved what a contrast and thin line it is between success and failure. As Morecambe celebrated, City players and fans were crestfallen, although the travelling red army did their best to lift the spirits of everyone concerned by applauding the efforts of their heroes.

City boss Paul Tisdale said they were undone by a wonder strike: 'The players have put in a great effort all season and to finish like that is frustrating. We tried our best, but in the end we have been beaten by a fantastic goal, and you have to put your hand up.

'We had a wonderful start, but then we didn't continue our positive start and they got hold of the game. The first half was theirs. But after half-time I changed the formation and we had more of the ball.

'The dressing room is very quiet – there was a stony silence. You can imagine how the players are feeling. But you have to ride these days and harness energy from it and use that for next year.'

Sammy McIlroy, manager of Morecambe, said he ranked the club's promotion among his greatest achievements:

'Today was a great advert for Conference football', he said. 'We had to stick in there after they scored, but in the end I thought we bossed the majority of the match.'

Exeter City: Paul Jones, Steve Tully, Chris Todd, Rob Edwards, Billy Jones, Wayne Carlisle (Richard Logan 53), Andy Taylor, Matthew Gill, Lee Elam (Jamie Mackie 56), Jon Challinor, Lee Phillips (Adam Stansfield 37).

Morecambe: Scott Davies, Adam Yates, Jim Bentley, Chris Blackburn, Danny Adams, Gary Thompson (Ged Brannan 86), Craig Stanley, Neil Sorvel, Michael Twiss (Gary Hunter 72), Wayne Curtis, Danny Carlton (David McNiven 88).

Adam Stansfield races away from Morecambe defender Adam Yates. (www.cheggerspics.co.uk)

Lee Phillips heads the Grecians into an early lead against Morecambe at Wembley. (www.cheggerspics.co.uk)

City on the attack against Torquay United in the play-off semi-final first leg at St James' Park.
(www.cheggerspics.co.uk)

Having reached the Blue Square Premier League play-off semi-finals for the second successive year, could the Grecians take advantage of the fact that they were once more at home for the first leg, played on Thursday 1st May 2008?

Having lost to Oxford United at this same stage at St James' Park 12 months earlier, but then gone on to produce a fabulous performance at the Kassam Stadium to win through to Wembley and face Morecambe, no one really wanted a repeat of that situation. A handsome home win was much more preferable.

But what happened? Yes, City duly lost to Devon rivals and play-off opponents Torquay United! Needless to say there was much build up in the press and amongst the respective sets of supporters leading up to the two matches.

With St James' Park and Plainmoor hosting virtual sell-out crowds there was huge anticipation for a cracking couple of games based on what had occurred earlier in the season at Exeter in the Blue Square Premier League, when City won a pulsating fixture, 4-3.

Whilst Exeter City enjoyed the lion's share of possession and the play in the first leg at the Park, they found themselves trailing to a 39th-minute header by Torquay's Tim Sills.

This was the first real attack that the visitors had mounted, so the lead was very much against the run of play.

It was a similar pattern in the second half and eventually the Grecians got a deserved equaliser when with 15 minutes to full time, Wayne Carlisle ghosted in behind the Torquay defence and crashed an unstoppable left-foot volley into the net.

With the game heading for an 'even stevens' finish, an uncharacteristic error by City keeper Paul Jones in stoppage time, saw his attempted clearance go straight to Chris Zebroski who prodded the ball into an empty net from 15 yards.

It was a sad way to lose the first leg tie and left the vast majority in a crowd of 8,276 stunned after the way their team had dominated so much of the game.

The City team had lined up: Paul Jones, Steve

*Wayne Carlisle, who ironically joined Torquay shortly after, slots home
another City goal at Plainmoor to send the Grecians on their way to Wembley. (www.cheggerspics.co.uk)*

Tully, Rob Edwards, Matt Taylor, George Friend, Danny Seaborne (Richard Logan), Dean Moxey, Ryan Harley, Matthew Gill, Wayne Carlisle (Lee Elam), Adam Stansfield (Ben Watson).

Despite the first leg defeat Grecians' manager Paul Tisdale was more than happy with the overall performance of the team:

'We played some good football and I am certainly proud of the players for having the confidence to play in such a huge game. For the first 30 minutes I thought we were absolutely fantastic. I was proud of the way we played and they scored two goals against the run of play.

'But that's football and it will be a different affair on Monday, I can assure you of that. We will have to wait and see what happens now. We have a big task ahead of us on Monday but it is one that we can achieve, I'm sure of that.'

City's sporting director Julian Tagg said: 'It was the sort of game you look back on afterwards and wonder how you have lost it. But we have got another opportunity on Monday, Paul will get the players right and we still have a fantastic opportunity to get back to Wembley.'

Could Exeter City pull the deficit back and reach their goal of Wembley? It seemed a tough task, especially in front of a partisan crowd at Plainmoor, even allowing for 1,500 or so City fans who would be in the ground.

When Torquay increased their advantage in the second leg with a goal from the long-serving Kevin Hill on the hour mark, many felt that the tie was beyond Exeter.

However, they were about to be proved wrong as Tisdale made an astute double substitution, and my, how it worked!

With 20 minutes to go, substitute Ryan Harley fired home from the edge of a crowded Torquay penalty area to reduce the overall deficit to 2-3.

Then in the 80th minute Richard Logan was bundled to ground by keeper Simon Rayner and Chris Zebroski, and up stepped City's second substitute, the on-loan Ben Watson from Grays Athletic, to coolly slot home the spot-kick and make it 2-1 to the Grecians on the day, but 3-3 on aggregate.

With their 'tails up', and the travelling Grecians roaring them on, City tore into Torquay but they had to wait until the 89th minute, and thus avoiding a period of extra-time, when Carlisle (Exeter's third

City are going back to Wembley! The supporters and players celebrate after winning the play-off semi-final second leg tie at Torquay United's Plainmoor. (www.cheggerspics.co.uk)

substitution) delivered a great cross for Logan who sent a downward header into the back of the net. Cue massive celebrations from the huge travelling support.

But it was far from all over, as City made sure of their second trip to Wembley in the space of 12 months when Rob Edwards played a pass from the left-back position into the Torquay half, releasing Watson against one defender.

Watson crossed for Carlisle. He took a touch and slotted past Rayner to make it 4-1 on the day, 5-3 to City on aggregate and it was the 94th minute. Game over.

The two matches, televised by Setanta, had been a tremendous advertisement for football in the Blue Square Premier League.

The fact that it was also a local derby just added spice to the occasion, and certainly the victory at Plainmoor will be long remembered by City fans.

Before an attendance of 6,015, the triumphant City team lined up: Paul Jones, Steve Tully, Rob Edwards, Matt Taylor, George Friend (Wayne Carlisle), Danny Seaborne, Dean Moxey, Bertie Cozic (Ryan Harley), Matthew Gill, Richard Logan, Adam Stansfield (Ben Watson).

Despite the euphoria of victory, Tisdale once again showed what a cool approach he has by saying the team had won nothing as yet.

'Of course we are very happy and it is hard not to celebrate', he said. 'We are all human and we love the feeling of victory and getting to a final. We know the bitter feeling we had last year and, off the back of that, we are not getting too carried away. But we are going to be happy about it and enjoy the occasion.

'This is about what the players did today, not me or anybody on the bench, they made the decisions not me. I asked the players for everything and then a little bit more and they gave me just that.

'I am just chuffed for them, the club and here we go again – we are back at Wembley. I really don't mind who we play in the final. Whoever we meet we will be prepared to win.'

It took Exeter City 103 years to get there, then they visited Wembley twice in the space of 12 months! Only unlike the first occasion, their Blue Square Premier League play-off final against Cambridge United ended in success and therefore the club won a place back in the Football League.

The whole approach to the game was completely different to that of one year earlier when the day ended in intense disappointment when losing to Morecambe.

This time, instead of the achievement of getting to the new Wembley Stadium, there was only one thing on everyone's minds – a victory! The game, despite its importance, was treated just like any other with the team opting to travel the day before, and there was no sign of the usual Wembley suits for the players, just their usual matchday wear.

This approach worked brilliantly, with manager Paul Tisdale rallying his players in the days leading up to the match and reminding them of the heartache of the Morecambe game.

'I want the players to give a good account of themselves', said Tisdale. 'They need to give it everything they have got. They can't have any fear of losing and, when the time is right, we need to take the game by the scruff of the neck.

'It is all to play for and the prize is big. The players need to play to the best of their ability, trust each other, trust themselves and don't be scared to lose. Let's go out and give it everything.'

With 20,000 City fans having travelled to the capital, there would be once again plenty of vocal encouragement for the players.

'The more fans the better', Tisdale added. 'It is something that has worked very well this year in terms of when the players have needed a push the supporters have been there to provide it.

'If we have got 20,000-plus supporters at Wembley I am sure that will be the push we need. And I think they have to enjoy the day because these days don't come around very often.

'If we go a goal up we shouldn't get too high and if we go a goal down we shouldn't get too down because it's going to be a long game.

'There are going to be lots of twists and turns and all we need is to be one goal better at the death. We all know this is a huge game and we have to deliver on the day. I have probably only said it three times in my two years here, but this is a must-win game.

'We don't under-estimate how big this game is but we can't start dreaming about winning until we have won. All we can do is prepare the best we can and be the best we can be.'

The defeat against Morecambe was clearly very much in the mind of both Tisdale and his players:

'We have still got that bitter disappointment at the back of our mind from last year. I can remember the coach going back from Wembley. We stopped on the M4 at the services and we all stood around like zombies and that is still pretty clear to mind. I don't want that feeling again.

'That feeling is still there and we have just have to take every bit of experience from last year and hopefully that will prepare us for what is coming. It gives you the determination that we want to win this game, not that we didn't want to win last year.

'Sometimes actually knowing what is coming is a good thing because there is no uncertainty or an element of the unknown on the day. The fact we were there last year and lots of players played in that game is a big plus for us. It doesn't give us the right to say we are going to win this game, though.

'I don't think there is a favourite going into this game. I think it is 50/50 and it is about what happens on the day. I just think it is too close to call. You can only influence certain things but you can't influence what your opponents are going to do or what decisions the referee is going to make.

'Every game has the potential to be tactical and my job is to have a lot of scenarios in place if I need to change it based on what unfolds. We have to be prepared for all angles. I will have a team of 11 and a bench of five who are all capable of playing two or three different ways.

'It is not a bigger game than last season because we wanted to win just as much last time. The fact that the lads lost against Morecambe can be turned into a positive because they know what they have got to do to get through it.

'It is not a day out, it is a job that needs to be done and we need to focus on that. As soon as they walk into the stadium they will have that same feeling as last year and hopefully everyone will say "we are not going to have that same feeling at the end of the game".'

The photograph that says it all ... EXETER CITY ARE BACK IN THE FOOTBALL LEAGUE! (www.cheggerspics.co.uk)

It was perhaps fitting that the player who scored the only goal of the play-off final, and thus sending Exeter City back to the Football League after an absence of five years, was someone who had been an ever-present all season, and what's more he was the oldest member of the team, not that you would have realised from his consistent performances throughout the season.

Rob Edwards had been magnificent all season, whether as a defender or in the midfield, but what better place to score a goal than at Wembley in such an important match?

In front of a crowd of 42,511, Exeter were determined to make up for the massive disappointment felt 12 months previous when they lost in the Blue Square Premier League play-off final to Morecambe.

Watching your team at Wembley means next to nothing if promotion is not won, especially when defeat extends your exile in the non-league wilderness.

The Grecians looked neat and composed and produced some excellent football, a trademark of Paul Tisdale's team that had been evident all season, whilst their opponents, Cambridge United, struggled to cope with the occasion early on.

City coped better with the pressure of such a big match and should have taken the lead after just six minutes, when Richard Logan nodded wide after being picked out by Dean Moxey's free-kick.

The big striker was defeated by the tight angle and put his header into the side netting.

The Grecians deservedly took the lead in the 22nd minute when Edwards headed in at the far post following Moxey's inswinging corner.

Needless to say this created an even louder noise from the massed following of City fans, decked out in red and white, although on this occasion (as at Torquay in the semi-final) the team played in their third-choice kit of all white.

The goal gave City even more confidence in their ability as they sprayed the ball around the big, wide open space of Wembley, with precision.

Daniel Gleeson had a decent chance to draw Cambridge level just before the break, but he fired over from the edge of the box with a volley.

It was a different story in the second half though as Cambridge pushed further and further forward in search of an equaliser, but the City defence held firm.

United substitute Magno Vieira raced clear in the 73rd minute and squared for Stephen Reed, but his shot was blocked by Steve Tully. A minute later, Mark Peters' close-range effort was cleared off the line by Matt Taylor.

It was a tense time for the team and supporters as the game entered its final phase, as Exeter had to deal with a constant aerial bombardment, however they still looked threatening on the counter attack.

Exeter could have sealed victory when one of

A relaxed Exeter City squad getting the 'feel' of Wembley prior to the play-off final. (www.cheggerspics.co.uk)

Rob Edwards – scorer of the goal that booked Exeter City's place back in the Football League.
(www.cheggerspics.co.uk)

the game's outstanding players, Moxey, burst into the box in the 89th minute only to see his shot blocked by former Grecian Danny Potter.

The final whistle blew moments later sending the 20,000 supporters from Devon into rapture. On the pitch, a squad that was on its knees 12 months ago danced with delight. The party was about to begin!

Exeter manager Paul Tisdale and director of football Steve Perryman saluted the loyalty of the fans who have stuck by the club since their relegation in 2003.

Goalscorer Edwards said: 'We're chuffed to bits and it means that much more given what the club has gone through. It's a huge day for everyone involved because there was a point when we thought we might not make it.

'This is a Football League club. We get four or five thousand gates when we're in the League and that is a lot more than many clubs already there.

'The people who have run the club in the last few years should take the credit for this rather than the players because they were the ones who made sure we survived.

'I don't score many goals so it's not bad, is it? We did our jobs well today, but I think the key was that we are mentally a totally different outfit to last year.

'We learnt that Wembley is not a place to come to and lose. The most important thing was to get Exeter back into the league. It was not about coming to Wembley and wearing a nice suit.'

Manager Paul Tisdale added: 'The club is well set to go on. We can be competitive now in League Two and, after that, who knows how far we can go?

'We have a good youth set-up, great support and a good stadium. We have the potential to go much, much further and hopefully we can.

'We were here last year and watched the opponents take to the steps and lift the cup; all we could do was believe that we'd come back. It's taken 12 months of incredibly hard work to achieve the opportunity again and we were determined not to waste that opportunity.'

'We played very well first half, but the second half was a bit nervy', he said. 'The emotions are one extreme to the other from last year, so I'll take this one. But on a day like this I have total sympathy for Cambridge.

'When we arrived at Wembley today, it felt different. There was a different atmosphere about the place. That was not something we tried to organise or contrive. It was how it was. It was about winning and doing a decent job and we knew we had to keep the ball.

'For me it wasn't a time to jump all over the place but instead to just be content and say, "We've done the job, well done everybody." I am very proud to be part of the football club that has made great strides and will continue to make them.

'We have had an up and down year this year and to get the same opportunity again – gosh – we didn't want to miss that opportunity a second time.

'It was a gigantic effort from the players, yes, it was edgy and it was backs to the wall in the second half. We told the players to make the right decisions and we are back in the Football League which is all that counts.

'I'm not sure of the exact financial implications of promotion but I know the club will receive a decent bonus. But it is a huge credit to the board that we are well set regardless of whether we stayed in the Conference or went up and that is why I have such an affinity with this club. It so well-run by people who really care about Exeter.'

Dejected Cambridge United boss Jimmy Quinn said: 'The better team won. We froze a little bit today, just like Exeter did a year ago, but we are miles better than that. It's disappointing.

'When you suffer the disappointment we've just suffered, it makes you more determined to do better next year. If we end up back here next year, that'll hold us in good stead. Exeter are proof of that.'

The day though belonged to Exeter City and their fans. It was a fitting reward for the players who suffered play-off heartbreak at the hands of Morecambe the previous year.

And it capped a remarkable rise for a club who were teetering on the brink of financial oblivion just five seasons ago. After falling into administration and finally seeing two of their former directors convicted of fraudulent trading in 2007, with John Russell receiving a 21-month custodial sentence and Mike Lewis being given 200 hours of community service, the club were

City manager Paul Tisdale with the Blue Square Premier League play-off trophy.
(www.cheggerspics.co.uk)

forced to go cap in hand to their supporters just to stay alive.

Long gone are the celebrities such as Michael Jackson and Uri Geller, along with Mike Lewis and John Russell, replaced by the Supporters' Trust led by Denise Watts, the chairman.

'There are plenty of challenges ahead of us', said club vice-chairman Julian Tagg. 'I am glad to get out of the Blue Square Premier as the league is getting harder and harder every year. You always need to stretch yourself to achieve success, but the trick is to get the balance right – which I think we have here.'

Finally manager Tisdale added: 'I am very proud to be given the opportunity to work here and work with such terrific people, with such a consistent approach to their business, be it lose, win or draw, and very proud to be supported by the fans, who have been fantastic towards me and the team over the last couple of years.'

Exeter City: Paul Jones, Steve Tully, Danny Seaborne, Matt Taylor, George Friend, Matt Gill, Ryan Harley, Rob Edwards, Dean Moxey, Adam Stansfield (Ben Watson 84), Richard Logan.

Cambridge United: Danny Potter, Daniel Gleeson (Leo Fortune-West 75), Mark Albrighton, Mark Peters, Wayne Hatswell, David Brown (Stephen Reed 66), Rob Wolleaston, Paul Carden, Courtney Pitt, Lee Boylan (Magno Vieira 69), Lee McEvilly.

Jack Edwards in 1964; Bobby Saxton in 1977; Terry Cooper in 1990; and now Paul Tisdale in 2008. All four men have led Exeter City to promotion, but the ultimate goal was achieved by Tisdale very differently to any of the previous three City managers.

To get to Wembley is everyone's dream, but to win there is even better. And when Tisdale and his players felt the utter disappointment of losing in the 2007 Blue Square Premier League play-off final to Morecambe, everyone hoped that the Grecians would get another opportunity to win a place back in the Football League.

To take the team to such a final once is an achievement, but to do it twice and win, is something rightly to be proud of, and that is exactly what Tisdale did, with the help of assistant manager Russell Osman and director of football Steve Perryman.

City were back at Wembley on 18th May 2008 and this time they didn't want to suffer defeat again, as they went on to defeat Cambridge United 1-0 with a goal from Rob Edwards. Thus the quietly spoken and thoughtful Tisdale earned a chance to manage a team – Exeter City – in the Football League.

He was appointed manager of Exeter City in June 2006 after making the shortlist of three, one of whom was ironically Jimmy Quinn, who tasted defeat against City when managing Cambridge United in the 2008 final.

Tisdale fitted the bill perfectly, for the Grecians were seeking not just a manger, but one who would continue to build on the community links that the club had built, one that would encourage youth players, and one that would hopefully lead them back into the Football League.

A former England Schools international player, Tisdale spent 11 years at Southampton. He also had experience at four other Football League sides, including Exeter City as a loan player, and had played at Premier League level in three European countries.

Tisdale began his playing career as a trainee at Southampton, but went on to make only a handful of appearances for the south coast club's first team. While at The Dell he spent time on loan at Northampton Town and Huddersfield Town, before joining Bristol City on a free transfer in 1997.

In December 1997 then Exeter manager Peter Fox signed Tisdale on loan. And he netted on his

City boss Paul Tisdale in typical, thoughtful mood. (www.cheggerspics.co.uk)

debut in a 3-0 win against Rochdale, going on to enjoy a productive ten-game stint in Devon. After leaving City he played a summer season in Finland for Helsinki-based side Finnpa before landing a one-year deal with Greek side Panionios. There he helped lead the Athens outfit to the quarter-finals of the 1999 European Cup, where they eventually bowed out at the hands of Lazio.

On his return to British shores, Tisdale was handed a route into coaching thanks to a new programme at the University of Bath and he prolonged his playing career on a part-time basis at Yeovil Town. But a back injury eventually forced him to hang up his boots, paving the way for him to carve out a career in management.

Tisdale guided Team Bath to four promotions in seven seasons and also gained an appointment as team coach to the England Universities side that won the British Universities championship in 2006.

His successful career as a manager has continued with the Grecians and it will take some beating for any other Exeter manager to have led the side out at Wembley twice in the space of 12 months.

Noted for his deep, thoughtful approach and methodical planning for matches, Tisdale is not averse to changing the formation of his starting line up from game to game, nor indeed during the course of a game. You certainly cannot argue against the success that he has brought to Exeter City.

It was time to take stock of the new situation that Exeter City found themselves in. After winning promotion back to the Football League, the planning began both on and off the field.

'I guess we have a new set of problems than we had when we were in the Conference', said City manager Paul Tisdale.

'We don't know what is to come because we haven't been in that situation, but whatever they are, we will approach them with great excitement. Hopefully we will get a few more days like the one at Wembley.

'It's wonderful to be back in the Football League. We tried not to dream and even at half-time against Cambridge United, we were saying – "Don't dream about it, we have to do what is necessary".

'This club can go forward. This is not a finished product now. I think the playing staff is progressing and hopefully things behind the scenes will continue at the same pace and we are going to be in good shape.

'I think we are good enough to be in the league above and, given time, who knows what will happen? We have certainly got the potential to not just rest in League Two but to move on and achieve further success in the future.'

From purely a financial point of view the Grecians were expecting a considerable amount of money to flow into the club's coffers with increased television and sponsorship money, youth funding, competing in more potentially lucrative competitions and a swell in visiting support.

There would also be a boost in commercial revenue through various sponsorship deals and hospitality packages.

'It is great on two levels', said City's commercial director Paul Morrish. 'One is for the profile of the club and the exposure this will give us is being reflected in the amount of new interest from new sponsors.

'And two there is more money to be made by being a league club from lots of different avenues and we are trying to ensure we capitalise on them. Most notably the pool of money that is dispersed

Exeter City commercial director Paul Morrish. (www.cheggerspics.co.uk)

to member clubs in the Football League, which comprises of TV and sponsorship money.

'We are not sure how much more we will get yet because the figures change year on year. It would appear that going back into the league, you get the money in two stages.

'So in the same way that you get the parachute payment when you come out of the league, you don't get the full amount in your first year when you come into the league.

'So we will be receiving 50 per cent in the first year which is a little bit more than we would have got had we stayed in the Conference.

'Obviously there are a number of other sources of income which we haven't had. Things like larger away support, access to both the F.A. Cup and the League Cup at a stage where we are more likely to be within a game or two of a big match.

'Then there is an opportunity with the work we do with our sponsors and our youth funding will be given a grant. The main story is we will see the real benefit in year two of being back in the league, not next year.'

The long wait was over. Some said it had been five years in a footballing wilderness, which is probably being very unkind to the Conference or Blue Square Premier League as it became known.

It was five years in which Exeter City Football Club was able to regroup and put in place various measures to ensure that a similar scenario to that which sent the club plummeting to near oblivion would never happen again.

The infrastructure of the club was completely reorganised and as a result the Grecians were in a far stronger position than they ever had been for a good number of years.

It was essential to have a firm base off the field and thriving commercial department to raise much-needed finance through various sponsorship and corporate deals to enable the club and the team go forward once again.

After a near promotion miss in 2007, when losing in the play-off final to Morecambe, the goal of regaining the Football League place that everyone so wanted was achieved 12 months later as Cambridge United were defeated 1-0 at Wembley.

So on to the day that everyone had been waiting for, ever since dropping out of the Football League in 2003.

The fixture could hardly have been much further afield as City found themselves having to make their longest trip of the season as they ventured to the north-east and the 'Land of the Prince Bishops' as the area is known – a journey that took them to the impressive stadium at Darlington F.C.

No matter how far the City supporters would have to travel, there is no doubt, such was their enthusiasm, they would have travelled anywhere.

A magnificent 604 supporters made it to Darlington, which was very impressive, especially when one considers that the attendance for the game was only 3,559 in total.

The fans travelled by car, coach, train and even a bike, the latter being ridden by supporter Pete Bishop, who rode from Exeter over the space of four days in order to raise money for charity.

Prior to the game City manager Paul Tisdale had told his players to go out and prove themselves at Football League level: 'It has been a long six weeks of pre-season but we are here now and raring to go', he said.

Looks like a painful landing during the game at Darlington for Adam Stansfield.
(www.cheggerspics.co.uk)

'It is very exciting for the playing squad who have worked so hard to get the club back in the Football League. The players have to make the most of it.

'We can't take it for granted and we have to make sure that we establish ourselves very quickly. Then we can set our sights on being successful at this level.

'We are relishing the prospect of travelling to Darlington but it's not going to be a party for us, it is business because there are three points at stake and you never know what those three points are going to mean to us come the end of the season.'

For the historic return to the Football League, City lined up as follows: Paul Jones, Steve Tully, George Friend, Matt Taylor, Danny Seaborne, Matthew Gill, Rob Edwards, Ryan Harley, Richard Logan, Adam Stansfield, Marcus Stewart.

City found themselves a goal in arrears in the first half as Friend brought down Billy Clarke in the box, and up stepped Rob Purdie to slot home the resultant penalty.

The second half proved to be much better for the Grecians as they began to get more accustomed to life in the Football League and they deservedly equalised on the hour mark when Danny Seaborne climbed high to nod home a Rob Edwards free-kick.

After that it was the Grecians who looked more likely to go on and claim the three points, although at the end of 90 minutes it was possibly fair to say that a point for each side was the right result.

At the final whistle the large City travelling

Danny Seaborne turns to celebrate scoring City's first goal back in the Football League and what proved to be the equaliser at Darlington. (www.cheggerspics.co.uk)

Celebrating City fans after the Grecians had scored at Darlington. (www.cheggerspics.co.uk)

support once again showed their appreciation to manager Paul Tisdale and his team, for Exeter City *really* were back in the Football League.

City boss Tisdale added: 'We have to make sure we start as best we can because we want to give ourselves an opportunity to settle into the season.

'The last thing we want is to be scrapping around the bottom of the table after the first ten games because we have not got ourselves going.

'So there is a different sort of pressure on us. But as a professional you have to demand certain things of yourself and those around you because

things can quickly slide. We have built real momentum around the place and we would like that to continue.'

Meanwhile, City defender Danny Seaborne was delighted to get on the score sheet as he added: 'It was an important goal and I am proud to have scored it. This was my first game in the Football League and hopefully it will be the first of many.

'It is always nice to get a result on the first day of the season. Obviously we would have loved to have come here and won, but realistically a draw is still a really good result and it can only get better from here.'

ST JAMES' PARK: HOW IT WAS

JUST THE TICKET

EXETER CITY F. & A. Co. LTD
ST. JAMES' PARK, EXETER
Third Division
EXETER CITY
VERSUS
PLYMOUTH ARGYLE
TUESDAY, 17th APRIL, 1978
Kick-off 7.30 p.m.
Secretary: P. R. WAKEHAM
Admit at   £1.80
WELL STREET ENTRANCE

BLOCK   **A**

Row   Seat No.

C 6

THIS PORTION TO BE RETAINED

*A selection of match tickets issued by Exeter City.
The one for the F.A. Cup tie against Middlesbrough
is a particularly interesting one, as the game was
never played, the Grecians having lost their third
round replay to Manchester United.*

EXETER CITY F. & A. Co., Ltd.
ST. JAMES' PARK EXETER
F.A. Cup—1st Round Replay

ADMIT AT
Well St.
ENTRANCE

EXETER CITY
VERSUS
CRAWLEY
Wed., 24th November, 1971
Kick-off 7.30 p.m.
Secretary : R. H. THOMAS, F.C.B.I.
Ticket 50p

BLOCK
A

Row/Seat
No.
037

TO BE RETAINED

FA CUP 3rd ROUND REPLAY
EXETER CITY
vs
MANCHESTER UNITED
TUESDAY 18th JANUARY 2005
KICK OFF 7.45pm
ST JAMES ROAD TERRACE
ADULTS: £11   CONCESSION: £6

01200

Ticket 1 — Exeter City v Torquay United

EXETER CITY FOOTBALL CLUB
St. James' Park, Exeter EX4 6PX
E.C.F.C. GRAPEVINE: 0891 44 68 68
Main Sponsor: Concept Incorporated

TORQUAY UNITED
Sunday 28th Dec
11.00am
GRANDSTAND
BLOCK C
ROW P SEAT 14

CONCESSIONARY
£7.00

ADULT
£10.00
CONCESSIONARY
£7.00

EXETER CITY V TORQUAY UNITED
NATIONWIDE LEAGUE DIVISION THREE
GRANDSTAND BLOCK C
ROW P SEAT 14
NO SMOKING IN THE GRANDSTAND

Sunday 28th Dec
11.00am KO

You are advised to take up your position
half an hour before the kick-off.
This ticket is valid for the above match
on whatever date it may be played.
Issued subject to the rules and
regulations of the Football League and
the Football Association.

TO BE GIVEN UP

TO BE RETAINED

Ticket 2 — Exeter City v Plymouth Argyle

EXETER CITY FOOTBALL CLUB
St. James' Park, Exeter EX4 6PX
Exeter City Clubcall: 0891 12 16 34

PLYMOUTH ARGYLE
Saturday 30th January
11.00am
GRANDSTAND
BLOCK C
ROW P SEAT 9

ADULT
£10.00

PLYMOUTH ARGYLE
Saturday 30th January
11.00am
GRANDSTAND
BLOCK C
ROW P SEAT 9

CONCESSIONARY
£7.00

ADULT
£10.00
CONCESSIONARY
£7.00

EXETER CITY V PLYMOUTH ARGYLE
NATIONWIDE LEAGUE DIVISION 3
GRANDSTAND BLOCK C
ROW P SEAT 9
NO SMOKING IN THE GRANDSTAND

Saturday 30th January
11.00am KO

Our Main Sponsor is:
EXETER FRIENDLY SOCIETY

You are advised to take up your position
half an hour before the kick-off.
This ticket is valid for the above match
on whatever date it may be played.
Issued subject to the rules and
regulations of the Football League and
the Football Association.

TO BE GIVEN UP   TO BE GIVEN UP

TO BE RETAINED

Ticket 3 — Exeter City v Middlesbrough

SECPRINT SECPRINT SECPRINT SECPRINT SECPRINT SECPRINT SECPRINT SECPRINT SECPR

EXETER CITY VS MIDDLESBROUGH
29.01.05
KICK OFF
5.20pm
EXPRESS & ECHO STAND
BLOCK C
L
36
TICKET OFFICE

EXETER CITY VS MIDDLESBROUGH
29.01.05
KICK OFF
5.20pm
EXPRESS & ECHO STAND
BLOCK C
L
36
TO BE GIVEN UP

EXETER CITY AFC LTD

EXETER CITY VS MIDDLESBROUGH
29.01.05
KICK OFF
5.20pm
EXPRESS & ECHO STAND
BLOCK C
L
36
TO BE GIVEN UP

FA CUP 4TH ROUND
EXETER CITY
VS
MIDDLESBROUGH
SATURDAY 29th JANUARY 2005
KICK OFF 5.20pm
EXPRESS & ECHO STAND
BLOCK C   ROW L   SEAT 36

Exeter City F.C. 2008–09

Back row: Ben Watson, Ryan Harley, Craig McAllister, Neil Saunders, Dean Moxey, Neil Martin, Liam Sercombe, Jack Obersteller, Chris Shephard.
Middle row: Tamer James (Physio), Scott Bennett, Manny Panther, Matt Taylor, Andy Marriott, Adam Stansfield, Paul Jones, George Friend, Richard Logan, Ian Andrews (Physio).
Front row: Steve Tully, Danny Seaborne, John Yems (Assistant Manager), Paul Tisdale (Manager), Steve Perryman (Director of Football), Mel Gwinnett (Youth Football Director), Matt Gill, Steve Basham.
(www.cheggerspics.co.uk)

RECOMMENDED BIBLIOGRAPHY

Garth Dykes, Maurice Golesworthy and Alex Wilson
Exeter City: A Complete Record 1904–1990
(Breedon Books, 1990 – ISBN 0–907–96968–2)

Dave Fisher and Gerald Gosling
Images of England: Exeter City Football Club 1904–1994
(Tempus Publishing, 1994 – ISBN 0–752–41167–5)

Lionel Francis
Seventy Five Years of Southern League Football
(Pelham Books, 1969 – ISBN 0–720–70262–3)

John Harman
Alliance to Conference: 1979–2004: The First 25 Years
(Tony Williams Publications, 2004 – ISBN 1–869–83352–X)

Barry J. Hugman
Football League Players Records 1946–2005
(Queen Anne Press, 2005 – ISBN 1–852–91665–6)

Michael Joyce
Football League Players' Records 1888–1939
(Soccer Data, 2002 – ISBN 1–899–46863–3)

Brian Knight
Plymouth Argyle: A Complete Record 1903–1989
(Breedon Books, 1989 – ISBN 0–907–96940–2)

Ian Laschke
Rothmans Book of Football League Records 1888–89 to 1978–79
(MacDonald & Jane's, 1980 – ISBN 0–345–08552–2)

Glenda and Jack Rollin
Sky Sports Football Yearbook 2007–08 (and all 37 previous editions of this footballing 'Bible')
(Headline, 2007 – ISBN 978–0–755–31664–9)

Phil Soar
The Hamlyn A–Z of British Football Records
(Hamlyn, 1981 – ISBN 0–600–34662–5)

Brian Tabner
Football Through the Turnstiles ... Again
(Yore Publications, 2002 – ISBN 1–874–42744–5)

Dennis Turner and Alex White
Football Managers
(Breedon Books, 1993 – ISBN 1–873–62632–0)

James Wright
The F.A. Cup: Club by Club Record Since 1945
(Tony Williams, 1993 – ISBN 1–869–83341–4)

Express & Echo – Heron Road, Sowton, Exeter, Devon EX2 7NF
Western Morning News – 17 Brest Road, Derriford, Plymouth, Devon PL6 5AA